D0276804

The 1984
Olympic Scientific
Congress
Proceedings
Volume 2

Sport, Health, and Nutrition

Series Editors:

Jan Broekhoff, PhD
Michael J. Ellis, PhD
Dan G. Tripps, PhD

*University of Oregon
Eugene, Oregon*

The 1984
Olympic Scientific
Congress
Proceedings
Volume 2

Sport, Health, and Nutrition

Frank I. Katch
Editor

Human Kinetics Publishers, Inc.
Champaign, Illinois

Library of Congress Cataloging-in-Publication Data

Olympic Scientific Congress (1984 : Eugene, Or.)
    Sport, health, and nutrition.

    (1984 Olympic Scientific Congress proceedings ;
v. 2)
    Bibliography: p.
    1. Sports—Physiological aspects—Congresses.
2. Nutrition—Congresses.   3. Health—Congresses.
I. Katch, Frank I.   II. Title.   III. Series:
Olympic Scientific Congress (1984 : Eugene, Or.).
1984 Olympic Scientific Congress proceedings ;
v. 2.
GV565.O46   1984 vol. 2   796 s   85-18117
[RC1235]   [613.2'088796]
ISBN 0-87322-010-2

Managing Editor: Susan Wilmoth, PhD
Developmental Editor: Susan Wilmoth, PhD
Production Director: Sara Chilton
Copyeditor: Olga Murphy
Typesetter: Theresa Bear
Text Layout: Cyndy Barnes
Cover Design and Layout: Jack Davis
Printed By: Braun-Brumfield, Inc.

ISBN: 0-87322-006-4   (10 Volume Set)
ISBN: 0-87322-010-2

Copyright © 1986 by Human Kinetics Publishers, Inc.

All rights reserved. Except for use in review, the reproduction
or utilization of this work in any form or by any electronic,
mechanical, or other means, now known or hereafter invented, including
xerography, photocopying and recording, and in any information retrieval
system, is forbidden without the written permission of the publisher.

Printed in the United States of America

10 9 8 7 6 5 4 3 2 1

Human Kinetics Publishers, Inc.
Box 5076, Champaign, IL 61820

Contents

Series Acknowledgments

The Congress organizers realize that an event as large and complex as the 1984 Olympic Scientific Congress could not have come to fruition without the help of literally hundreds of organizations and individuals. Under the patronage of UNESCO, the Congress united in sponsorship and cooperation no fewer than 64 national and international associations and organizations. Some 50 representatives of associations helped with the organization of the scientific and associative programs by coordinating individual sessions. The cities of Eugene and Springfield yielded more than 400 volunteers who donated their time to make certain that the multitude of Congress functions would progress without major mishaps. To all these organizations and individuals, the organizers express their gratitude.

A special word of thanks must also be directed to the major sponsors of the Congress: the International Council of Sport Science and Physical Education (ICSSPE), the United States Olympic Committee (USOC), the International Council on Health, Physical Education and Recreation (ICHPER), and the American Alliance for Health, Physical Education, Recreation and Dance (AAHPERD). Last but not least, the organizers wish to acknowledge the invaluable assistance of the International Olympic Committee (IOC) and its president, Honorable Juan Antonio Samaranch. President Samaranch made Congress history by his official opening address in Eugene on July 19, 1984. The IOC further helped the Congress with a generous donation toward the publication of the Congress papers. Without this donation it would have been impossible to make the proceedings available in this form.

Finally, the series editors wish to express their thanks to the volume editors who selected and edited the papers from each program of the Congress. Special thanks go to Frank I. Katch of the University of Massachusetts for his work on this volume.

Jan Broekhoff,
Michael J. Ellis, and
Dan G. Tripps

Series Editors

Series Preface

Sport, Health, and Nutrition contains selected proceedings from this inter-disciplinary program of the 1984 Olympic Scientific Congress, which was held at the University of Oregon in Eugene, Oregon, preceding the Olympic Games in Los Angeles. The Congress was organized by the College of Human Development and Performance of the University of Oregon in collaboration with the cities of Eugene and Springfield. This was the first time in the history of the Congress that the event was organized by a group of private individuals, unaided by a federal government. The fact that the Congress was attended by more than 2,200 participants from more than 100 different nations is but one indication of its success.

The Congress program focused on the theme of Sport, Health, and Well-Being subdisciplines of sport science such as sport medicine, biomechanics, sport psychology, sport sociology, and sport philosophy. For the first time in the Congress' history, these disciplinary sessions were sponsored by the national and international organizations representing the various subdisciplines. In the afternoons, the emphasis shifted toward interdisciplinary themes in which scholars and researchers from the subdisciplines attempted to contribute to crossdisciplinary understanding. In addition, three evenings were devoted to keynote addresses and presentations, broadly related to the theme of Sport, Health, and Well-Being.

In addition to the scientific programs, the Congress also featured a number of associative programs with topics determined by their sponsoring organizations. Well over 1,200 papers were presented in the various sessions of the Congress at large. It stands to reason, therefore, that publishing the proceedings of the event presented a major problem to the organizers. It was decided to limit proceedings initially to interdisciplinary sessions which drew substantial interest from Congress participants and attracted a critical number of high-quality presentations. Human Kinetics Publishers, Inc. of Champaign, Illinois, was selected to produce these proceedings. After considerable deliberation, the following interdisciplinary themes were selected for publication: Competitive Sport for Children and Youths; Human Genetics and Sport; Sport and Aging; Sport and Disabled Individuals; Sport and Elite Performers; Sport, Health, and Nutrition; and Sport and Politics. The 10-volume set published by Human Kinetics Publishers is rounded out by the disciplinary proceedings of Kinanthropometry, Sport Pedagogy, and the associative program on the Scientific Aspects of Dance.

Jan Broekhoff,
Michael J. Ellis, and
Dan G. Tripps,

Series Editors

Preface

This volume contains a wealth of recent information gleaned from the world literature as it relates to nutrition in a broad sense and application to exercise performance in a more specific way. One apparent thread in the nutrition literature relative to exercise is the diversity and interpretation of the available basic and applied research and "so-called" research. Unlike some of the more mature physical and biological sciences where it is relatively simple to gather factual information and test the resulting hypotheses and theories, the situation in the area of nutrition and human performance is not as clear cut. Two main reasons account for the slow emergence of "hard facts": (a) considerable intravariation in human biologic response patterns, and (b) difficulty from an experimental standpoint in controlling the many interrelated factors that exert their influence during such experiments. In terms of biovariation and experimental design, it is virtually impossible to carry out even a "near perfect" experiment. The tools for statistical analysis of results poses no problem, nor is there a problem in setting up a proper experimental design. The problem is in narrowing the extent of biovariation and extraneous "noise" that prevents clean interpretation. This latter factor is certainly operative in several of the papers in this volume.

I decided early in the review and editing process to allow the authors total freedom in their presentation of material. The authors had been invited as guests to participate in the Scientific Congress, or their papers had been accepted for presentation by a committee established by the scientific organizing committee of the Congress. Many readers may disagree with a particular author's viewpoint or interpretation or with the adequacy of the experimental design. However, diversity in science has its place if for no other reason than to illuminate the pitfalls of a mutilated experimental design or inaccuracy of data interpretation. Colgan's paper on the "Effects of Multinutrient Supplementation on Athletic Performance" is the salient example where strict peer review of his presentation of experimental data would probably prohibit publication. Colgan might argue that the scientific establishment is not really tuned in or ready for the types of studies he conducts; he might even think that conventional science has no place in intrepretation of nutritional research as he conducts it. Nevertheless, he should have a forum even though many would argue about the adequacy of his data, his method of control, and the subsequent statistical analysis. Publication of his material was permitted for this very reason: to foster dialogue concerning many of the strategies he employs as "research." Graduate students and others, for example, should be able to contrast Colgan's treatment of the subject matter with Keen and Hackman's paper "Trace Elements in Athletic Performance," or with the Demopolus et al. treatise, "Free Radical Pathology," or the other studies that rely heavily on the scientific method to conduct and carry out their research.

There is ample room in the scientific arena to permit those who believe they are contributing to science to make their case. For those who don't agree with this premise, please keep in mind that publication in a volume such as this does not confer sainthood on their written word. It is hoped that those who are critical of such studies can distinguish fact from fiction and will dramatize such contrasts in their own published work. We must continually be on the alert to recognize the charlatan and snake oil salesmen who pontificate about the virtues of their nutritional truths in the absence of any.

The volume is divided into two sections: (a) The Role of Nutrition in Athletic Performance, and (b) Nutrition, Health, and Health Behaviors. Each section contains considerable factual, relevant, and new material on the role of nutrition and athletic performance. The emerging subdisciplines in the nutrition and exercise sciences have the potential to contribute significantly to our understanding of the broad role of nutrition as it relates to sport and performance. There is a tremendous need to carry out collaborative studies with colleagues in diverse fields. This would greatly accelerate new facts and understandings and would begin to diminish the plethora of nutritional pseudoscience and hucksterism that seems to flourish within this area.

I extend my gratitude to Sue Wilmoth of Human Kinetics Publishers for her perseverance and technical assistance and to the many contributors who met their deadlines and were so gracious and eloquent in their presentations at the Eugene meetings.

In my opinion, the Congress was a smashing success! I hope you enjoy the volume.

Frank I. Katch,
Editor

The 1984
Olympic Scientific
Congress
Proceedings
Volume 2

Sport,
Health,
and
Nutrition

PART I

The Role of Nutrition in Athletic Performance

1

The Leading Edge: Nutrition and Athletic Performance

Robert M. Hackman
UNIVERSITY OF OREGON
EUGENE, OREGON, USA

Many athletes operate under the false assumption that adequate training procedures are sufficient to optimize their athletic performance. Evidence accumulates that nutritional status can significantly influence performance, yet this information has not seemed to reach many athletes. For example, in studying runners' diets in Eugene and in Honolulu, many runners were found to have unbalanced diets: high in sugar and low in vegetable fiber, fluid intake, and likely, inadequate vitamin and mineral intake. What are the implications of improper nutrition for sports performance? and how can the nutritional scientist devise protocols to adequately assess the association between diet and performance?

Experimental Design

Many difficulties arise in designing research protocols that adequately address the impact of nutrition on performance. A major difficulty with humans is the potentially compounding variable of the training effect; that is, people who are training can improve their performance independent of diet, and diet can improve their performance, possibly independent of training. In fact, it is likely that an interaction between training and diet exists, yet in research design, single variables are ideally isolated and manipulated to determine correlations or cause-and-effect associations. Current protocols here at the University of Oregon involve screening individuals for a narrow range of miles run per week and insisting that the subjects adhere to the same training schedule during the course of the experiment. However, this situation is not as controlled as the consistent manipulation of physical activity in laboratory rats; people are free to live as they please and there will be some variation in their physical activity.

Another potential variable influencing outcome data is the psychological or motivational component of the individual. For example, if a subject is run to exhaustion on a treadmill or bicycle ergometer, the time it takes before the person quits might be influenced by training effect, dietary patterns, and the motivation to perform until complete exhaustion. This variable depends upon the indivudual's ability and desire to work through increasing pain and fatigue. Because no two people are alike in their ability to work through fatigue, this suggests that using the person as his or her own control and measuring pre-to poststudy changes in performance is more desirable than assessing group data.

The placebo effect is an important consideration as well. The fact that a person takes a pill may influence outcome performance. Clinical trials demonstrate that placebos work in a surprisingly large number of cases. Beecher (1955) reviewed 15 studies involving more than 1,000 patients and found that, on the average, placebos helped one third of the people who received them. Effectiveness ranged from a low of 15% in a study of pain to 58% in a study of seasickness. Placebos helped treat postoperative pain, angina, anxiety, and the common cold.

Benson and McCallie (1979) have reviewed numerous studies of several treatments for angina. In the past 200 years there have been various treatments, but the diagnosis and severity measurement for angina has basically remained the same. Success rates of up to 90% for drugs and surgical procedures were reported in the past. However, it is now believed these treatments had no physiological effectiveness. According to Benson and McCallie, the high success rates came from the placebo effect, the belief that improvement occurs in response to the treatment.

Although few examples of the placebo effect have been documented for athletic performance, it is reasonable to assume that a similar influence of the person's belief system can influence physiological parameters. The importance of using placebos when nutrient supplements are used in research cannot be overemphasized. This may present some difficulties to the investigator because twice the number of subjects are needed if a placebo group is utilized. However, the influence of taking a supplement over and above the taking of a pill must be accounted for.

Nutrient Supplementation

Is any information available that suggests athletes might improve performance by taking nutrient supplements? A growing number of researchers are exploring this area, and some recent findings suggest that vitamin and mineral supplementation can normalize physiological parameters.

A compromised riboflavin status has been demonstrated in college females during exercise (Belko et al., 1983). Using the enzymatic marker, erythrocyte glutathione reductase activity (EGRAC), the riboflavin intake required to keep the activity coefficient at 1.25 (approximately in balance) was significantly greater when the women jogged for 20 to 50 min per day for 6 weeks, compared to when they were sedentary over a 6-week period.

The authors conclude that healthy young women require more riboflavin to achieve biochemical normality than the 1980 RDAs suggest and that exer-

Table 1. Individual riboflavin and Kilocalorie requirements for an EGRAC of 1.25

Subject	Riboflavin (mg/1000 kcal)	kcal	Riboflavin (mg/1000 kcal)	kcal
1	0.62	2240	0.85	2480
2	0.63	1700	0.63	1940
3	0.84	2240	1.30	2480
4	0.98	2000	1.21	2240
5	0.86	2240	0.98	2480
6	1.09	2000	1.15	2240
7*	>1.0 *	2720	1.33	2960
8*	>1.0 *	2240	1.4*	2480
9	0.98	2240	1.21	2720
10	0.96	2000	1.01	2240
11	0.90	2480	1.23	2720
12	1.21	2240	1.24	2480
Mean + SD	0.92 ± 0.17	2195 + 257	1.12 + 0.21	2455 ± 270

*Estimates for subjects 7 and 8 are approximated; there was not a clear relationship between riboflavin intake and EGRAC.
Note. From "Effects of Exercise on Riboflavin Requirements of Young Women" by A.Z. Belko et al, 1983, American Journal of Clinical Nutrition, **37**, p. 512. Reprinted by permission.

cise increases riboflavin requirements. Because riboflavin is essential for the metabolism of carbohydrates and the production of energy at the cellular level, it can be assumed that a compromised riboflavin status can impair the efficiency of fuel metabolism.

Lonsdale and Shamberger (1980) have demonstrated compromised thiamin status in individuals ingesting high amounts of sucrose. Twenty patients presented with symptoms of chest pains, sleeplessness, depression, anorexia, peripheral neuropathy, and elevated temperature were found to have significantly depressed erythrocyte transketolase levels. All patients consumed copious amounts of sugar, especially soft drinks. Upon supplementation, 18 of the patients were asymptomatic within 90 days, and the other 2 improved substantially. Many athletes ingest high quantities of sucrose, partially out of ignorance about what constitutes a balanced diet and partially as a means of achieving caloric balance for someone burning 3,000 to 5,000 kcal per day. The potential depletion of vitamins and minerals as a combination of exercise and inadequate intake must be considered. More research is needed to elucidate these relationships.

Normal Values

The zinc status in runners has been studied during the past 2 years. A screening assessment in Eugene and Honolulu indicated that serum zinc levels of 30 to 48% of runners were below 0.8 ug/100 ml or parts per million (ppm) (Hackman & Keen, 1983). This value is regarded as marginal zinc deficiency by accepted clinical standards; that is, zinc deficiency has been documented in humans based on stunted growth, reduced taste and smell acuity, depressed immune function, and impaired wound healing, and these physiological signs were accompanied by serum zinc values of 0.8 ppm or less.

Dressendorfer and Sockolov (1980) found that many runners in a 20-day road race in Hawaii also displayed hypozincemia. The runners appeared healthy and had no overt signs of zinc deficiency. However, marginal zinc status might be occurring in these runners with low serum zinc levels. Analysis of diets indicated that roughly two-thirds of all runners studied had dietary zinc intakes of 10 mg or less, suggesting that low zinc intake might be one component of marginal zinc status. Furthermore, increased zinc losses through kidney and sweat might account for the low serum zinc levels.

However, whether low serum zinc levels represent true loss of zinc stores or merely a redistribution of zinc into muscle and liver is uncertain because it is difficult to obtain muscle biopsies in humans and nearly impossible to obtain liver biopsies to confirm whether there is merely a redistribution of body zinc or a true loss. This situation is further complicated by the problem of uncertainty regarding which tissue or tissues need to be assessed for body zinc status. While serum is the generally accepted tissue of assay, other investigators have explored zinc concentration in whole blood, hair, urine, saliva, white blood cells, and muscle. A dynamic model which considers zinc levels from all of the mentioned tissues represents total body zinc status more accurately than any one measure. However, due to time and financial constraints researchers must estimate zinc status based on access to one or two tissue samples per person and must believe that serum values meet this need.

Athletes may be moved by our preliminary finding to take zinc supplements and may believe that if a bit of zinc is helpful, more may be even better. This assumption is dangerous for two reasons: First, zinc in high doses is toxic; and second, as nutrition is better understood, we realize that the interaction between two nutrients is just as important, if not more important than examination of single nutrient values. The zinc:copper interaction is well documented, and a zinc:iron interaction has also been shown. Thus, a person taking high levels of zinc through dietary supplementation might impair copper or iron absorption. When assessing an individual's nutritional status, especially for the trace elements, the interaction and relationship between two nutrients must be considered. Unfortunately, most research data has considered nutrients separately and therefore, little normative data is available upon which to draw new understanding. More attention must be given to the interactions and relationship among nutrients in addition to examination of single variables. In the future, more complex interactions among three, four, or more nutrients will probably be discovered.

Furthermore, the interaction between genetic and environmental factors where nutrition is one of many environmental factors must be considered. For example, Hurley (1976) has demonstrated that manganese deficiency in prenatal development results in ataxia, a middle-ear defect resulting in a loss of balance. Ataxia is also found in the homozygous *pallid* mouse that has a genetic abnormality also manifesting in this middle-ear defect.These genetically susceptible mice, supplemented with manganese during their pregnancy, can bear normal young, demonstrating the potential for nutrition to overcome abnormal genetic tendencies. This concept may also be relevant to athletes, not in terms of genetic tendencies for impaired function, but rather in terms of optimizing performance. World-class and highly skilled athletes are genetically endowed for athletic performance in terms of body composition, neuromuscular coordination, and metabolism. Many of these individuals are superior in their athletic ability relative to most other adults, and have little apparent need to concern themselves with the potential impact of nutrition on improving their athletic performance. They are so much better than everybody else as it is, so why worry about nutrition? The answer lies in the knowledge of nutrition/environmental interactions. Optimal nutrition for any person, whether or not genetically endowed, has the potential to change biochemical and physiological parameters to approach the person's genetic limitations.

Physiological Correlates

Much of the previous discussion has centered around theoretical metabolic and biochemical concepts. One of the reasons so few examples can be given regarding nutrition and athletic performance is that few examples exist. Normalizing biochemical and physiological parameters is a useful way of approaching nutrition research related to human performance. However, the bottom line is performance, and few well-controlled studies other than those on fuel metabolism address the aspect of improving performance. What is needed to advance the leading edge of nutrition and athletic performance is a variety of performance outcome measurements that are able to relate nutritional status and physiological function in athletes; namely, running faster, working for longer periods of time, reducing fatigue at a given workload, extension of anaerobic threshold, increased strength, and so on.

Furthermore, understanding the correlations between nutritional status and wound healing is beneficial, for many athletes are injured during much of their competitive season. Also important is the knowledge of the relationship between nutrition and immune function in humans. Many athletes have reported that their level and frequency of illness increases as the season progresses. This is quite a paradox, for the end of the season—a time when the athlete is normally peaking and engaged in championship events—is also often the time when the athlete is ill. Without substantial scientific evidence, this illness propensity at the end of the season might be a result of long-term marginal nutritional depletion. The relationship among injury, illness, and nutritional status must be further evaluated in order to better assist athletes to perform optimally when it counts most.

Ergogenic Aids

Potential ergogenic aids include polymerized glucose replacement fluids, octacosanol, carnitine, and neurotransmitter precursors. Initial studies on polymerized glucose solutions indicate that they are isotonic, not drawing fluid into the stomach, and have a gastric emptying rate similar to that of water itself. Polymerized glucose has the potential to maintain blood glucose levels during long-term aerobic exercise, thereby reducing the depletion of glycogen stores, and thus enabling an athlete to perform longer before the onset of fatigue. Studies by Macaraeg (1983) indicate that relative to no fluids or water itself, the ingestion of a polymerized glucose replacement fluid resulted in an increase in work time until exhaustion in well-trained men from 58 to 78 to 103 min for the three treatments, respectively. Unfortunately, there was no group that received a dilute sucrose or fructose solution, making an interpretation of these data difficult. While research studies on polymerized glucose to date have been done in laboratory settings, and the results appear promising, actual field trials for this new product are also needed; in essence, testing whether the ingestion of polymerized glucose can help endurance athletes perform faster, reduce their fatigue at the end of a competition, or recover more quickly.

Substances which facilitate the uptake and catabolism of fatty acids might also be important in preserving glycogen stores and in facilitating the ease with which long-term aerobic activity can be conducted. Two such potential ergogenic compounds are octacosanol and carnitine. The octacosanol studies conducted by Cureton (1972) provide some interesting insights into how exercise physiology research was conducted during those years. By current research standards, measurements simply of work time until exhaustion, speed with which a person can complete a half-mile run, and coordination responses seem indirect. However, these techniques are still of some merit, and the results might shed some useful insight into this often maligned substance. While the generally accepted thinking is that octacosanol, a wheat germ oil extract, is useless in improving performance, some preliminary studies recently conducted in our laboratory indicate that male runners taking octacosanol for 6 weeks have improved work time until exhaustion compared to those taking a placebo or nothing at all.

Runners in all three groups ran approximately 22 min before the intervention. After 6 weeks, those receiving no tablet or placebo again ran for 22 min, while those taking octacosanol ran for 24.5 min. These pilot data were conducted with six or seven subjects in each group, making it difficult to draw firm conclusion regarding the efficacy of octacosanol. However, this data is intriguing in the sense that an improved endurance time might represent a shift in metabolic efficiency, and further studies will hopefully elucidate whether or not this is occurring.

Carnitine is also a substance which might facilitate the combustion of fats, thereby preserving glycogen stores. While carnitine is naturally occurring, primarily in skeletal muscle, some European scientists maintain carnitine supplementation can facilitate the uptake and metabolism of free fatty acids and prolong work time until exhaustion. While pure L-carnitine is not available in the United States at the present time, the D, L-form is available. However, the D-isomer impairs the absorption and utilization of the L-isomer, thereby making the D, L- form much less biologically potent than the pure L-form.

Substances which can maintain the level of neurotransmitters at the neuromuscular junction, basal ganglia, and sympathetic nervous system have a potential of reducing fatigue and improving performance. Angrist and Sidelovsky (1978) studied highly trained college swimmers, runners, and weight throwers taking d-amphetamine in a double-blind, placebo-controlled study. An improvement of 0.6% to 4% was found in performance when subjects took the amphetamine. This substance, of course, has deleterious side effects, and its use in athletics is both unhealthy and illegal. Phosphatidycholine (lecithin) can also maintain neurotransmitter levels and might be beneficial to athletes. Harless and Turbes (1982) provide 10 case studies in dogs which showed dramatic improvement in neuromuscular coordination after choline loading. While case studies give no definitive answers, positive reports suggest the need for a more detailed examination.

Nourishment as Nutrition

In conclusion, a broad concept of nutrition which accommodates mental, emotional, and spiritual factors must be considered. The human body feeds not only on biochemicals; we cannot ignore the dynamic interplay of mind/body/spirit interactions that exert an effect on an individual's metabolism. For example, a study (which I call the bunny rabbit experiment) sheds new light about the complex interactions that affect plaque formation (Nerem, Levesque, and Cornhill, 1980). In this study, rabbits were assessed for plaque formation as a function of consuming a 2% cholesterol diet. This diet proved extremely atherogenic in rabbits, as assessed by removal of the aorta and staining for lipid infiltration. Rabbits fed this diet for 6 weeks under standard laboratory conditions showed approximately 36% of their intimal area stained. Amazingly, however, a second group of rabbits also fed a 2% cholesterol diet for 6 weeks demonstrated only a 6% staining of arterial surface with lipids after an identical dietary regimen. When the investigators reviewed the case report forms and interviewed the technicians, they discovered an interesting corollary. The rabbits that demonstrated a signficantly reduced plaque formation had all been treated by a woman veterinarian in following way: Every morning the woman came into the animal room and removed each rabbit from its cage, played with it, petted it, touched it, whispered in its ears, and then returned it to its cage. This "treatment" took approximately 10 min per rabbit twice a day. How could playing with and touching a rabbit have such a profound influence on arterial plaque accumulation? The study was repeated, this time with the same intervention of touching and human contact with rabbits being controlled as the experimental variable. Almost identical results were found in the repeat study: Animals fed the 2% cholesterol diet had 36% of their aorta stained with plaque, whereas those rabbits touched and petted had only 6% of their area stained.

The implications of such findings demonstrate the importance of emotional and even spiritual contact amongst organisms and how this emotional and spiritual contact can alter physiological functions. This actually is not surprising, for we intuitively and intellectually know that when we are centered and spiritually awakened, we feel better and function better physiologically. These concepts can also be applied to nutrition, or nourishment.

Nourishment includes those factors and processes that stimulate the organism to achieve its full potential on a biological, intuitive, and spiritual level. Too often nutritionists think in strictly biochemical terms; we must consider broader questions of nourishment and recognize that mental, emotional, and spiritual factors can have an equally profound impact on a person's physiological functioning. Many athletes are in a competitive situation for the emotional and perhaps even spiritual stimulation. We hear about the runner's high, which is not merely a manifestation of high endorphin levels; perhaps the high endorphin levels are actually secondary to other processes that are occurring on the emotional and spiritual levels. Thus, the entire concept of nutrition and athletic performance must be reframed. It should include the nourishment provided to the competitive athlete, or merely the recreational individual, so that the physical activity itself has intrinsic rewards that are fulfilling and therefore nourishing to the individual.

As sports nutritionists, or as those interested in this field, we are likely to see an explosion in our understanding of the dynamic interplay of factors involved to help individuals achieve their full biological potential. This should provide us all with the inspiration to help advance the frontiers of this field and be on the leading edge.

References

Angrist, B., & Sidelovsky, A. (1978). Central nervous system stimulants-historical aspects and clinical effects. In L. L. Iversen, S.D. Iversen, & S.H. Snyder (Eds.), *Stimulants, handbook of psychopharmacology* (Vol. 11, pp. 96-165). New York: Plenum Press.

Beecher, H.K. (1955). The powerful placebo. *Journal of the American Medical Association,* **159,** 1602-1606.

Belko, A.Z., Obarzanke, E., Kalkwarf, H.J., Rotter, M.A., Bogusz, S., Miller, D., Haas, J.D., Roe, D.A. (1983). Effects of exercise on riboflavin requirements of young women. *American Journal of Clinical Nutrition,* **37,** 509-517.

Benson, H., & McCallie, D.P. (1979). Angina pectoris and the placebo effect. *New England Journal of Medicine,* **300,** 1424-1429.

Cureton, T.K. (1972). *The physiological effects of wheat germ oil on humans in exercise.* Springfield, IL: Thomas.

Dressendorfer, R.H., & Sockolov, R. (1980). Hypozincemia in runners. *Physician and Sportsmedicine,* **8,** 97-100.

Hackman, R.M., & Keen, C.L. (1983). Trace element assessment in runners. *Federation Proceedings,* **37,** 44.

Harless, S.J., & Turbes, C.C. (1982, August). Choline-loading: Specific dietary supplementation for modifying neurologic and behavioral disorders in dogs and cats. *Veterinary Medicine/Small Animal Clinician,* pp. 1223-1231.

Hurley, L.S. (1976). Interaction of genes and metals in development. *Federation Proceedings,* **35,** 2271-2275.

Lonsdale, D., & Shamberger, R.J. (1980). Red cell transketolase as an indicator of nutritional deficiency. *American Journal of Clinical Nutrition,* **33,** 205-221.

Macaraeg, P.V.J. (1983). Influence of carbohydrate electrolyte ingestion on running endurance. In E.L. Fox (Ed.), *Nutrient hydration during exercise* (pp. 91-98). Ross Symposium, Columbus, OH: Ross Laboratories.

Nerem, R.M., Levesque, M.J., & Cornhill, J.F. (1980). Social environment as a factor in diet induced atherosclerosis. *Science,* **208,** 1475-1476.

2
Weight Control and the Athlete

Janet L. Walberg
VIRGINIA TECH
BLACKSBURG, VIRGINIA, USA

Having a lean body composition is an advantage for most athletic events. Excess body fat increases the energy cost of exercise and therefore explains the negative correlation of percent body fat and performance in events where the body is moved through space. The studies describing the body composition of successful athletes have shown that male endurance runners can be as low as 3% fat. Because they require more essential fat, women athletes are rarely less than 10% fat. However, large individual variations in body composition exist for both sexes.

Wilmore (1983) summarizes the results of a large number of studies that involved assessment of body composition of male and female athletes of various sports and events. Just as it is difficult to define ideal body weight for the general population, no rigid, absolute standards have been developed for body fat content. Each individual probably has a range of acceptable percent fat that is related to his or her body type and metabolism. Therefore, although body composition can affect success, pressure to force the athlete to conform to a particular body fat value may be unnecessary and have unfavorable effects on performance. However, athletes often feel pressure from coaches and parents as well as from peers to attain an optimum body composition. This is reflected in the high concern with eating habits and diet among athletes and is even more apparent in female than male competitors (Snyder, Spreitzer, & Hoy, 1982). While some athletes are interested in weight loss, some want to gain weight. Costill (Moore, 1981) surveyed 360 college athletes and discovered that 33% dieted to lose weight, and 29% changed their habits to gain weight.

Several researchers have attempted to determine the nutrition knowledge of athletes and the sources of this information. Parr, Porter, and Hodgson (1984) found that 61% of high school coaches questioned had no formal background in nutrition. Their primary nutritional concern for their athletes was fluid consumption and balance. However, their athletes' most prominent nutritional interest was weight control. In a more recent survey of Big Ten coaches (Wolf, Wirth, & Lohman, 1979), 39% of the female coaches and 20% of the male coaches were basing their recommendations on objective methods of body structure assessment including skinfold measurements. The majority of the responding Big Ten coaches, however, used no method of body structure assessment, and very few measured nutritional status of their teams. In fact, only 2 teams of the 153 who responded used dietary surveys even though 22% were prescribing vitamin supplements to their athletes. The pressure to lose weight, in conjunction with the relative lack of guidance in proper methods to achieve weight gain or loss safely, has resulted in unusual and sometimes dangerous weight-control techniques.

Several athletic groups are traditionally vulnerable to abnormal nutritional practices to reduce body weight. Wrestlers, for example, are notorious for rapid weight loss schemes to qualify for a lower weight class. Eighty-eight percent of the college wrestlers surveyed by Costill (Moore, 1981) changed their diet to lose weight. These competitors routinely subject themselves to fasting, saunas, diuretics, and other means to achieve amazing weight losses within a few days. This can obviously cause a multitude of physiological and metabolic deviations including electrolyte depletion, blood volume depression, impairment of thermoregulation, tachycardia, and loss of lean body mass (Tipton, 1980). These may have particularly negative consequences for the still growing high school wrestler. Freischlag (1984) followed one high school wrestling team over a season. While the wrestlers had an average 4% drop in body weight, similar control students gained 5.4% of their body weight during this period. This weight loss was concurrent with an impaired grip strength as well as a depressed subjective energy level in these wrestlers during the competitive season. Thus, although the athletes may disregard warnings of health consequences, they may respond to facts concerning effects on athletic performance.

Studies documenting impairments in strength, muscular endurance, and aerobic capacity resulting from rapid weight loss in wrestlers have been summarized in a position statement by the American College of Sports Medicine (1976). A controlled study by Houston, Marrin, Green, and Thompson (1981) demonstrated that a 66% decrease in food intake of a wrestler for 48 hours caused a decrease in quadricep peak torque plus a 25% depression in muscle glycogen stores that were not replenished by a 32-hour fluid/carbohydrate ingestion period. Thus, all of the disturbances incurred as a result of the weight loss cannot be rapidly reversed during the period after weigh-in but before the match.

Ballet dancers are also pressured to achieve extremely thin physiques. Although some have naturally lean body types, Cohen, Chung, May, and Ertel (1982) report that 69% of the dancers dieted for weight loss during the year. Analysis of nutritional intake indicated the average dancer consumed 70% of the recommended dietary allowance (RDA) for energy in spite of the increased energy utilization associated with prolonged workouts. This may be partly to blame for the high incidence of menstral dysfunction in this group.

Cohen et al. (1982) discovered that 37% of a group of professional ballet dancers had a history of amenorrhea. This subgroup had significantly lower body weights for their height than those not exhibiting this abnormality. Some dancers even develop serious eating disorders. Peterson (1982) clearly describes several case studies of ballet dancers with anorexia nervosa or bulimia that appeared to be directly related to their participation in dance.

Runners can also become excessively concerned about their body weight and diet. Smith (1980) and Nelson (1982) describe cases of extreme weight loss resulting from food-aversion behavior simulating anorexia nervosa in young competitive athletes. Smith (1980) noted that this occurred primarily in perfectionistic, rigid athletes who may have been encouraged to lose weight to improve performance by coaches or parents. He suggests that "losing fat becomes a challenge...and food becomes 'the opponent' in a contest" for these athletes. A more recent description of middle-aged male runners (Yates, Leehey, & Shisslak, 1983) depicts an unusual concern over diet and body fat content in "obligatory" runners.

Although these are extreme examples, they illustrate the real concern many athletes have about their body weight and composition.

Unfortunately, most coaches and athletes are not well-informed on nutrition and weight-control techniques. Unrealistic goals may be set. Thus, there is a need to increase assessment of body composition plus provide guidance in proper and effective weight-control techniques for athletes.

Assessment

The body composition method generally accepted as most valid is hydrostatic weighing. This technique requires expensive special equipment usually found in an exercise physiology lab, but equipment may also be purchased for use in an available swimming pool. The density of the body is determined using the change that occurs in body weight from land to total water submersion. Lung residual volume must also be determined or estimated and accounted for. The accuracy of this method is dependent on a cooperative subject whose expulsion of lung air must be complete, or body fat will be overestimated.

Other limitations of this method exists for some athletes. For example, one study (Adams, Mottola, Pagnall, & McFadden, 1982) calculated body fat for some professional football players as less than 0%, which is obviously impossible. Wilmore (1983) suggests that this may be explained by higher density of the lean component of body mass in some athletes. In other words, bone-to-muscle ratio or actual bone mineralization may be higher than the general population. This should be considered when interpreting the results of hydrostatic weighing.

An easier method of body composition assessment, but one that requires an experienced assessor, is skinfold measurement. Various equations call for caliper measurement of the thickness of several skinfold sites and use these to compute body density. Traditionally, equations have been population-specific for age and sex. However, Jackson and Pollock (1978) and Jackson, Pollock, and Ward (1980) have developed generalized equations for each sex based on data from many subjects of different ages and body compostion.

An even easier, yet admittedly less accurate technique is girth measurement. Katch and McArdle (1983) provide equations to estimate body fat based only on three girth measurements. These equations include an adjustment for physically active versus sedentary individuals.

Any of these methods is certainly better than no objective assessment. Even if absolutely valid body fat values cannot be guaranteed, these methods are especially useful longitudinally and for goal setting of individual athletes. Once percent body fat has been determined, a body weight goal can be estimated for the following equation:

$$\text{body weight goal} = \frac{100 \text{ x current lean body weight}}{\text{percent lean body mass desired}}$$

Diet

Nutritional recommendations for weight control must center on total calories but must also consider the sources of calories. Depending on the athlete's sport or activity, energy requirements may be very high. This is most obvious for endurance sports where many hours each day are spent in continuous aerobic exercise. Kirsch and von Ameln (1981) observed the eating patterns of endurance runners and cyclists. The runners were consuming 3,316 kcal while the cyclists ate 5,281 kcal to maintain their body weight while training. However, a javelin competitor, for example, may need no more calories than a moderately active nonathlete.

Exercise has been shown to stimulate as well as depress food intake in humans and animals depending on age, sex, and exercise intensity/duration. Oscai (1973) and Wilmore (1983) review this complex area. However, most work in this field has looked at obese individuals and may not be applicable to average weight athletes.

Wood et al. (1983) noted a decrease in percent fat and body weight in a group of 48 initially sedentary middle-aged men who participated in a year-long running program without dietary recommendations. This suggests that appetite did not keep up with enhanced energy requirements related to the running. Several mechanisms have been suggested to explain the decrease in appetite after exercise. Proposed factors include lactate accumulation (Baile, Zinn, & Mayer, 1971), increased glucose utilization (Christoph & Mayer, 1958), increased body temperature, and hormonal variations (Russek, 1962). Some individuals will later compensate for this negative energy balance while others do not. For example, Edholm, Fletcher, Widdowson, and McCance (1955) noted that food intake was depressed in a group of cadets on days of high-physical activity, but the average food intake increased 2 days later to compensate for the negative energy balance. However, Garrow (1974) interprets the data differently. He points out that if one computes the individual values rather than looking at the aggregate means, only 2 of the 12 cadets actually achieved energy balance. Thus, certain individual athletes may not compensate for the extra energy expenditure of training and will inadvertently lose weight.

Energy needs are difficult to assess. The Food and Nutrition board of the National Academy of Science lists RDAs for calories by sex and age. They point out that these are rough estimates and cannot be used on an individual basis. A more practical method to determine energy need is with a dietary record. Recording of food consumed over a 3- to 7-day period, while body weight is stable, allows calculation of calories required for weight maintenance. Athletes must receive instruction on the record-keeping procedure including portion sizing to ensure accurate estimates. Next, a calorie goal should be set depending on the desire for weight loss or gain. An approximate energy deficit of 3,500 calories must be achieved to lose a pound of fat, while an excess of the same number of calories is necessary to accumulate a pound of muscle. (Although the final energy content of the muscle tissue is less than this amount, extra energy is required for the synthetic process.) Nutritionists recommend limiting expectations of weight gain or loss to 1 to 2 lbs per week. This translated into a 500 to 1,000 calorie adjustment per day. Overzealous losers may inadvertently lose muscle tissue as well as fat. Trying to accelerate weight gain will likely add fat tissue instead of lean tissue. A diet containing fewer than 1,200 cal is generally not recommended because it is virtually impossible to acquire all needed nutrients on a lower energy intake. In fact, while consuming a low-calorie diet, a supplement containing the RDA of vitamins and minerals may be recommended if the athlete is consistently not making wise food choices. Chronic intake of micronutrients below the RDA level may have repercussions on the health and performance of the athlete.

Once a calorie goal has been defined, the composition of the diet should be prescribed. Diets with only a few foods should be avoided. A variety of foods following the four food groups (4 servings fruits and vegetables, 4 servings bread and cereal, 2 to 4 servings dairy, 2 servings meat and protein) is most likely to be satisfying and provide the necessary nutrients. On a percentage basis, the diet should be composed of approximately 10-20% protein, 55-60% carbohydrate, and 25-30% fat.

Athletes are likely to inquire about special protein needs for weight gain. Although the individual's average protein intake should be examined from his or her dietary records, most Americans consume substantially more than the RDA for protein. An existing protein intake buffer is especially likely for an individual consuming a high-calorie diet. Because most Americans consume 10-15% of their calories as protein, few individuals would fall below the RDA of 0.8 gm/kg body weight.

Some researchers suggest that the protein requirement is higher for the athlete than for the sedentary individual. Recommendations of up to 2 gm/kg body weight have been made (Evans, Fisher, Hoerr, & Young, 1983; Laritcheva, Yalovaya, Shubin, & Smirnov, 1978; Yoshimura, 1961). Their reasons for suggesting the increase in the protein requirement include increased muscle protein catabolism, increased muscle protein synthesis, increased red blood cell synthesis, and increased loss of nitrogen through sweat. Considering the last factor, Consolazio et al. (1975) found a positive nitrogen balance in athletes participating in a vigorous training schedule whether they were given 100 or 197 grams of protein per day. Although no benefit was demonstrated on work performance, there was more nitrogen retention in the high-protein consumers. Measurement of nitrogen loss in sweat identified this to be a significant consideration when calculating nitrogen balance in all athletes. This was especially important in the high-protein consumers because nitrogen loss in sweat was accentuated by a high-protein diet. Thus, protein consumption must be evaluated on an individual basis.

Expensive protein supplements are not recommended. The unique individual whose dietary records demonstrate a consistently low-protein intake should increase consumption of foods from the meat and protein or dairy groups. The disadvantages of an excessively high-protein intake include possible anorexia, dehydration, and impaired kidney function. Many popular weight loss diets severely restrict carbohydrate intake. Although weight loss is often rapid on low-carbohydrate diets, a large portion of the weight change is due to body water that had been associated with muscle and liver glycogen (Yang & Van Itallie, 1976). Thus, the athlete gets a false sense of successful fat loss over a short time period. This weight will be quickly regained when carbohydrate is again included in the diet and glycogen is resynthesized. In addition, adequate liver and muscle glycogen stores are important to excercise performance. Although an individual can adapt and regain exercise endurance capacity over a period of weeks on a low-carbohydrate diet (Bogardus, LaGrange, Horton, & Sims, 1981), fatigue occurs more quickly in individuals with recently depleted carbohydrate stores (Bergstrom, Hermansen, Hultman, & Saltin, 1967). Other reasons to avoid a low-carbohydrate diet include the ketosis and lethargy that usually accompany these diets. Therefore, low-carbohydrate diets are self-defeating for the athlete interested in optimal performance.

Athletes working on weight loss should chose nutrient dense foods; these provide large amounts of nutrients per calorie. This generally translates into a decreased intake of high-fat and sugar foods and an increase in less processed high-fiber foods. Again, the four food groups and the USDA/HHS Dietary Guidelines can serve as a baseline for food choices. Continuous dietary intake records may be somewhat inconvenient for the athlete but will allow individualization fo the diet prescription. In addition to noting total calories and nutrients consumed, attention can be paid to parameters like meal spacing. This is especially important to the individual on a weight gain regimen. He or she will need to have a "nibbling" food consumption pattern with many small meals in order to consume the extra calories (Kirsch & von Ameln, 1981). For the athlete who has difficulty ingesting enough calories through normal meals, calorie supplements may be necessary in the form of canned liquid high-energy products. Record keeping also serves to maintain the athletes awareness of their present food consumption and how it relates to their prescription. Someone other than the coach, ideally a nutritionist, could be involved with the athletes to regularly monitor body weight changes, develop diet goals and prescription, examine dietary records, and be a general counselor in these areas. This individual would also be in charge of initial analysis and later reanalysis of body composition changes. Goals and treatments must be tailored to these adaptations.

Exercise

Exercise is also an important component in a weight-control program. Physical activity can aid weight loss or gain. Exercise alone can decrease body weight and fat (Gwinup 1975; Wood et al., 1983), but very gradually. For example, across 55 studies reviewed by Wilmore (1983) that used just exercise training, only a 1.6% average decrease in body fat was noted in programs of 6 to 104 weeks duration. Combining exercise with diet changes can have more rapid and dramatic consequences. Advantages of adding exercise to diet control have been noted in animal (Oscai 1973; Walberg, Mole, & Stern, 1982) as well as human research (Zuti & Golding, 1976). While diet alone causes loss of some lean tissue, exercise helps to decrease muscle tissue loss during weight reduction. This is an important consideration for the athlete.

The exercise prescription must include information on type, intensity, frequency, and duration of exercise. The American College of Sports Medicine has published a position statement on weight loss programs that includes exercise recommendations (1983). The type of exercise most likely to cause a decrease in body fat is continuous exercise stressing the aerobic energy system because fat can only be oxidized aerobically. Examples of good exercises for fat reduction are running, swimming, and bicycling. Although intensity of exercise is a key factor in improvement of cardiovascular function and endurance performance, it is less critical if the goal is weight reduction. A minimal level of 60% of maximum heart rate is recommended. Very intense exercise (greater than 90% $\dot{V}O_2$ max) can only be continued for a short time period and would rely more on carbohydrate than fat as fuel sources. Pollock et al. (1972) compared the anthropometric changes resulting after a 20-week program of exercise conducted 2 days per week for 45 min at either 90% or 80% of maximal heart rate. Although the increase in fitness was the same, the lower intensity exercise group decreased percent fat more than the higher intensity group. However, the change was minimal. The authors suggest that increasing the frequency of the aerobic workout might accentuate body fat loss. In fact, the same research group (Pollock, Cureton, & Greninger, 1969) found this to be the case when they noted a larger decrease in body fat in a group exercising 30 min with interval training 4 days per week compared to a group doing the same training regimen 2 days per week. Increased duration was also beneficial because a comparison between two studies looking only at the groups exercising 2 days per week showed that those going 45 min per session lost body fat while those exercising only 30 min per session did not show a significant change in percent fat over a 20-week program. Gwinup (1975) also did not see a decrease in body weight of overweight women until exercise was continued for at least 30 min per session. Thus, exercise prescription for weight loss should be aerobic and of moderately high intenisty; the duration must be at least 30 minutes, and must be pursued as frequently as can be tolerated by the individual.

Exercise should also accompany dietary recommendations for weight gain. Although aerobic exercise of 30 min per day, 5 days per week caused a slow but steady weight gain and an increase in lean body mass in chronically underweight women (Wilmore, 1973), most exercise programs designed to increase body weight utilize resistance weight training. Mayhew and Gross (1974) put untrained women on a circuit weight-training routine of 40 min per session, three times per week for 9 weeks. Lean body mass plus bicep and forearm girths increased while percent fat declined in these women. Wilmore (1974) tested the adaptations to a similar weight-training program in men and women. Body weight remained stable for both groups, but lean body mass increased by 2.4% in men and 1.9% in women. Upper body girths also increased for both sexes. Weight training may have a different effect depending on initial body weight of the athlete. Brown and Wilmore (1974) followed seven nationally ranked track and field female athletes over a 6-month training program of high volume strength training and general conditioning. Three of the heaviest women (2 were technically obese with body fat greater than 34%) decreased their body weight through a decrease in fat and some gain in lean body mass. Conversely, 3 of the 4 lightest women increased their body weight during this training period.

In summary, increased assessment of body composition, diet, and physical activity of athletes is recommended. Body weight goals can then be developed based on objective criteria specific to the individual. Counseling must include dietary recommendations on calorie content, composition, and spacing of food consumption as well as prescription of appropriate exercise intensity, duration, type, and frequency. Desirable weight changes will result for the athelete through guided moderate modification of diet and exercise patterns.

References

Adams, J., Mottola, M., Bagnall, K.M. & McFadden, K.D. (1982). Total body fat content in a group of professional football players. *Canadia Journal of Applied Sports Science, 7*, 36-40.

American College of Sports Medicine (1976). Position stand on weight loss in wrestlers. *Sports Medicine Bulletin, 11*, 1-2.

American College of Sports Medicine (1983). Position statement on proper and improper weight loss program. *Medicine and Science in Sports and Exercise. 15*, ix-xiii.

Baile, C., Zinn, W., & Mayer, J. (1970). Effects of lactate and other metabolities on food intake of monkeys. *American Journal of Physiology, 219*, 1606-1613.

Bergstrom, J., Hermansen, L., Hultman, E., & Saltin, B. (1967). Diet muscle glycogen and physical performance. *Acta Physiologica Scandinavia, 71*, 140-150.

Bogardus, C., LaGrange, B., Horton, E., & Sims, E. (1981). Comparison of carbohydrate-containing and carbohydrate-restricted hypocaloric diets in the treatment of obesity. *Journal of Clinical Investigation, 68*, 399-404.

Brown, C.H., & Wilmore, J.H. (1974). The effects of maximal resistance training effects on the strength and body composition of women athletes. *Medicine and Science in Sports and Exercise, 6*, 174-177.

Christoph, J., & Mayer, J. (1958). Effect of exercise on glucose uptake in rats and man. *Journal of Applied Physiology, 13*, 269-272.

Cohen, J.L., Chung, S.K., May, P.B., Ertel, N.H. (1982). Exercise, body weight, and professional ballet dancers. *The Physician and Sports Medicine, 10*, 92-101.

Consolazio, C.F., Johnson, H.L., Nelson, R.A., Dramise, J.G., & Skala, J.H. (1975). Protein metabolism during intensive physical training in the young adult. *The American Journal of Clinical Nutrition, 28*, 29-35.

Edholm O., Fletcher, J., Widdowson, E.M., & McCance, R.A. (1955). The energy expenditure and food intake of individual men. *British Journal of Nutrition, 9*, 286-300.

Evans, W.J., Fisher, E.C., Hoerr, R.A., & Young, V.R. (1983). Protein metabolism and endurance exercise. *The Physician and Sportsmedicine, 11*, 63-72.

Freischlag, J. (1984). Weight loss, body composition, and health of high school wrestlers. *The Physician and Sportsmedicine, 12,* 121-126.

Garrow, J.S. (1974). *Energy Balance and Obesity in Man.* New York: American Elsevier.

Gwinup, G. (1975). Effect of exercise alone on the weight of obese women. *Archives of Internal Medicine, 135,* 676-680.

Houston, M. E., Marrin, D.A., Green, H.J., & Thompson, J.A. (1981). The effect of rapid weight loss on physiological functions in wrestlers. *The Physician and Sports Medicine, 9,* 73-78.

Jackson, A.S., & Pollock, M.L. (1978). Generalized equations for predicting body density of men. *British Journal of Nutrition, 40,* 497-504.

Jackson, A.S., Pollock, M.L., & Ward, A. (1980). Generalized equations for predicting body density of women. *Medicine and Science in Sports and Exercise, 12,* 175-182.

Katch, F.I., & McArdle, W.D. (1983). *Nutrition, Weight Control, and Exercise.* Philadelphia: Lea and Febiger.

Kirsch, K.A., & von Ameln, H. (1981). Feeding patterns of endurance athletes. *European Journal of Applied Physiology, 47,* 197-208.

Lavitcheva, K.A., Yalovaya, N.I., Shubin, V.I., & Smirnov, P.V. (1978). Study of energy expenditure and protein needs of top weight lifters. In J. Parizkova & V.A. Rogozkin (Eds.), *Nutrition, physical fitness, and health* (pp 155-164). Baltimore: University Park Press.

Mayhew, J.L., & Gross, P.M. (1974). Body composition changes in young women with high resistance weight training. *Research Quarterly, 45,* 433-440.

Moore, M. (1981). Athletes' diets lack guidance survey says. *The Physician and Sportsmedicine, 9,* 28.

Nelson, R.A. (1982). Nutrition and physical performance. *The Physician and Sports Medicine, 10,* 55-63.

Oscai, L.B. (1973). The role of exercise in weight control. In J. Wilmore (Ed.), *Exercise and sport science reviews* (Vol. 1, pp. 103-123). New York: Academic Press.

Parr, R.B., Porter, M.A., & Hodgson, S.C., (1984). Nutrition knowledge and practice of coaches, trainers, and athletes. *The Physician and Sportsmedicine, 12,* 127-138.

Peterson, M.S. (1982). Nutritional concerns for the dancer. *The Physician and Sportsmedicine, 10,* 137-143.

Pollock, M.L., Broida, J., Kendrick, Z., Miller, H.S., Janeway, R., & Linnerud, A.C. (1972). Effects of training two days per week at different intensities on middle-aged men. *Medicine and Science in Sports and Exercise, 4,* 192-197.

Pollock, M.L., Cureton, T.K., & Greninger, L. (1969). Effects of frequency of training on working capacity, cardiovascular function, and body composition of adult men. *Medicine and Science in Sports and Exercise, 1,* 70-74.

Russek, M. (1962). Conditioning of adrenalin anorexia. *Nature, 193,* 1296-1297.

Smith, N.J. (1980). Excessive weight loss and food aversion in athletes simulating anorexia nervosa. *Pediatrics, 66,* 139-142.

Snyder, E.E., Spreitzer, E., & Hov, C. (1981). A psychosocial profile of adult participants in running and racquetball. *Journal of Sports Behavior, 4,* 186-201.

Tipton, C.M. (1980). Physiological problems associated with the "making of weight." *American Journal of Sports Medicine, 8,* 449-450.

Walberg, J.L., Mole, P.A., & Stern, J.S. (1982). Effect of swim training on the development of obesity in the genetically obese rat. *American Journal of Physiology, 242,* R204-R211.

Wilmore, J.H. (1973). Exercise-induced alterations in weight of underweight women. *Archives of Physical and Medical Rehabilitation, 54,* 115-119.

Wilmore, J.H. (1974). Alterations in strength, body composition, and anthropometric measurements consequent to a 10-week weight training program. *Medicine and Science in Sports and Exercise,* **6**, 133-138.

Wilmore, J.H. (1983). Body composition in sport and exercise: Directions for future research. *Medicine and Science in Sports and Exercise,* **15**, 21-31.

Wolf, E.M.B., Wirth, J.C., & Lohman, T.G. (1979). Nutritional practices of coaches in the Big Ten. *The Physician and Sportsmedicine,* **7**, 113-124.

Wood, P.D., Haskell, W.L., Blair, S.N., Williams, P.T., Krauss, R.M., Lindgren, F.T., Albers, J.J., Ho, & Farquhar, J.W. (1983). Increased exercise level and plasma lipoprotein concentrations: A one-year, randomized, controlled study in sedentary, middle-aged men. *Metabolism,* **32**, 31-39.

Yang, M. & Van Itallie, T.B. (1976). Metabolic responses of obese subjects to starvation and low calorie ketogenic and nonketogenic diets. *Journal of Clinical Investigation,* **58**, 722-730.

Yates, A., Leehey, K., & Shisslak, C.M. (1983). Running—an analogue of anorexia? *New England Journal of Medicine,* **308**, 1251-1255.

Yoshimura, H. (1961). Adult protein requirements. *Federation Proceedings,* **20** (Suppl. 7), 103-110.

Zuti, W.B., & Golding, L.A. (1976). Comparing diet and exercise as weight reduction tools. *The Physician and Sports Medicine,* **4**, 49-53.

3

Effects of Multinutrient Supplementation on Athletic Performance

Michael Colgan
COLGAN INSTITUTE OF NUTRITIONAL SCIENCE
ENCINITAS, CALIFORNIA, USA

Only a few examples of the research of the last decade on effects of nutrient supplementation and dietary changes on physical performance can be covered. The work has developed differently from traditional beliefs about optimal nutrition, the food groups, food exchange lists, the easy availability of the good mixed diet in America, and the Recommended Dietary Allowances (RDAs). (National Research Council, 1980; Recommended Dietary Allowances, 1980). These beliefs still form the basis of most information on nutrition given to athletes and to the public. Yet national nutritional surveys show that Americans of all ages and income levels eat deficient diets.

The First Health and Nutrition Examination Survey (HANES I, 1976) studied 28,000 people, aged 1 to 74, in 65 different areas of the United States.

The survey examined both what people ate and the levels of certain nutrients in their blood and symptoms of malnutrition. Even at the RDA levels that, as we will see for some nutrients, are insufficient for athletes, huge dietary deficiences existed. Nine females out of every 10 had insufficient iron in their diets. One in every 2 females are deficient in calcium. These deficits occurred despite the common "enrichment" of American foods with added iron and calcium. Overall, more than 60% of those surveyed showed at least one nutrient deficit.

The Ten-State Nutritional Survey (1972) of 86,000 people found similar evidence of dietary deficits. This survey was aimed at people on lower incomes, and the findings have sometimes been used to suggest that the deficits were associated with being too poor to afford a sufficient quantity of food. Detailed examination of the data shows that this view is incorrect. To review one example, despite sufficient caloric intake obtained from a wide daily variety of usual American foods, 1 person out of 3 in Southern California was deficient in riboflavin, a nutrient supposedly abundant in milk, eggs, breads, and cereals. Another example is vitamin A. In Texas and Washington, 1 out of 4 men and 1 out of 3 women were deficient in this available nutrient. Overall, two thirds of those tested showed nutrient deficits, even though testing was confined to only 8 of the 49 nutrients essential for human health.

More recent data from the Nationwide Food Consumption Survey (1980) of 15,000 households showed that 1 out of 3 households had diets deficient in calcium (Ca) and pyridoxin. One out of 4 had diets deficient in magnesium (Mg), and 1 out of 5 had diets deficient in iron (Fe) and vitamin A. These data indicate a considerable problem of nutrient deficiency in America despite the easy availability and supposed nutrient sufficiency of "the good mixed diet". Our laboratory regularly finds dietary and physiological evidence of nutrient deficits in people from throughout America who are very conscious of their food and make considerable efforts to eat a healthy diet. In testing approximately 400 adults per year at the RDA levels, we find evidence of deficits in 34%.

One major problem is that the nutrient content of common foods does not accord with the tables commonly used as standards by hospitals and other agencies responsible for dietary planning and advice. Since 1973, we have analyzed multiple samples of 170 different foods. For example: Vitamin C in oranges varies from a trace to 116 mg per 100 grams, over a 100-fold variation.

Vitamin E in fresh wheat germ samples varies from 3.21 mg alpha-TE to 21 mg alpha-TE per 100 grams, a 6-fold variation. Pantothenic acid in samples of stone-ground whole wheat flour varies from 0.3 mg to 3.3 mg per 100 grams, an 11-fold variation. Beta carotene from samples of poor quality pale carrots to samples of excellent quality red-orange carrots, varies from 70 mcg RE (an extreme sample) to 1,850 mcg RE per 100 grams. With a current RDA of 1000 mcg RE, carrots can provide either a completely inadequate supply of vitamin A or an overabundance, depending on the carrots. Ranges for some other common foods tested are shown in Table 1. The American Medical Association (1974) and the U.S. Department of Argriculture (Watt & Merrill, 1963) have published similar findings.

A similar story attends the mineral content of foods. Selenium (SE), for example, varies 200-fold in crops and soils in America (Colgan, 1981b; Patrias & Olson, 1967). Consequently, daily bread intake (six slices of whole wheat) can contain from 200 mcg Se (the tentative RDA) to 12 mcg. Processing of foods also removes minerals. Canning of carrots, for example, removes 70% of their cobalt (Co); canning of tomatoes removes 80% of their zinc (Zn) (Schroeder, 1971).

Such wide variations in the nutrient content of foods are probably a major factor in the high incidence of nutritional deficiencies in American hospitals (Bistrian, Blackburn, Hallowell, & Heddle, 1974; Bistrian, Blackburn, Vitale, Cochran, & Naylor, 1976; Bollet & Owens, 1973; Butterworth, 1974, Klevay, Reck, & Barcome, 1979; Weinsier, Hunker, Krumdieck, & Butterworth, Jr., 1979) where there is no reason to suppose that patients are given anything but the most conscientious nutritional care. A false sense of security in the good mixed diet (on which hospitals usually rely) has been generated

Table 1. Variations in vitamin content of common foods supposedly high in particular vitamins (per 100 grams of fresh raw food)

Vitamin Content	Oranges	Carrots	Tomatoes	Cheddar cheese	Wheat germ	Calf liver	Whole wheat flour
Vitamin A (mcg Re)	-	70-1850	64-302	73-159	-	15-36	-
Vitamin C (mg)	trace-116	trace-8	9-38	-	-	-	-
Vitamin E (mg alpha-TE)	-	trace-1.6	-	-	3.2-21	-	0.8-9.8
Thiamin (mg)	-	-	-	-	0.7-2.1	trace-0.4	trace-0.6
Riboflavin (mg)	-	-	-	-	0.5-1.7	1.0-3.6	-
Niacin (mg)	-	-	-	-	2.0-5.5	8.5-13.4	2.9-7.0
Pantothenic acid (mg)	-	-	-	-	0.9-4.0	5.2-8.8	0.3-3.3
Pyridoxin (mg)	-	-	-	-	0.8-1.1	0.5-0.7	trace-0.4
Cobalamins (mcg)	-	-	-	-	-	55-82	-
Folic acid (mcg)	-	-	-	-	109-362	210-313	33-149

by widely used figures from the United States Department of Agriculture (USDA, 1974) that indicate that the nutrients available per capita per day in Amercia exceed the RDAs for micronutrients (a not entirely coincidental correlation). Even many researchers seem unaware that the USDA figures are based on raw, unprocessed foods. They make no allowances for the losses of nutrients that occur during storage, processing, or food preparation. In contrast, the RDAs do allow for losses and are based on foods as eaten (Recommended Dietary Allowances, 1980). Consequently, if the losses are substantial, the food available will not provide sufficient nutrients.

Thiamin and riboflavin are two micronutrients that athletes may require in amounts greater than the RDAs. USDA figures estimate thiamin and riboflavin available in fresh, raw, unprocessed food, per capita per day as 1.94 mg and 2.33 mg, respectively (USDA, 1974). However, losses before the food is eaten may be considerable. Losses of B vitamins in grapes in cool storage range from 10% to 30% per month (Krochta & Feinberg, 1975). Losses of thiamin in canning of vegetables range from a low of 17% in tomatoes to 83% in lima beans. Losses of riboflavin range from 25% in tomatoes to 67% in lima beans (Watt & Merrill, 1963). Losses in preparation for freezing in peas range from 16% to 34% for thiamin, and from 30% to 50% for riboflavin (Lund, 1975). Losses of thiamin in baking can be almost 100% if PH rises above 6, as it does in most bakery goods that are chemically leavened (Matz, 1975). Even drying meat can destroy 50-70% of its thiamin (Calloway, 1962). Home cooking of vegetables can destroy three quarters of both thiamin and riboflavin (Lachance & Erdman, 1975). Given even this small sampling of possible sources of loss, it is clear that the usual interpretation of USDA figures presents a falsely optimistic picture of available nutrients.

Similar losses in storage and preparation occur for most other vitamins (Harris & Karmas, 1975; Harris & Von Loesecke, 1960). Coupled with large variations in nutrients found for fresh unprocessed foods (see Table 1) and the reduction in absorption and increased excretion of minerals caused by the composition of the American diet (e.g., the high protein level increasing calcium excretion)(Margen, Chu, & Kaufman, 1974) the widespread nutrient deficiencies found in America are not surprising.

Principles of Nutrient Supplementation

In attempting to design optimum nutrition programs for athletes, one must allow for the previously mentioned food problems. The 20 major variables underlying our system of analysis are as follows. Most are self-explanatory, but numbers 1, 2, and 20 require more explanation.

1. Synergy. Nutrients operate by multiple interactions
2. Biochemical individuality
3. Race
4. Family medical history
5. Individual medical history
6. Current medication
7. Lifestyle and environment

8. Living and working environment
9. Exercise
10. Individual diet
11. Bioavailability of nutrients
12. Current nutritional status
13. Air and water pollution
14. Food pollution
15. Food degradation
16. Food processing
17. Food additive combinations
18. Food storage and preparation
19. Excretion of nutrients
20. Physiological dynamics

Synergy

From the influence of Pasteur, medicine still has an emphasis on the use of single substances to affect single conditions. This emphasis has been erroneously carried over into nutrition because the human body evolved to use a *mix* of certain nutrient substances common in nature for its growth, development, and repair. It is the multiple interactions of nutrients, not their single actions, that determine their biological functions (Lavender & Cheng, 1980).

We are all familiar with the controlling role that vitamin D plays in the metabolism of calcium and phosphorus (P) (e.g., Norman, 1977, 1979) and of the synergistic action of the B vitamins (Sauberlich, 1980). We may not be so familiar with the equally important synergy between vitamins E and B_{12}; and vitamin E and zinc (Machlin & Gabriel, 1980); or between trace elements nickel (Ni) and iron; and nickel and copper (Cu) (Nielsen, Hunt & Uthus, 1980; or calcium and magnesium (Shils, 1980); or copper and zinc (Klevay, 1980), or vitamins C, B_6, B_{12}, folic acid, choline, and zinc (Phillips & Baetz, 1981). After plotting the known interactions of nutrients, it becomes more than plausible that every known nutrient may affect the metabolism of every other. Even the known interactions make it clear that supplementing diets with one or other nutrient in arbitrary fashion, as has been the case for most studies of supplementation in athletics (Colgan, 1982; Williams, 1981) is an inadequate approach. Consequently, we use only complete multinutrient supplements.

Biochemical Individuality

The second principle of biochemical individuality was proposed first by Roger Williams in 1950 (Williams, Beerstecher, & Berry, 1950; Williams, 1956). In animals he has shown 20-to-40-fold intersubject variations in nutrient requirements (Williams, 1950, 1967). Data on human subjects are more limited. But Williams, Heffley, Yew, and Bode (1973) found 2-to-7-fold variations in needs for different amino acids, and Hegsted (1963) found a mean 5-fold variation in amino acid needs in normal "healthy" women. Anderson, Perry, Modell, Child, and Mollin (1979) and Clements and Anderson (1980) have further shown that rates of conversion of pyridoxin to their coenzymes may differ significantly in normal individuals and that these differences may be genetically controlled. I suggest that established genetic deficits, such as the deficient binding of thiamin pyrophosphate to its apoenzyme in Wernicke-Korsakoff syndrome, which greatly increases thiamin requirement, are the tip of a genetic iceberg of individual differences in nutrient needs; most of these needs remain to be investigated *because the physiological and behavioral deficits they create are currently accepted as normal human health.*

The RDAs make no allowance for such diversity. Owing to the dearth of appropriate measurements on human subjects, they are based on a wide variety of guesses, assumptions, and speculations, yet come to extraordinarily precise conclusions which generally allow for less than a 2-fold range in human requirements.

In addition to genetic sources of variation in nutrient needs, there are environmental sources of biochemical individuality. The RDA handbook repeatedly acknowledges that temperature, heavy sweating, heavy exercise, and a wide variety of other physiological stressors increase nutrient needs, such as a 4-fold increase in the need for vitamin C (Recommended Dietary Allowances, 1980, p. 74). Because of both genetic and environmental sources of variation, little use is found for the RDAs in attempting to design nutrition programs for athletes.

Physiological Dynamics

Most past experiments in sport nutrition have been single nutrient studies over short time periods that look for pharmacological or ergogenic effects (e.g., Bailey, Carron, Teece, & Wehner, 1970; Grey, Cooper, & Bottenberg, 1970; Howald & Segesser, 1975). Not only do these studies violate the principles of synergy and biochemical individuality, but they fail to address the question of nutritional effects at all. The aim of nutrient supplementation is to build a better body. This action is slow, requiring the turnover of generations of cells. It has to wait for the natural death of suboptimal cells and the growth of new cells in what has become an enriched nutrient medium of body fluids. Red blood cells, for example, live from 60 to 140 days. Therefore, they are completely replaced three to four times per year. Their minimum time scale for replacement is about 3 months.

Deficiency studies provide excellent examples of the time scales involved for nutrient effects. Iron deficiency after pregnancy takes up to 6 months to correct with supplementation (Fairbanks, Fahey, & Beutler, 1971). Diets lacking vitamin C reduce blood levels of ascorbate significantly within 3 weeks. But it takes 4 months for enough cells to die and new defective cells to grow before the first degenerative signs of scurvy appear (Marks, 1968). In addition, nutrition for athletes has to encompass the physiological stresses and probable specific nutrient deficits caused by training and competition, for elite athletes today, even sprinters, are all endurance athletes because they need to train for 4 hours or more daily.

Water

Water is the most important nutrient in the body—and often the most neglected. Even the bones are a quarter water. Brain and muscles are three-quarters water. A 150-lb athlete holds about 90 pints of plain water. During medium intensity training all of it must be replaced every 8 days (Consolazio, Metoush, Nelson, Harding, & Canham, 1963). Thankfully, athletes are now advised to drink freely during training and competition, but there still lingers a shadow of the old madness that water might somehow inhibit performance, add weight, or cause cramps. In addition, thirst sensors in the throat and gut are inhibited during strenuous exercise (Costill & Miller, 1980). Uninformed athletes tend to neglect fluid intake. During marathons and triathlons and over very long training sessions, many laboratories (e.g., Costill, Krammer, & Fisher, 1970) have recorded losses of 8 to 9% (12- to 16-lb bodyweight) in athletes who compete "dry."

Even a small level of dehydration reduces performance. Using a diuretic, Fink (1982), purposely dehydrated runners by only 2-3% (3-to-4-lbs bodyweight). They then raced over 1,500, 5,000, or 10,000 meters. This small level of dehydration reduced performance by 3% at 1,500 meters and 6 to 7% at the longer distances. It is not surprising that performance deteriorates with dehydration. Even if body temperature remains below 104°F because of advantageous external temperature and humidity, a loss of 5% body water means twice that loss of water from the blood because blood plasma is the major source of water for sweat. The attendant problems caused for oxygenation of brain and muscles are amply documented (e.g. Greenleaf, 1982). Even though most elite athletes now realize the dangers of dehydration, many are still unaware how difficult it is to drink sufficiently to offset the effects of dehydration during competition. Consider the marathon as an example. A runner drinks at Miles 4, 7, 10, 13, 16, 19, and 22, seven drinks in all of about 5 to 6 oz for a total of about 40 oz. Average sweat loss at best marathon effort under temperate conditions is about 6 oz per mile. The total requirement is at least 160 oz, leaving a huge 120 oz deficit.

Ways to ensure prehydration are by copious drinking of water every day and up to 20 min before an event and by carbohydrate loading, which is discussed later. Maximum prehydration for a 150-lb athlete is estimated to be 40 oz by water loading and 50 oz by carbohydrate loading; this reduces weight loss in a marathon to 4%. Our findings agree with earlier studies (e.g., Moroff & Bass, 1965). To date we have measured 18 male and 5 female marathoners with and without prehydration under similar conditions of temperature, humidity, training, and course; these subjects ranged in age from 21 to 47, and their times varied from 2:21 to 3:38. Of course, effects of water and carbohydrate supplementation are inextricably confounded, but overall mean performance improvement with prehydration was 9.1 min.

Simple and Complex Carbohydrates

Most athletes should be advised to eat a diet of 80% complex carbohydrates, 10% fats, and 10% proteins. Four related aspects of this diet deserve note here: stability of blood glucose, use of fiber, chromium supplementation, and maintenance of muscle glycogen stores. Keller and Schwarzkopf (1984) have shown that *preexercise* snacks of simple carbohdryates (sugar) cause a rapid rise in blood glucose, then a rapid fall; these snacks increase the rate of muscle glycogen depletion and generally impair performance (Bonen, Malcolm, Kilgour, MacIntyre, & Belcastro, 1981; Costill, Coyle, Dalsky, Evans, Fink, & Hoopes, 1977; Foster, Costill, & Fink, 1979). Those elite athletes who spend most of their waking hours either in preexercise periods or exercising should be advised to avoid simple carbohydrates altogether.

Other reasons why athletes (and everyone) should avoid sugar includes increased uric acid levels (Kelsay, Behall, Moser, & Prather, 1977; Solyst, Michaelis, Reiser, Ellwood, & Prather, 1980) and reduced glucose tolerance (Cohen, Teitelbaum, Balogh, & Groen, 1966; Reiser, Handler, Gardner, Hallfrisch, Michaelis, & Prather, 1979). High-sugar diets disorder lipid metabolism. In both animal and human studies, sugar feeding raises cholesterol and triglycerides (Reiser, 1983). Apart from the established risk of cardiovascular disease (Tzagournis, 1978; Kolata, 1984) it is believed that raised levels of blood lipids are associated with impaired athletic performance, although the hard data to confirm it is not available as yet. However, in 12 years of testing more than 1,700 people, I have not found a single case of an athlete who is performing well with cholesterol level over 200 mg/dl or a triglyceride level over 125 mg/dl.

Not all simple carbohydrates have the same yo-yo effect on blood glucose, and not all supposedly complex carbohydrates avoid this effect. It is now established that the simple sugar fructose does not cause a large or rapid rise in blood glucose, whereas the supposedly complex starches of potato and wheat do (Crapo, Insel, Sperling, & Kolterman, 1981; Bantle, Laine, Castle, Thomas, Hoogwerf, & Goetz, 1983). Jenkins, Wolever, and Taylor, (1981) proposed that carbohydrates be classified into a glycemic index based on the blood glucose response evoked and compared to the response to an equivalent amount of glucose. I have used a modified form of this index with all athletes (since 1981). Table 2 advises athletes to avoid refined flours, certain fruits and vegetables, honey and glucose, and to eat all types of beans, some whole grains, apples, and oranges.

Fructose is also included in the advised list because during competition, it spares glycogen stores. Levine, Evans, Cadarette, Fisher, & Bullen, (1983), for example, found that if fructose is taken even immediately prior to exercise, it hardly affects blood glucose levels and significantly spares muscle glycogen. In a 30-minute treadmill test, subjects used less than 50% of the glycogen used by control subjects who were fed glucose or plain water.

Fructose poses other problems, however, and athletes should be cautioned against its use as a regular part of the daily diet. It seems to be more rapidly converted to triglycerides than to glucose and readily raises triglyceride levels in primates (Kritchevsky, et al., 1980). It also raises uric acid levels above normal ranges in human subjects (Emmerson, 1974; Heuckenkamp & Zollner, 1971).

Fiber

Low intake of dietary fiber, which occurs in most diets low in complex carbohydrates, causes detrimental physiological changes (Painter, 1964). However, until the report of the British Royal College of Physicians in 1980 it was not clear just how detrimental these changes are to human functioning. Dietary

Table 2. Comparison of common foods with an equivalent substitute having a lower glycemic index

Eat less of these foods	Glycemic index	Eat more of these foods	Glycemic Index
Sugars		*Sugars*	
Glucose	100	Fructose	20
Honey	87		
Vegetables		*Vegetables*	
Parsnips	98	Soybeans	15
Carrots	90	Kidney Beans	30
White potatoes	70	Lentils	25
		Sweet Potatoes	48
Fruit		*Fruit*	
Bananas	65	Apples	36
Raisins	68	Oranges	40
Dates	72		
Grains		*Grains*	
White flour spaghetti	56	Whole wheat spaghetti	40
Cornflakes	85	Oats	48
White rice	70	Brown rice	60
White flour pancakes	66	Buckwheat pancakes	45
White bread	76	Whole wheat bread	64

Table 3. Fiber "10" each contains 10 grams of dietary fiber

Grains	Vegetables	Fruits
½ cup All Bran	½ cup mixed beans	3 pears
1 cup rolled oats	½ cup peas, lentils	3 bananas
1 cup whole grain cereal	1 cup peanuts	4 peaches
2 cobs sweet corn	2 cups soybeans	4 oz blackberries
3 slices whole rye bread	3 cups steamed vegetables	5 apples
3 cups puffed wheat	4 servings mixed salad	6 oranges
4 slices whole wheat bread	4 large carrots	6 dried pear halves
4 shredded wheat	4 cups sunflower seeds	10 dried figs
4 oz bag popcorn	5 cups raw cauliflower	20 prunes

fiber stabilizes blood glucose. Studies with prediabetics and diabetics leave little doubt that daily dietary fiber intake at about the level recommended by Trowill & Burkitt (1981) stabilizes blood glucose so effectively that many patients do not have to succumb to the use of insulin or can reduce or even eliminate this medication (e.g., Camarini-Davalos & Hanover, 1979; Spiller & Kay, 1980). To simplify athletes' use of fiber the "Fiber 10" list on Table 3 is provided with the advice to eat 40 grams per day.

Chromium

Chromium (Cr) also stabilizes blood glucose (Mertz, 1979); however, it is not abundant in our food, so Cr deficiencies are common in America (Glinsmann & Mertz, 1966; Liu & Morris, 1978). Body Cr is used up rapidly in glycogen metabolism and is likely to be even more deficient in athletes. If the norm is set at the upper level of the tentative RDA of 50-200 micrograms per day (Recommended Dietary Allowances, 1980), 70% of the athletes are deficient in this essential mineral. The upper limit is taken because of the high use of Cr during exercise. Running a 10 K race, for example, increases urinary excretion of Cr almost 5-fold. Total daily urinary CR of runners per running day is twice that of a nonrunning day (Anderson, Polansky, Bryden, Roginsky, Patterson, & Reamer, 1982). Also Riales and Albrink (1981) have shown that 200 micrograms of supplemental Cr per day improves blood glucose stability and blood insulin stability in healthy males on normal diets.

Carbohydrate Loading/Maintaining Glycogen Stores

It is possible for a club level athlete to double his or her usual level of muscle glycogen by a hard-depletion run of 90 min, then a high-carbohydrate diet for the next 48 to 72 hours. For an elite athlete, depletion requires a longer effort and the loading effect is smaller. Nevertheless, anyone entering a long event who does not use this technique is at serious disadvantages regarding both energy and fluid stores. For every gram of extra glycogen stored, the body also retains 2.7 grams of water. Metabolism of the glycogen during exercise yields another 0.6 grams of water per gram (Greenleaf, Olsson, & Saltin, 1969; Locksley, 1980). Doubling the muscle glycogen store from about 400 to 800 grams for a 150-lb athlete yields about 50 oz of extra water.

Costill (1979) and others agree that the commonly used, uncomfortable, and possibly detrimental high-protein phase following depletion is unnecessary. In fact, the question for elite athletes is not isolated carbohydrate loading at all, or phases of this or that form of diet, but a continuous stable diet to ensure the continuous maintenance of glycogen stores necessary for long daily training.

This need for continuous maintenance is another reason complex carbohydrates are strongly recommended because they restore muscle glycogen better than simple carbohydrates. Costill, Sherman, Finks, Maresh, Witten, and Miller (1981) fed male runners either a 70% simple or 70% complex carbohydrate diet for 48 hours following a depletion run. The result was 20% greater glycogen repletion for those on the complex carbohydrates. The list shown in Table 4 provides athletes a basis of a continuous diet of up to 80% complex carbohydrates. The mean achieved level is 68% for athletes tested over 1 year on this program by the Colgan Institute.

Table 4. Top twenty grains and legumes for athletes

Best protein sources over 20% protein under 20% fat	Best carbohydrate sources under 5% fat over 70% carbohydrate
Soybeans	Brown Rice
Split Peas	Whole Barley
Kidney Beans	Whole Buckwheat
Dried Whole Peas	Whole Rye
Wheatgerm	Foxtail Millet
Lima Beans	Wild Rice
Black-Eyed Peas	Whole Corn
Lentils	Pearl Millet
Black Beans	Whole Wheat
Navy Beans	Rolled Oats

Toxic Metals

In 1979 the surgeon general indicted the hundreds of pollutants that now contaminate the food, water, and air as major causes of degenerative diseases. As such, they also must be detrimental to athletic performance. Various sources have indicated that urban cadmium (Cd) pollution of air, water, and food is approximately 50 micrograms intake per urban person daily, a level that is toxic to all mammal systems (National Academy of Sciences, 1974-78, Underwood, 1977). The prevalent practice of using fertilizers made from dried sewage sludge results in high concentrations of Cd (and other metals) in vegetables (e.g., Stoewsand, 1980) that became another source of unavoidable food pollution.

Aluminum (Al) is also a prevalent pollutant because of its use in food containers, cooking utensils, foil wrap, baking powders, antacids, toothpastes, and cosmetics. Long-term contamination is associated with bone mineral loss and neurological impairments (Crapper, Krishman, & Quittkat, 1976; Spencer, Kramer, Osis, Waitrowski, Norris, & Lender, 1980). Athletes must have essential mineral balances, and evidence from animal studies indicates that Al interferes with incorporation of phosphorus (P) into ribonucleic and deoxyribonucleic acids and also disrupts the balance of adenosine mono-, di-, and tri-phosphates (Ondreicka, Kortus, & Ginter, 1971).

Mercury (Hg) pollution from multiple sources is also well known. Like Al, it rarely causes clear-cut disease in America today. However, it is associated with clinical depression, muscle tremor, dizziness, and diarrhea at levels above 5.0 ppm in hair or 0.20 micrograms/gram in whole blood (Underwood, 1977); these same levels are sometimes found in urban athletes. The concerns with athletes is in the preferential incorporation of Hg into erythrocytes (Aberg, Ekman, Falk, Greitz, Persson, & Snihs, 1969). It is of special concern when one 8-oz serving of fish can deliver in excess of the tentative maximum safe daily intake of 0.03 mg (Bradley & Hugunin, 1980).

Supposed "safe" levels of lead (Pb) pollution have been progressively lowered over the years because of health problems connected with it. Although the 1980 guidelines of 150 micrograms per day for a 5-year-old child are still quoted, the FDA no longer quotes any level as safe. Every sample of canned food I have tested (seamed cans) has been lead contaminated. Mitchell and Aldous (1974) bought 122 canned foods and beverages over the counter in upstate New York. Average lead contamination was 80 micrograms per pound. In 1981, *Consumer Reports* found that an 8-oz serving of canned beans can also contain 100-120 micrograms of lead.

These examples illustrate that athletes frequently carry body burdens of toxic metals, which medical evidence indicates are detrimental to health. These toxic metals must be assessed and removed. Elevated levels of the essential metals Cu and Ni and of the toxic metals Hg and Al in the hair of eight runners living in New York City are shown in Figure 1. Shaded areas are norms for athletes who have been on my program for more than 1 year.

These athletes are issued lists of contamination sources to avoid. Those on tap water are switched to distilled water. Vitamins and minerals known to neutralize or aid excretion of specific metals are used, and micronutrient deficits that facilitate body absorption of specific metals are corrected. For example, Fe and vitamin C reduce body Cd (Spivey, Fox, Jacobs, Lee Jones, Fry, & Stone, 1980); Se and Zn reduce Cd toxicity (Mason & Young, 1967); Se and vitamin E detoxify Hg in the body (Ganther, 1980); and marginal deficits of Zn, Fe, and Ca facilitate Pb absorption. Conversely, supplementation with Fe, Zn, and vitamin E reduces body Pb (Mahaffey & Rader, 1980; Levander, Welch, & Morris, 1980).

Results illustrated in Figure 1 show significant reductions in all four metals, although Cu and Hg remained well above acceptable levels (shaded). Five of the 8 runners showed significant improvements in 10 K performance compared with their improvements over the 6 months prior to the study, and with improvements of a matched pairs control group who were given a general multivitamin and mineral supplement without regard to specific levels of vitamins or metals. The study was not blinded. That effects of reductions in levels of toxic metals are inextricably confounded with any beneficial effects of the supplements and dietary changes is also clear.

Figure 2 is derived from a study on 16 New Zealand children with learning and behavior problems (Colgan & Colgan, 1984). Over 21 weeks of nutrient supplementation, plus avoidance of sources of toxic metal contamination, the group showed significant improvement in both behavior and learning compared with a control group treated identically except for the nutritional manipulations. As illustrated in the figure, there were significant reductions in body burdens of Cd, Pb, and Hg. Levels of Cu increased slightly, although they remained within the reference range, an indication that the effect was not a general leaching of metals from the body.

I would like to present more direct data that reduction of toxic metals improves athletic performance, but our case studies, however dramatic, have little scientific weight. Nevertheless, it seems more than a reasonable inference that the body performs better when it is not being poisoned.

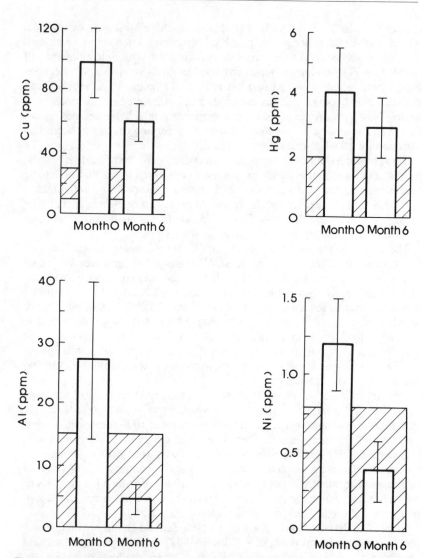

Figure 1. Hair concentrations of toxic metals in 8 male runners over a 6-month nutrition program. Shaded areas are reference ranges for healthy adults commonly cited by reference laboratories

Iron, Folic Acid, B$_{12}$

Since 1974 computerized records of blood fractions of athletes going through my nutritional programs have been kept. From these reference ranges for a variety of blood fractions under various conditions have been derived on first examination, at 1 year, 2 years and so on, and during periods of greatest gains

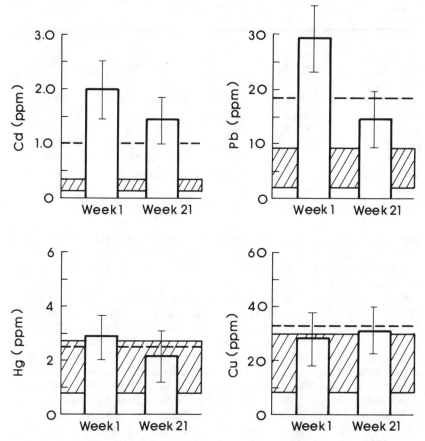

Figure 2. Hair concentrations of Cd, Pb, Hg, and Cu in 16 children with learning difficulties and behavior problems, on referral and after 21 weeks nutritional intervention. Shaded areas are means ± 2SD for 192 healthy, non-smoking adults. Dashed lines are maximum safe concentrations commonly cited by reference laboratories

in performance. In Table 5 are shown the ranges for serum iron, RBC, hematocrit, and hemoglobin compared with reference ranges commonly used in medicine. Performance ranges relate only to accurately measureable improvements, that is, times, weights, or distances.

Note that the ranges are narrower than the medical ranges and that the trend is for levels of all variables to rise with time on the program and during periods of best performance increments. Earlier versions of these tables indicated that the average diets of athletes possibly may not provide a sufficient amount of the hematopoietic factors (Fe, folic acid, vitamin B_{12}) to offset losses of red blood cells with heavy training, losses of iron in sweat, and a consequent decline of the body's capacity to use oxygen. The surveys reviewed indicate

Table 5. Reference ranges for athletes' serum iron, RBC, hematorcrit, and hemoglobin (*N* = 124 males, 79 females)

Fraction	Medical ranges (metpath)	1st exam ranges	1-Year exam ranges	Performance high ranges
Serum Iron mcg/dl	45-200	95-184	113-179	129-186
RBC Mill/cu mm	3.8-6.8	3.6-5.6	4.1-6.0	4.5-6.6 (M)
	3.9-5.8	3.3-5.1	3.9-5.9	4.3-5.9 (F)
Hematocrit %	35-54	40-49	41-49	42-48 (M)
	36-46	33-42	36-44	39-46(F)
Hemoglobin gm/dl	11.5-18.5	13.0-16.3	13.6-16.8	14.2-17.4 (M)
	11.0-16.0	12.1-14.7	12.0-15.2	13.5-15.8 (F)

that Fe is deficient in the usual American diet, even at the RDA level (Hanes, 1976; Nationwide Food Consumption Survey, 1980). In fact 1 out of every 2 American women is likely to be Fe deficient most of her adult life (Sturgeon & Shoden, 1975).

Athletes are likely to be doubly deficient, because even if they did get the RDA of 10 mg for men and 18 mg for women, it is not enough to offset training losses. These may be 0.5 mg per hour or more (Consolazio, Johnson, & Pecora, 1963; Veller, 1968). A maximum effort in a marathon has been reported to result in losses of 4.5 mg Fe per liter of sweat (Williams, 1981). With 3 liters sweat loss being not uncommon, Fe loss might total 13.5 mg in one race. Because athletes' diets tend toward low meat, therefore a low intake of the better absorbed heme iron, high fiber, high phytates, high calcium, and magnesium—all of which inhibit Fe absorption—overall absorption can be estimated at about 6%. To replace 13.5 mg Fe under these conditions, the athletes would need to eat 225 mg Fe, a difficult task unless very carefully supplemented. From the principle of synergy covered earlier, simply popping iron pills is ineffective although a common practice among athletes. It is not surprising therefore that numerous reports on athletes show low iron stores (e.g., Ehn, Carlmark & Hoglund, 1980), iron deficiency (e.g., Parr, Bachman, & Moss, 1984) and low hemoglobin levels (e.g., Clement, Asmundson, Medhurst, 1977).

Folic acid is also commonly deficient in American males and females. (Ten-State Nutritional Survey, 1972). This deficit occurs despite evidence from assays of American diets that folacin content ranges from 379 mcg, just below the RDA of 400 mcg, to 1097 mcg (Butterworth, Santini, & Frommeyer, 1963). Unfortunately, determination of the RDA has been unduly influenced by the work of Herbert (1962, 1968, 1971) who estimates the total body pool of folacin in an adult male at 7.5 $\pm$ 2.5 mg. This figure is probably far too low because autopsy analysis of folacin in human livers shows that the liver alone contains this amount (Food and Nutrition Board, 1977). Even at the RDA of 800 mcg advised during pregnancy, folic acid is deficient in about one third of pregnant women, even among those taking folacin supplements (Baker & De Maeyer, 1979). Also, the RDA is based only on minimum amounts of folacin that prevent megaloblastic anemia and that maintain serum levels over short periods (6 weeks) (Recommended Dietary Allowance, 1980). It is unwise to place confidence in the figures, especially for athletes with their high level of blood replacement caused by the physiological damage of heavy training. After extensive reviews of the literature (Food and Nutrition Board, 1977; Rodriguez, 1978) and from my own data, folacin requirements of athletes can be estimated at 2.0-6.0 mg ingested per day. I have used supplements between these levels daily with athletes for periods of 1 to 11 years without side effects and with beneficial results.

The essential interactions between folic acid and vitamin B_{12} in erythrocyte function and in immune function are well documented (e.g. Minson, Piczfalusy, Glover & Olson, 1976; Lavoie, Tripp & Hoffbrand, 1974). However, unlike folic acid, B_{12} is poorly absorbed. The optimal body store, hence the optimal intake, is unknown (Recommended Dietary Allowances, 1980). The RDA of 3.0 micrograms is based on scant data, an extraordinarily low figure in the face of the huge reported injected amounts of up to 1000 mg (Williams, 1981) commonly used in athletics. Although no scientific justification exists for such injections, their persistent use by intelligent coaches and physicians with reported highly beneficial results, suggests there is much to learn about B_{12} metabolism. Unfortunately, controlled studies of B_{12} with athletes (Williams, 1981) suffer from the single nutrient and short term course faults discussed earlier. I use oral B_{12} supplements between 100 and 300 micrograms. Absorption at this level of intake occurs not only by the medium of Castle's intrinsic factor, but also by simple diffusion (Herbert, 1972). An absorption of 6% reducing to 4% at the highest dosage can be estimated.

Red Blood Status

As Table 6 indicates, levels of hemoglobin, hematocrit, and RBC tend to rise with the length of time athletes are on the nutritional programs and tend to be highest during periods of greatest improvements in performance; these are often periods of heaviest training. Such trends are directly contrary to studies of athletes who enter a heavy training period on average or unsupplemented diets. These athletes tend to show reductions in iron stores and losses of red blood status (e.g., Frederickson, Puhl, & Runyan, 1983).

Evidence for development of this "sports anemia" is a study of Dressendorfer, Wade, and Amersterdam (1981). Twelve experienced male marathoners ran 312 miles over a 20-day period, averaging 17 miles a day (double their usual mileage) at 8.5 min/mi. Although required running speed was not stressful, all subjects showed large reductions in hemoglobin, hematocrit, and RBC count, as shown in Figure 3. Referring the final figures for Day 20 to reference ranges for athletes on the programs (Table 6), RBC count is at the low end of the range for the 1-year exam range and below the range for periods of high performance. Hematocrit and hemoglobin are below the low end of both ranges. Dressendorfer, et al., did not test the effects of the deficient red blood status on maximum performance.

Depriving a control group of athletes of hematopoietic supplementation in order to confirm that our programs prevent sports anemia cannot be justified, so I might be forgiven for using the data from Dressendorfer, et al. Since 1975

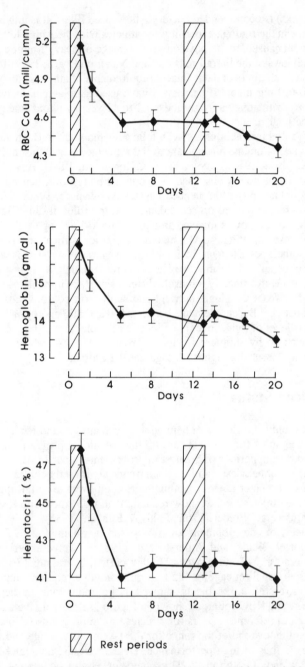

Figure 3. Red blood cell concentration hematocrit and hemoglobin during 312-mile road-running race held over 20 days. Values are means ± SEM (vertical bars) for 12 marathon runners (Redrawn from Dressendorfer, R.H. et: JAMA 1981, **246**, 1215-1218)

not one of my athletes has shown the sort of reduction in red blood status Dressendorfer et al. found, no matter how much training was increased. On the contrary, the athletes usually show the opposite trend. The records of 10 male and 6 female distance runners over the first 6 months of nutritional supplementation is illustrated in Figure 4. As is usual in enthusiastically starting a new program, all subjects documented *increased* training regimens and maintained them throughout to a reasonable degree. Despite the heavier training, the three blood fractions did not show a significant decline in the first 30 days and in

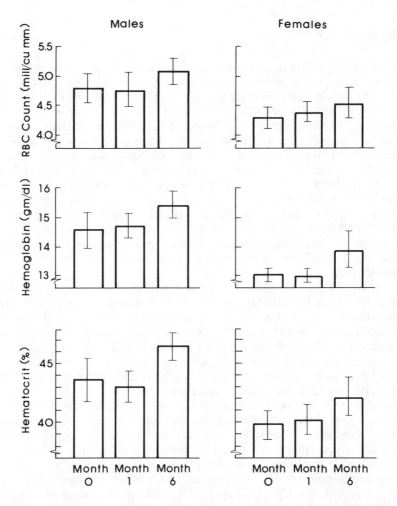

Figure 4. Changes in red blood cell count, hemoglobin and hematocrit after 1 month and 6 months nurtitional supplementation and increased levels of training in 10 male and 6 female distance runners

6 months showed substantial increases. For males all three increases were statistically significant at the $p < 0.05$ level (t-test). For females, hemoglobin and hematocrit increases were significant at the $p < 0.05$ level (t-test).

Because of wide variations in training, it was not possible to determine whether performance improvements were significant. Nevertheless, resulting similar hematological changes with altitude training are associated with improved oxygen uptake and improved running performance (Margaria, 1967); thus a reasonable inference can be made: the "improvements" in red blood status, which can be reliably achieved with nutritional supplementation, are beneficial to athletes. Also, unlike the very temporary effects of altitude training, the supplementation effects can be maintained indefinitely.

Performance

Other reliable effects of nutritional supplementation can be found, including reductions in resting pulse and blood pressure, and improvements in blood liped status. Briefly, it is plausible that there is an optimal level for each nutrient for each individual at any give time. Compilation of the variables began 12 years ago. The variables from the literature (including the veterinary literature) and from cases in two clinics suggested possible vitamin and mineral deficits and possible optima of human functioning. Testing many hundreds of variables over the years, I have gradually reduced the number to about 270 I now use. From these a matrix of the weighted principle relations between each was developed; then computer programs were devised to solve this matrix and to calculate a nutrient supplement and diet designed specifically for an individual subject. Ranges of nutrients used are shown in Table 6.

The matrix has enabled me to carry out some studies with nutrients that have provided startling data: one on explosive effort performance and two on endurance performance.

For the first study, (Colgan, 1982) four experienced marathon runners were used (See Figure 5). Individual supplements were designed for each, who were then randomly assigned in pairs of two groups of 2. Group 1 was given supplements during the first 3 months. Group 2 was given supplements during the second 3 months. During the first 3 months, Group 2 was given placebos which looked and tasted like the supplements. (The same was given to Group 1 in the second 3 months.) Changes in performance (seconds/mile) were measured over 20+ mile runs or marathon races. A similar study was conducted on explosive power performance using 4 experienced weight lifters. (Colgan 1982)(Figure 6). For supplemented lifters, there was a percentage increase in strength in the military press and clean and jerk combined of between 4 and 8%, compared with 0 to 2% for unsupplemented lifters.

The final study was a double-blind performed with 10 marathon runners. However, complete data was available only for 8 subjects. (Table 7). The subjects were matched in pairs for age, for the number of previous marathons, and for their best marathon times. Individual supplements were designed for each; they were then randomly assigned to either an experimental or a control group. The experimental group received supplements and the control group was given placebos. Best marathon times before the study and at its conclu-

Table 6. Vitamins, co-factor, and trace elements used for supplementation

Substance	U.S. RDA 1980-male 23-50	U.S. RDA 1980-female 23-50	Ranges used for supplements/diem
Retinol/Beta Carotene	1000 mcg RE	800 mcg RE	1000-9000 mcg RE
Thiamin	1.4 mg	1.0 mg	40-600 mg
Riboflavin	1.6 mg	1.2 mg	30-250 mg
Niacin/Niacinamide	18 mg	13 mg	100-1000
Pantothenic Acid			50-1000 mg
Pyridoxin	2.2 mg	2.0 mg	40-300 mg
Cobalamins	3.0 mcg	3.0 mcg	100-300 mcg
Folacin	400 mcg	400 mcg	2-30 mg
Biotin			2-100 mg
Inositol			100-1000 mg
P-Amino-Benzoic Acid			100-500 mg
Phosphatidyl Choline			200-2000 mg
Ascorbates	60 mg	60 mg	2000-16,000 mg
Cholecalciferol	5 mg	5 mg	5-62 mcg
Tocopherols	10 mg TE	8 mg TE	200-1600 mg TE
Zinc	15 mg	15 mg	50-150 mg
Iron	10 mg	18 mg	30-60 mg
Iodine	150 mcg	150 mcg	0.15-1.0 mg
Calcium	800 mg	800 mg	1000-3500
Magnesium	350 mg	300 mg	1000-2000 mg
Maganese			20-100 mg
Phosphorus	800 mg	800 mg	200-2000 mg
Potassium			198-5000 mg
Copper			0-5 mg
Molybdenum			50-500 mg
Chromium			0.3-1.0 mg
Selenium			0.2-1.0 mg

Note. Some essential elements are not used or are used in only small quantities because of evidence of ample or excessive amounts of these substances in the diet or the tissue of a majority of subjects. Nickel and copper are two examples.

sion are shown in Table 7. The experimental group (supplemented) showed improvements of between 9.7 min and 28.4 min in the marathon. Between the two groups, the experimental group improved 17.73 min, and the control group improved 6.72 min. The 11.02 min superiority of the supplemented group was significant ($t=4.03$, $df=3$, $p < 0.05$). Some improvement of the control group was expected because of the placebo effect and effects of the training. (In general, people improve with training.) The improvement of the control group is comparable to improvements shown in the running literature for long-distance runners who are taken into studies on rates of improvement and simply follow their usual training patterns (See Figure 7).

Other differences between the groups were also found. Supplemented athletes had 35% fewer injuries and 81% fewer infections over a period of the study than the athletes on placebos. Supplemented athletes showed a reliable drop in their already low resting pulse rates of 9.1 beats per min. The pulse rates of the control group did not change significantly. Resting blood pressure

of supplemented athletes also dropped reliably. Their already low cholesterol levels also dropped reliably for the supplemented athletes but did not change for those on placebos. Also, the rate of performance improvement was significantly greater for supplemented athletes than were their improvements over the 12 months prior to the study (Figure 7). The rate of performance improvement of the control group remained unchanged.

In sum, six forms of measurement were taken and the following changes were found:

- a reliable change in physiological variables;
- a significant improvement in performance over the control group;
- a significant increase in rate of performance improvement compared with performance improvement over the 12 months prior to the study;
- a reliable reduction in cholesterol levels;
- a reduction in illnesses; and
- a reduction in injuries.

All these changes suggest that supplementation conferred a decided advantage. This paper has summarized some of the important changes over the last decade in an attempt to provide athletes with optimum nutrition. This new approach, which incorporates principles of synergy, biochemical individuality,

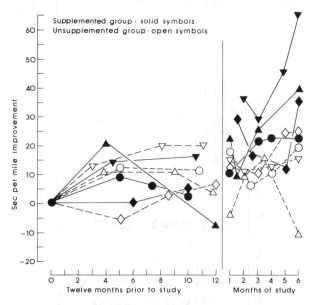

Figure 7. Seconds per mile improvement in time trials or races of 20± miles (including marathons for 8 athletes for 12 months prior to supplementation and for 6 months supplementation of subjects E1-E4

physiological dynamics, and the special nutrients needs of athletes, bears no relation to past work relying on studies of single nutrients over short-term courses and arbitrary levels of nutrient needs for a mythical average man. Though slim, the controlled data are growing. After 12 years of work, I firmly conclude that if others tell you that nutrients have little effect on athletic performance, do not believe them.

References

Aberg, B.L., Ekman, L., Falk, B., Greitz, U., Persson, G., & Snihs, J. (1969). Metabolism of methyl mercury (203 Hg) compounds in man. *Archives of Environmental Health, 19*, 478.

American Medical Association, Council on Foods and Nutrition. (1974). *Nutrients in Processed Foods.* Acton, MA: Publishing Science Group.

Anderson, B.B., Perry, G.M., Modell, C.B., Child, J.A., & Mollin, D.L. (1979). Abnormal red-cell metabolism of pyrodoxine associated with B-thalassaemia. *British Journal of Haematology, 41*, 497.

Anderson, R.A., Polansky, M.M., Bryden, N.A., Roginski, E.E., Patterson, K.Y., & Reamer, D.C. (1982). Effect of exercise (running) on serum glucose, insulin, glucagon and chromium excretion. *Diabetes, 31*, 212.

Bailey, D.A., Carron, A.V., Teece, R.G., & Wehner, H.J. (1970). Vitamin C supplementation related to physiological response to exercise in smoking and nonsmoking subjects. *American Journal of Clinical Nutrition, 23*, 905.

Baker, S.J., & DeMaeyer, E.M. (1979). Nutritional anemia: Its understanding and control with special reference to the work of the World Health Organization. *American Journal of Clinical Nutrition, 32*, 368.

Bantle, J.P., Laine, D.C., Castle, G.W., Thomas, J.W., Hoogwerf, B.J., & Goetz, F.C. (1983). Postprandial glucose and insulin responses to meals containing different carbohydrates in normal and diabetic subjects. *New England Journal of Medicine, 309*, 7.

Bistrian, B.R., Blackburn, G.L., Hallowell, E., & Heddle, R. (1974). Protein status of general surgical patients. *Journal of the American Medical Association, 230*, 858.

Bistrian, B.R., Blackburn, G.L., Vitale, J., Cochran, D., & Naylor, J. (1976). Prevalence of malnutrition in general medical patients. *Journal of the American Medical Association, 235*, 1567.

Bollet, A.J., & Owens, S. (1973). Evaluation of nutritional status of selected hospitalized patients. *American Journal of Clinical Nutrition, 26*, 931.

Bonen, A., Malcolm, J.A., Kilgour, R.D., MacIntyre, K.P., & Belcastro, A.N. (1980). Glucose ingestion before and during intense exercise. *Journal of Applied Physiology, 50*, 766.

Bradley, R.L., & Hugunin, A.G. (1980). Mercury in food, food stuffs and environment. *Safety of Foods, 350.*

Butterworth, C.E. (1974). The skeleton in the hospital closet (iatrogenic malnutrition in our nation's hospitals is a cause of rising medical concern). *Nutrition Today, 9*, 4.

Butterworth, C.E., Santini, J.R., & Frommeyer, W.B. (1963). The Pterolyglutamate components of American diets as determined by chromatographic fractionation. *Journal of Clinical Investigation, 42*, 1929.

Calloway, D.H. (1962). Dehydrated foods. *Nutrition Review, 20,* 257.

Camarini-Davalos, R.A., & Hanover, R. (Eds.), (1979). *Treatment of early diabetes: Advances in experimental medicine and biology* (Vol. 119). New York: Plenum.

Clement, D.B., Asmundson, R.C., & Medhurst, C.W. (1977). Hemoglobin values: comparative survey of the 1976 Canadian Olympic team. *Canadian Medical Association Journal, 117,* 614.

Clements, J.E., & Anderson, B.B. (1980). Glutathione reductase activity and pyridoxine (pyridoxamine) phosphate oxidase activity in the red cell. *Biochimica et biophysica acta, 632,* 159.

Cohen, A.M., Teitelbaum, A., Balogh, M., Groen, J.J. (1966). Effect of interchanging bread and sucrose as main source of carbohydrate in low fat diet on glucose tolerance curve of healthy volunteer subject. *American Journal of Clinical Nutrition, 19,* 59.

Colgan, M. (1981a, March). Effects of vitamin and mineral supplementation of physiology and performance of athletes. Paper presented at the Rockefeller University, New York.

Colgan, M. (1981b). Trace Elements. *Science, 214,* 744.

Colgan, M. (1982). *Your personal vitamin profile.* New York: Marrow.

Colgan, M. (1983a, April). *Effects of nutrient supplements on athletic performance.* Paper presented to the U.S. Navy Research and Development Center. Carlsbad, CA: Colgan Institute.

Colgan, M. (1983b). *Copper contamination of drinking water in Upper East Side Manhattan.* Carlsbad, CA: Colgan Institute.

Colgan, M., & Colgan, L. (1984). Do nutrient supplements and dietary changes affect learning and emotional reactions of children with learning difficulties? A controlled series of 16 cases. *Nutrition and Health, 3,* 1.

Consolazio, C.F., Johnson, R.E., & Pecora, L.J. (Eds.). (1963). *Physiological measurement of metabolic function in man.* New York: McGraw-Hill.

Consolazio, C.F., Matoush, L.O., Nelson, R.A., Harding, R.S., & Canham, J.E. (1963). Excretion of sodium, potassium, magnesium and iron in human sweat and the relation of each to balance and requirements. *Journal of Nutrition, 79,* 407.

Consumer Reports. (1981, July). P. 376.

Costill, D.L. (1979). A scientific approach to distance running. Los Altos, CA: Track and Field News.

Costill, D.L. (1982). Fats and carbohydrates as determinants of athletic performance. In W. Haskel (Ed.), *Nutrition and athletic performance* (p. 16). Palo Alto, CA: Bull.

Costill, D.L., Coyle, E., Dalsky, G., Evans, W., Fink, W., & Hoopes, D. (1977). Effects of elevated plasma FFA and insulin on muscle glycogen usage during exercise. *Journal of Applied Physiology, 43,* 695.

Costill, D.L., Kammer, W.F., & Fisher, A. (1970). Fluid ingestion during distance running. *Archives of Environmental Health, 21,* 520.

Costill, D.L., Sherman, W.M., Finks, W.J., Maresh, C., Witten, M., & Miller, J.M. (1981). The role of dietary carbohydrates in muscle glycogen resynthesis after strenuous running. *American Journal of Clinical Nutrition, 34,* 1831.

Crapo, P.A., Insel, J., Sperling, M., & Kolterman, O.G. (1981). Comparison of serum glucose, insulin and glucagon responses to different types of complex carbohydrate in noninsulin-dependent diabetic patients. *American Journal of Clinical Nutrition, 34,* 184.

Crapper, D.R., Krishman, S.S., & Quittkat, S. (1976). Aluminium, neurofibrillary degeneration and Alzheimer's disease. *Brain, 99,* 67.

Dressendorfer, R.H., Wade, C.E., & Amersterdam, E.A. (1981). Development of pseudoenemia in marathon runners during a 20-day road race. *Journal of the American Medical Association, 246,* 1215.

Ehn, L., Clarlmark, B., & Hoglund, S. (1980). Iron status in athletes involved in intense physical activity. *Medicine and Science in Sports and Exercise, 12,* 61.

Emmerson, B.T. (1974). Effect of oral fructose on urate production. *Annals of Rheumatic Disorders, 33*, 276.

Fairbanks, V.F., Fahey, J.L., & Beutler, E. (Eds.). (1971). *Clinical disorders of iron metabolism* (2nd ed.). New York: Grune and Stratton.

Fink, W. (1982). In Haskell, W. (Ed.), Fluid intake for maximizing athletic performance. *Nutrition and athletic performance* (p.52). Palo Alto, CA: Bull.

Food and Nutrtion Board. (1977). *Folic acid.* Washington, DC: National Academy of Sciences.

Foster, C., Costill, D.L., & Fink, W.J. (1979). Effects of preexercise feedings on endurance performance. *Medicine and Science in Sports and Exercise, 11*, 1.

Frederickson, L.A., Puhl, J.L., Runyan, W.S. (1983). Effects of training on indices of iron status of young female cross-country runners. *Medicine and Science in Sports and Exercise, 15*, 271.

Ganther, H.E. (1980). Interactions of vitamin E and selenium with mercury and silver. In O.A. Levander & L. Cheng, *Micronutrient interactions* (p. 212). New York: New York Academy of Sciences.

Glinsmann, E., & Mertz, W. (1966). Effect of trivalent chromium on glucose tolerance. *Metabolism, 15*, 510.

Greenleaf, J.E., Olsson, K., & Saltin, B. (1969). Muscle glycogen content and its significance for the water content of the body. *Acta physiologica scandinavia, 330*, 86.

Grey, G.O., Cooper, K.H., & Bottenberg, R.A. (1970). Effect of ascorbic acid on endurance performance and athletic injury. *Journal of the American Medical Association, 211*, 105.

Hanes I. (1976). *First health and nutrition examination survey, United States 1971-72* (DHEW Publication 76-1219-1). Rockville, MD: DHEW.

Harris, R.S., & Karmas, E. (1975). *Nutritional evaluation of food processing.* Westport, CT: Avi.

Harris, R.A., & Von Loesecke, H. (Eds.). (1960). *Nutritional evaluation of food processing.* Westport, CT: Avi.

Hegsted, D.M. (1963). Variations in requirements of nutrients—amino acids. *Federation Proceedings, 22*, 1424.

Herbert, V. (1962). Experimental nutritional folate deficiency in man. *Transactions of the Association of American Physicians, 75*, 307.

Herbert, V. (1968). Nutritional requirements of vitamin B_{12} and folic acid. *American Journal of Clincial Nutrition, 21*, 743.

Herbert, V. (1971). Predicting nutrient deficiency by formula. *New England Journal of Medicine, 284*, 976.

Herbert, V. (1972). Detection of malabsorption of vitamin B_{12} due to gastric or intestinal dysfunction. *Seminars in Nuclear Medicine, 2*, 220.

Heuckenkamp, P.U., & Zollner, N. (1971). Fructose induced hyperuricaemia. *Lancet, 1*, 808.

Howald, N., & Segesser, B. (1975). Ascorbic acid and athletic performance. *Annals of the New York Academy of Sciences, 258*, 458.

Jenkins, D.J., Wolever, T.M., & Taylor, R.H. (1981). Glycemic index of foods: a physiological basis for carbohydrate exchange. *American Journal of Clinical Nutrition, 34*, 362.

Keller, K., & Schwarzkopf, R. (1984). Pre-exercise snacks may decrease exercise performance. *Physician and Sports Medicine 4, 12*, 89.

Kelsay, J.L., Behall, K.M., Moser, P.B., & Prather, E.S. (1977). The effect of carbohydrate in the young woman. I. Blood and urinary lactate, uric acid and phosphorus. *American Journal of Clinical Nutrition, 30*, 2016.

Klevay, L.M. (1980). Interactions of copper and zinc in cardiovascular disease. In O.A. Levander & L. Cheng (Eds.), *Micronutrient interactions.* New York: New York Academy of Sciences. 140.

Klevay, L.M., Reck, J.J., & Barcome, D.F. (1979). Evidence of dietary copper and zinc deficiencies. *Journal of the American Medical Association,* **241**, 1916.

Kolata, G. (1984). Lowered cholesterol decreases heart disease. *Science,* **223**, 381.

Kritchevsky, D., Daridson, L.M., Kim, H.K., Krendil, D.A., Malhotra, S., Mendelson, D., Watt, J.J., duPlessis, J.P., & Winter, P.A.D. (1980). Influence of type of carbohydrate on atherosclerosis in baboons fed semipurified diet plus 0.1% cholesterol. *American Journal of Clinical Nutrition,* **33**, 1869.

Krochta, J.M., & Feinberg, B. (1975). Effects of harvesting and handling on fruits and vegetables. In R.S. Harris & E. Karmas (Eds.), *Nutritional evaluation of food processing.* Westport, CT: Avi.

Lachance, P.A., & Erdman, J.W. (1975). Effects of home food preparation practices on nutrient content of foods. In R.S. Harris & E. Karmas (Eds.), *Nutritional evaluation of food processing,* Westport, CT: Avi.

Lavoie, A., Tripp, E., & Hoffbrand, A.V. (1974). The effect of vitamin B_{12} deficiency on methylfolate metabolism and pteroylpolyglutamate synthesis in human cells. *Clinical Science and Molecular Medicine,* **47**, 617.

Levendar, O.A., & Cheng, L. (Eds.). (1980). *Micronutrient interactions.* New York: New York Academy of Sciences.

Levander, O.A., Welch, S.O., & Morris, V.C. (1980). In O.A. Levander & L. Cheng (Eds.), *Micronutrient interactions.* New York: New York Academy of Sciences. 227.

Levine, L., Evans, W.J., Cadarette, B.S., Fisher, E.C., & Bullen, B.A. (1983). Fructose and glucose ingestion and muscle glycogen use during submaximal exercise. *Journal of Applied Physiology,* **55**, 1767.

Liu, A., & Morris, S. (1978). Relative chromium response as an indicator of chromium status. *American Journal of Clinical Nutrition,* **31**, 972.

Locksley, R. (1980). Fuel utilization in marathons: Implications for performance. *Western Journal of Medicine,* **133**, 493.

Lund, D.B. (1975). Effects of commercial processing and storage on nutrients. In R.S. Harris & E. Karmas (Eds.), *Nutritional evaluation of food processing.* Westport, CT: Avi. 205.

Machlin, J., & Gabriel, E. (1980). Interaction of vitamin E with vitamin C, vitamin B_{12} and zinc. In O.A. Levander & L. Cheng (Eds.), *Micronutrient interactions.* New York: New York Academy of Sciences. 98.

Mahaffey, K.R., Rader, J.I. (1980). Metabolic interactions: Lead, calcium and iron. In O.A. Levander & L. Cheng (Eds.), *Micronutrient interactions.* New York: New York Academy of Sciences. 285.

Margaria, R. (Ed.). (1967). *Exercise at altitude.* Amsterdam: Excerpta Medica.

Margen, S.J., Chu, J.Y., & Kaufman, N.A. (1974). Studies in calcium metabolism. I. The calciuretic effect of dietary protein. *American Journal of Clinical Nutrition,* **27**, 584.

Marks, J. (1968). *The vitamins in health and disease.* London: Churchill.

Mason, K.E., & Young, J.O. (1967). Effectiveness of selenium and zinc in protecting against cadmium induced injury of the rat testes. In O.H. Muth (Ed.), *Selenium in biomedicine.* Westport, CT: Avi.

Matz, S.A. (1975). Effects of baking on nutrients. In R.S. Harris & E. Karmas (Eds.), *Nutritional evaluation of food processing.* Westport, CT: Avi.

Mertz, W. (1979). In D. Shapcott & J. Hubert (Eds.), *Chromium in nutrition and metabolism.* Amsterdam: Elsevier North Holland. 1.

Minson, P.L., Piczfalusy, E., Glover, J., & Olson, R.E. (Eds.). (1976). *Vitamins and hormones* (Vol. 34). New York: Academic Press.

Mitchell, D.G., & Aldous, K.M. (1974). Lead in canned foods. *Environmental health perspectives,* **7**, 59.

Moroff, S.V., & Bass, D.E. (1965). Effects of overhydration on man's physiological responses to work in the heat. *Journal of Applied Physiology, 20,* 267.

National Academy of Sciences. (1974-1978). *Reports of the Sub-committee on the Geochemical Environment in Relation to Health and Disease.* (1980). Washington, DC: National Academy of Sciences.

National Research Council, (1980). *Toward healthful diets.* Washington, DC: National Academy of Sciences.

Nationwide food consumpton survey, 1977-1978 (Preliminary Report No. 2). Washington, DC: USDA.

Nielsen, F.H., Hunt, C.D., & Uthus, E.O. (1980). Interactions between essential trace and ultratrace elements. In O.E. Levander & L. Cheng (Eds.), *Micronutrient interactions.* New York: New York Academy of Sciences. 152.

Norman, A.W. (Ed.). (1977). *Vitamin D: Biochemical, chemical and clinical aspects related to calcium metabolism.* Berlin: Walter de Gruyter.

Norman, A.W. (Ed.), (1979). *Vitamin D: basic research and its clinical applications.* Berlin: Walter de Gruyter.

Norms for hair concentrations of Cu, Ni, Cd, Hg, Al, Pb, in subjects who avoid sources of metal contamination of food water and air. (1983). Carlsbad, CA: Colgan Institute of Nutritional Science.

Ondreicka, R., Kortus, J., & Ginter, E. (1971). Aluminum. In S.C. Skoryna & D. Waldron-Edwar (Eds.), *Intestinal incorporation of metal ions, trace elements and radionuclides.* Oxford: Pergamon. 293.

Painter, N. (1964). The etiology of diverticulosis of the colon with special reference to the action of certian drugs on the behavior of the colon. *Annals of the Royal College of Surgeons* (England), **34,** 98.

Parr, R.B., Bachman, L.A., & Moss, R.A. (19 4). Iron deficiencies in female athletes. *Physician and Sports Medicine,* **4,** 81.

Patrias, B., & Olson, O. (1967). Selenium distribution in crops and soils. *Journal of Agriculture and Food Chemistry,* **15,** 448.

Paul, A.A., & Southgate, D.A. (1978). *The composition of foods, (4th Ed.).* Oxford: Elsevier/North-Holland.

Philips, M., & Baetz, A. (Eds.). (1981). *Diet and resistance to disease: Advances in experimental medicine and biology* (Vol. 35). New York: Plenum.

Recommended Dietary Allowances (9th rev. ed.). (1980). Washington, DC: National Academy of Sciences.

Reiser, S., Handler, H.B., Gardner, L.B., Hallfrisch, J.G., Michaelis, O.E., & Prather, E.S. (1979). Isocaleric exchange of dietary starch and sucrose in humans. II. Effect on fasting blood insulin, glucose, and glucagon and on insulin glucose response to a sucrose load. *American Journal of Clinical Nutrition,* **32,** 2206.

Reiser, S. (1983). Physiological differences between starches and sugars. In G. Bland (Ed.), *Medical aspects of clinical nutrition.* New Canaan, CT.

Riales, R., & Albrink, M.J. (1981). Effect of chromium chloride supplementation on glucose tolerance and serum lipids including high-density lipoprotein of adult men. *American Journal of Clinical Nutrition,* **34,** 2670.

Rodriguez, M.S. (1978). A conspectus of research on folacin requirements of man. *Journal of Nutrition,* **108,** 1983.

Royal College of Physicians. (1980). *Medical aspects of dietary fiber.* London: Pitman.

Sauberlich, H.E. (1980). Interaction of thiamin, riboflavin and other B-vitamins. In O.A. Lavender & L. Cheng (Eds.), *Micronutrient interactions.* New York: New York Academy of Sciences. 80.

Schroeder, H.A. (1971). Losses of vitamins and trace minerals resulting from processing and preservation of food. *American Journal of Clinical Nutrition,* **24,** 362.

Shils, M. (1980). Mangesium, calcium and parathyroid hormone interactions. In O.A. Levander & L. Cheng (Eds.), *Micronutrient Interactions,* New York: New York Academy of Sciences, 165.

Solyst, J.T., Michaelis IV, OE., Reiser, S., Ellwood, K.E., & Prather, E.S. (1980). Effect of dietary sucrose in humans on blood uric acid, phosphorus, and lactic acid responses to a sucrose load. *Nutrition and Metabolism,* **24,** 182.

Spencer, H., Kramer, L., Osis, D., Waitrowski, E., Norris, C., & Lender, M. (1980). Effect of calcium, phosphorus, magnesium and aluminum on fluoride metabolism in man. In O.A. Levander & L. Cheng (Eds.) *Micronutrient Interactions,* New York: New York Academy of Sciences, 181.

Spiller, G.A., & Kay, R.P. (Eds.). (1980). *Medical aspects of dietary fiber.* New York: Plenum.

Spivey, M.R., Fox, R.M., Jacobs, A.O., Lee Jones, B.E., Fry, B.E., & Stone, C.L. (1980). Effects of vitamin C and iron on cadmium metabolism. In O.A. Levander & L. Cheng (Eds.), *Micronutrient interactions.* New York: New York Academy of Sciences, 249.

Stoewsand, G.S., (1980). Trace metal problems with industrial waste materials applied to vegetable producing soils. In H.D. Graham (Ed.), *The safety of foods.* Westport, CT: Avi. 423.

Sturgeon, P., & Shoden, A., (1975). Total liver storage iron in normal populations of the USA. *American Journal of Clinical Nutrition,* **24,** 469.

Ten-state nutritional survey, (DHEW Publications 72-8130 Nos. 1, 2, and 3). (1972). Rockville, MD: DHEW.

The Surgeon General. (1979). *Healthy people,* (DHEW Publications Nos. 79-55071 and 79-55071A). Washington, DC: Government. Printing Office.

Trowell, H.C., & Burkitt, D.P. (Eds.). (1981). *Western diseases: Their emergence and prevention.* Cambridge, MA: Harvard University Press.

Tzagornis, M., (1978). Triglycerides in clinical medicine: A review. *American Journal of Clinical Nutrition,* **31,** 1437.

Underwood, E.J., (1977). *Trace elements in human and animal nutrition* (4th Ed.). New York: Academic Press.

USDA. (1974). *National food situation* (USDA Circular No. 150). Washington, DC: USDA.

Veller, O. (1968). Studies on sweat losses of nutrients. *Scandinavian Journal of Clinical Investigation,* **21,** 157.

Watt, B.K., & Merrill, A.L. (1963). *Composition of foods.* Washington, DC: USDA.

Weinsier, R.L., Hunker, E.M., Krumdieck, C.L., & Butterworth, Jr., C.E. (1979). Hospital malnutrition. A prospective evaluation of general medical patients during the course of hospitalization. *American Journal of Clinical Nutrition,* **32,** 418.

Williams, M.H. (1981). Vitamin, iron and calcium supplementation: Effect on human physical performance. In W.L. Haskell (Ed.), *Nutrition and athletic performance.* Palo Alto, CA: Bull. 106.

Williams, R.J., Beerstecher, E., & Berry, L.J. (1950). The concept of genetotrophic disease. *Lancet,* **258,** 287.

Williams, R.J. (1956). *Biochemical individuality.* New York: Wiley.

Williams, R.J., & Deason, G. (1967). Individuality in vitamin C needs. *Proceedings National Academy of Sciences U.S.A.,* **57,** 1638.

Williams, R.J., Heffley, J.D., Yew, M., & Bode, C.W. (1973). A renaissance of nutritional science is imminent. *Perspectives in Biology and Medicine,* **17,** 1.

4

Trace Elements in Athletic Performance

Carl L. Keen
UNIVERSITY OF CALIFORNIA
DAVIS, CALIFORNIA, USA

Robert M. Hackman
UNIVERSITY OF OREGON
EUGENE, OREGON, USA

An increasing emphasis has been placed on the role of trace elements in human health and disease. By definition, the essential trace elements are those metal ions required in very small amounts for optimum body function. The concentration of these elements in biological tissues is in the range of micrograms per gram to nanograms per gram. Trace elements can have as many as four roles in biological systems. First, they can be components of body fluids (i.e. electrolytes); second, they can be cofactors in enzymatic reactions; third, they can serve to bind, transport, and release oxygen; and fourth, they can be structural components of nonenzymatic macromolecules. An example of the fourth role would be the presence of silicone as a component of the organic matrix of bone. To date, 15 trace elements have been reported to be essential for the growth and health of animals. The list of these elements includes arsenic, cobalt, copper, chromium, fluorine, iodine, iron, lead, manganese, molybdenum, nickle, selenium, vanadium, and zinc. Although a deficiency of some of these elements such as arsenic, fluorine, lead, silicone, and vanadium has only been demonstrated in experimental animals under rigidly controlled environments, deficiencies of others such as copper, iodine, iron, selenium, and zinc have been reported to occur in domestic animals and humans under natural conditions (Table 1).

Table 1. Trace elements essential for the development and health of mammals and birds

A*	B*
Cobalt	Arsenic
Copper	Chromium
Iodine	Fluorine
Iron	Lead
Manganese	Nickel
Molybdenum	Silicon
Selenium	Vanadium
Zinc	

*A Deficiency known to occur under natural conditions.
*B Deficiency induced experimentally using purified diets in a rigidly controlled environment.

This review will concentrate on three elements—zinc, copper, and iron—to exemplify the concepts involved in trace element metabolism and nutrition. These elements have been chosen as examples because growing evidence indicates that their deficiencies in humans may be widespread, and perturbations in their metabolism have been reported in the trained athlete. In a recent survey by Parr and co-workers (Parr, Porter, & Hodgson, 1984) of high school and college coaches and athletes, minerals were found to be the least important concern with regard to diet. The intent of this review is to demonstrate the need for greater awareness of mineral nutrition in such individuals.

Zinc Metabolism and Nutrition

An average 70 kg man contains between 1.4 and 2.3 grams of zinc (Widdowson, McCance, & Spray, 1951). Next to calcium and magnesium, zinc is the most concentrated intracellular cation. In the adult a large portion of zinc is present in bone; however, unlike calcium, bone zinc is not mobilized in response to zinc deficiency. Thus, the consumption of a zinc-deficient diet can result in a significant reduction in circulating levels of the element. In some species this reduction can be quite dramatic. In the rat, for example, consumption of a severely zinc-deficient diet can result in a 50% reduction in plasma zinc levels within 24 hours of introduction of the diet (Hurley, Gordon, Keen, & Merkhofer, 1982). Muscle contains about 65% of the total body zinc. Although similar to bone, zinc in muscle is not released in response to low circulating levels of the element. Thus, muscle catabolism can result in the release of significant amounts of zinc into circulation in relatively short time periods. This can be an important consideration because severe zinc deficiency can result in depressed food intake that in turn results in increased tissue (muscle) catabolism (Masters, Keen, Lonnerdal, & Hurley, 1983).

Zinc is essential for the function of more than 90 enzymes from different species. Zinc-containing enzymes are found in all of the major metabolic pathways; they are involved in carbohydrate, lipid, protein, and nucleic acid metabolism. Zinc can function as a structural component of the enzyme away from the active site, as a proton donor at the active site, and as a bridging atom between the substrate and the enzyme. Mammalian zinc enzymes include carboxypeptidases, aminopeptidases, alkaline phosphatase, alcohol dehydrogenase, carbonic anhydrase, superoxide dismutase, and thymidine kinase. With the variety of enzymes which contain zinc, it is reasonable to expect that a cellular deficiency of this element would have profound consequences. Thus the status of an individual with regard to zinc becomes an important issue.

The importance of zinc in human nutrition has received increasing attention during the last decade; this is partially due to the growing recognition that its intake may often be less than optimal. It is estimated that the average adult in the United States consumes about 10 mg of zinc/day, although this amount can be considerably less. This level of intake should be compared to the recommended daily allowance (RDA) for zinc that is currently set at 15 mg for adults. The first human zinc-deficiency syndrome was identifed in the early 1960's by Prasad and co-workers who found that symptoms of growth retardation, delayed sexual maturation, and skin lesions in a group of young malnourished men in Egypt and Iran could be ascribed to long-term nutritional zinc deficiency (Prasad, Miale, Farid, Schulent, & Sanstead, 1963). Individuals with this syndrome respond favorably to dietary zinc supplementation and show significant increases in growth rate and sexual maturation occurring shortly after zinc treatment (Halsted et al., 1972).

The occurrence of severe acute zinc-deficiency syndromes in humans was subsequently demonstrated in 1973 by Moynahan and Barnes who made the important discovery that the clinical manifestations of the potentially lethal genetic disorder *acrodermatitis enteropathica* were resolved with dietary zinc supplementation (Moynahan, 1974; Moynahan & Barnes, 1973). Severe acute zinc deficiency can also occur in some patients receiving long-term total parenteral nutrition (Phillips, 1982). Zinc deficiency has also been reported as a complication of several disease states that include protein calorie malnutrition, malabsorption syndromes, alcoholism, chronic liver disease, and nephrotic syndrome (Prasad, 1983).

In addition to severe zinc deficiency, it is currently recognized that marginal zinc deficiency may be common in some population groups. In 1972, Hambidge and co-workers reported that a large number of young children from middle-class families living in Denver, Colorado, were marginally zinc deficient. These children exhibited symptoms of growth retardation, poor appetite, and impaired taste acuity. Zinc supplementation corrected the above symptoms (Hambidge, Hambidge, Jacobs, & Baum, 1972). It has been suggested that one factor contributing to the poor zinc status of these children was the low concentration of the element in some infant formulas (Walravens & Hambidge, 1977). Current practice now is to supplement infant formulas with zinc; however, a considerable number of infant formulas continue to be deficient in this element (Lonnerdal, Keen, Ohtake, & Tamura, 1983). Recently, Buzina, Jusci, Sapunar, and Milanovic (1980) provided additional evidence that suboptimal zinc status can be a problem in young children. In their study they showed an increased incidence of retarded growth in children between the ages of 9 and 12 who also had low hair plasma zinc levels.

Suboptimal zinc status has also been associated with poor pregnancy outcome. Jameson (1983) has provided data that poor zinc status during pregnancy can be correlated to increased maternal morbidity, abnormal taste sensations, prolonged gestation, prolonged labor, atonic bleeding, and poor fetal outcome, including prematurity, stillbirths, and congenital malformations. That suboptimal zinc status during pregnancy would have such severe effects in humans is consistent with studies in several experimental animal models documenting the severe teratogenicity of maternal dietary zinc deficiency (Hurley, 1981). Based on this information, it is evident that the zinc status of some individuals may be less than optimal under noncontrolled conditions. Thus, dietary zinc intake may not always meet the requirements of the individual.

Zinc in Athletes

The first report that exercise could affect zinc metabolism was made by Lichti, Turner, Deweese, and Henzel (1970) who found that plasma zinc levels in dogs could fluctuate considerably after a 10 min treadmill run. Subsequently, the same authors reported that intense, brief exercise in man, achieved by running up four flights of stairs, could result in a sharp increase in plasma zinc levels (Lichti, Turner, & Henzel, 1971). As a result of the finding by Lichti et al. on the effects of acute exercise on plasma zinc, Hetland, Brubak, Refsum, and Stromme (1975) examined the change in zinc concentration in serum and erythrocytes after heavy exercise of long duration. These investigators followed serum and erythrocyte zinc changes in a group of men who participated in a 5 hour 70 km cross-country skiing competition. Samples were taken prerace, immediately postrace, and on days 1 and 2 postrace. They observed that postrace serum zinc levels were significantly higher by 19% than prerace levels; however, by Day 1 postrace, zinc levels were back to prerace values. Interestingly, on Day 2 postrace, serum zinc levels tended to increase over initial levels. In contrast to serum, erythrocyte zinc levels did not change with exercise. However, it is important to point out that erythrocyte zinc levels are 10 times higher than serum zinc levels, so even a moderate degree of hemolysis would result in an increase in serum zinc. In studies of this kind, the degree of hemolysis in all samples must be noted. The increase in serum zinc could not be attributed to hemoconcentration as average hematocrits only dropped 4% during the race. Therefore, the increase in serum zinc observed after intense exercise may be the result of muscle leakage of zinc into the extracellular fluid. Consistent with this possibility is the observation that a significant increase in serum levels of muscle lactic dehydrogenase, a zinc enzyme, occurs following intense exercise (Karlson, Diamant, & Saltin, 1968).

An additional point can be drawn from the report by Hetland et al. (1975) who found that the change in serum zinc following exercise is dependent on the time the zinc sample is obtained. Ohno et al. (1983) recently have provided data that under certain condition with acute exercise, there can be a leakage of zinc from the erythrocyte into the serum. To what extent this contributes to the rise in serum zinc observed with acute exercise is not yet clear.

These studies clearly show that exercise can have an immediate short-term effect on circulating zinc levels. However, it was not evident from these studies if the trained athlete is suboptimal with regard to zinc status. Dressendorfer and Sockolov (1980) suggested that a high level of constant exercise could have a more long-lasting effect on zinc status. These investigators observed that long-distance runners had significantly lower average serum zinc levels compared to sedentary control (76 and 94 μg/dl, respectively). Furthermore, they observed that the serum zinc was inversely related to training distance with average serum zinc levels of 81 μg/dl and 67 μg/dl for runners training 6 to 12 and 40 to 84 mi/week, respectively. Thus, the short-term perturbations seen in zinc metabolism following exercise may have long-lasting effects for the individual. In support of these observations, Haralambie in 1981 reported that in a survey of 160 training athletes (57 women and 103 men), 23% of the men and 43% of the women athletes had serum zinc levels lower than the limit accepted for the normal range. The presence of hypozincemia in trained athletes has since been reported by other laboratories (Dressendorfer, Wade, Keen, & Scaff, 1982; Hackman & Keen, 1983).

At least three possibilities can be considered in regard to the observation of low serum zinc levels in some trained athletes. The first is that the low serum zinc reflects a poor zinc status of the individual due to high zinc losses and/or inadequate zinc intake. Second, the results may reflect a transient fall of serum zinc levels after exercise. Data on the changes in serum zinc in trained athletes for several days postexercise have not been published. Third, other factors such as plasma volume expansion or a reduction in serum zinc binding ligands (such as α_2-macroglobulin) may be the cause of the low values observed. The third possibility does not seem likely as the change in plasma volume is not correlated to changes in serum zinc levels and the levels of the principal ligands that bind zinc in serum are only slightly changed or indeed increased in the trained individual (Haralambie, 1981). Thus, it would appear that the first possibility is the most likely explanation. The athlete's increased sweat loss of zinc may be one reason underlying an excessive loss of the element from the body (Consolazio, Nelson, Matoush, Huges, & Uroné, 1964; Uhari, Pakarinen, Hietala, Nurmi, & Kouralainen, 1983). Excessive zinc loss may also occur due to proteinuria, a problem which can occur in many trained individuals (Halsted, Smith, & Irwin, 1974; Wade, Dressendorfer, O'Brian, & Claybaugh, 1982).

In addition to the loss of zinc from the body, a redistribution of zinc within the body may in part explain the serum levels seen in some individuals. Oh, Deagen, Whanger, and Weswig (1978) have reported that drop in plasma zinc levels in rats after acute endurance swimming was related to increased synthesis of hepatic metallothionein, a zinc-binding protein. An increase in the synthesis of this protein during exercise may be attributed to increased production of leukocyte endogenous mediator, a hormone-like substance released for phagocytes during exposure to stressors (Oh et al., 1978) or to ACTH (Falchuk, 1977), the production of which is also increased during exercise. Increases in body temperature may also produce a shift of plasma zinc to the liver (Keen, Lonnerdal, & Fisher, 1981).

The changes in serum zinc with exercise may (a) be a transitory increase in zinc levels due to muscle breakdown and leakage and erythrocyte leakage and (b) be caused by a decrease in serum zinc level due to increased body loss of the element via sweat and urine coupled with a redistribution of serum zinc to the liver.

It seems evident that low serum zinc levels can be found in a large number of trained athletes. Although there is considerable debate over the value of serum zinc levels in determining the zinc status of an individual, prolonged low serum zinc levels would be indicative of suboptimal zinc status under most conditions. Brooks and co-workers (1984) have suggested that suboptimal zinc status may be one of the etiologic agents of athletic amenorrhea in vegetarians. With prolonged suboptimal zinc status, it would be predicted that muscle zinc levels would decrease. Furthermore, because zinc is required for the activity of several enzymes of energy metabolism and is a component of lactate dehydrogenase, it could be predicted that suboptimal muscle zinc levels could negatively affect muscle strength and endurance. Consistent with this reasoning, Richardson and Drake (1979) have reported that rats given dietary zinc supplementation had gastrocnemius muscles that took longer to fatigue than did muscles taken from control rats. Unfortunately, dietary zinc levels and muscle zinc levels were not reported. Consistent with the findings of Richardson and Drake is the report by Krotkiewski, Gudmundsson, Backstrom, and Mandroukas (1982). They found that women who supplemented for 14 days with 135 mg zinc/day showed a significant increase in isokinetic leg strength at high angular velocities and in isometric endurance. Krotkiewski et al., (1982) suggested that the effects of zinc supplementation may be due to either an effect of zinc in increasing lactate dehydrogenase activity or through an effect of zinc on glucose transport into, and its metabolism in, muscle. Unfortunately, serum zinc was not measured either before or after zinc supplementation. Recently, Lukaski, Bolonchuk, Klevay, Milne, and Sandstead (1983) studied the relationship between maximal oxygen cosumption and plasma levels of several trace elements in athletes and untrained men who underwent maximal treadmill exercise. They found no relationship between plasma zinc levels and maximum oxygen uptake; however, the plasma zinc levels of their athletes were similar to those of an untrained group.

The studies on the potential positive effects of zinc supplementation on muscle function are intriguing; however, considerable caution must be used in advocating massive zinc supplementation for improvement of athletic performance. Although zinc is considered to be among the least toxic of the trace elements, adverse effects can occur at pharmacological levels of zinc supplementation. One potential negative effect of excessive zinc supplementation is that excess zinc may inhibit the absorption of copper due to their similar physio-chemical characteristics (Hurley, Keen, & Lonnerdal, 1983). That high dietary zinc can potentiate copper deficiency in experimental animals is well accepted (Reinstein, Lonnerdal, Keen, & Hurley, 1984). In humans, long-term (2 years) zinc supplementation at 150 mg/day (for treatment of sickle-cell anemia) has been reported to result in hypocupremia (Prasad, Brewer, Shoomaker, & Rabbani, 1978). Young men treated with 160 mg of zinc/day for 16 weeks were found to have a significant decrease in high-density lipoprotein cholesterol concentrations (Hooper, Visconti, Garry, & Johnson, 1980). As this type of cholesterol is thought to be protective against cardiovascular disease, such an effect of zinc is certainly not beneficial. Recall that the level of zinc supplementation used in the study on muscle function by Krotkiewski et al. (1982) was 135 mg of zinc/day. Recently Fisher, Giroux, & L'Abbe (1984) have reported that zinc supplementation of adult men with 50 mg/day for 6 weeks resulted in a decrease in erythrocyte copper levels. Hackman and Keen (1984) observed the levels of 23 mg of zinc/day for 4 weeks tend to have a slight lowering effect on plasma copper levels during the first 3 weeks; however, this effect was not evident at the end of the study. Thus, zinc supplementation at a high level in an attempt to improve athletic performance may not be beneficial to the individual. Zinc supplementation at a level of 23 mg/day for 4 weeks tended to affect serum copper, but this effect was transitory. Based on current information, therefore, zinc supplementation should be on the order of 15 mg/day, the current U.S. RDA for adults. Although levels of daily zinc supplementation as high as 23 mg may be safe, long-term studies of the effects of such supplementation need to be done.

Copper Metabolism and Nutrition

An average 70 kg man contains between 60 and 80 mg of copper. In the adult about one-third of total body copper is found in the liver and brain. Skeletal muscle, although considered low in copper, also contains about one-third of total body copper due to its mass. The remainder of the copper is fairly evenly distributed throughout the body (Cartwright & Wintrobe, 1964). Similar to zinc, there is little storage of copper which can be utilized if the diet is inadequate. However, in contrast to zinc, there is a very effective recycling of body copper because it takes considerably longer to induce a copper deficiency than a zinc deficiency.

Copper is associated with a number of oxygenases, including cytochrome oxidase, the terminal component of the electron transport chain. The two other major copper enzymes (with regard to amounts found) are copper-zinc superoxide dismutase, which catalyzes the reaction of superoxide anion to hydrogen peroxide, and ceruloplasmin (Ferroxidase I), a copper transport protein that has weak oxidizing properties and that may be required for the incorporation of iron from liver into transferrin for its transport to extrahepatic tissues. An additional key copper enzyme is lysyl oxidase. This enzyme catalyzes the oxidation of specific lysyl and hydroxylysyl residues in soluble collagen and elastin, a step which is critical for cross-linking of connective tissue. Other copper enzymes include tryptophan oxygenase, needed for tryptophan degradation; dopamine β-hydroxylase, needed for catecholamine production; tyrosinase, needed for melanin production, and possibly some fatty acid desaturase enzymes, such as $C^{18}\Delta - ^9$ desaturase (O'Dell, 1984). Pathological signs of copper deficiency include anemia, skeletal and other connective tissue defects, depigmentation, lipid abnormalities, and neurological disturbances. Similar to zinc, a deficiency of copper during pregnancy can result in congenital abnormalities (Keen, Lonnerdal, & Hurley, 1982).

It is estimated that the average adult in the United States consumes between 1.0 and 1.5 mg of copper/day. Theoretically, recommended intake levels include a margin of safety. Similar to zinc, cases of copper deficiency in humans are not uncommon; however, the majority of cases have been reported in infants and young malnourished children (Williams, 1982), although se-

vere copper deficiency has been reported in adults on long-term total parenteral nutrition (Dunlap, James, & Hume, 1974). Although the number of cases
of severe adult copper deficiency are few, many think that the number of individuals with marginal copper deficiency may be quite large (Klevay, 1980).
As discussed, the excessive use of zinc supplements may precipitate functional copper deficiency in some individuals.

Copper in Athletes

Exercise can have a pronounced effect on copper metabolism as it does on
zinc. Haralambie (1975) has shown that shortly after the initiation of intense
exercise on an ergometer, untrained men first show a slight increase, and then
a decrease in serum copper after 30 min. This decrease was shown to be correlated to a decrease in the level of ceruloplasmin, the principal protein that
binds copper in serum. After the drop in serum copper levels, there was a
constant increase in serum copper for the remaining 1.5 hours of exercise.
At the end of 2 hours, serum copper was considerably higher than the level
recorded at the start of the experiment. The increase in copper was due to
an increase in the concentration of ceruloplasmin.

The effects of acute exercise on serum copper levels in the untrained individual have also been reported for the athlete. Olha, Klissouras, Sullivan,
and Skoryna (1982) found that with 90 min of intense exercise on an ergometer, serum copper increased 35% in the trained athlete and only 15% in the
untrained athlete. This effect of intense exercise on increasing serum copper
levels can continue for prolonged time periods. In the study by Dressendorfer
et al. (1982), plasma copper levels increased constantly during the first week
of a 20-day, 500 km race. After this point, levels remained fairly constant.
The increased copper output into the serum with exercise seems to have a long-
lasting effect in that serum copper levels at rest tend to be higher in athletes
than in untrained individuals (Haralambie, 1975; Haralambie & Keul, 1970;
Lukaski et al., 1983; Olha et al., 1982). In contrast to the above, Dowdy and
Burt (1980) have reported that serum ceruloplasmin and serum copper significantly decreased in competitive swimmers over a 6-month training period.
The reason for the difference between the findings of Dowdy and Burt and
others is not clear. In studies with rats, Dowdy and Dohm (1972) showed a
significant increase in serum ceruloplasmin levels in trained and untrained
animals with acute exercise. The increase was larger in the trained rats.
Haralambie's (1975) results in humans were similar.

At least two explanations account for the increased serum ceruloplasmin levels seen with exercise. First, ceruloplasmin is an acute phase protein whose
production in the liver is increased by various nonspecific stressors including
physical trauma (Mason, 1979). By this mechanism, the increase in serum
ceruloplasmin with exercise could be viewed as being indicative of tissue
damage. The second possible explanation is that the increased ceruloplasmin
output from the liver, and hence increased levels in the serum, is an adaptive
response by the body to an increased requirement for extrahepatic copper. It

is known that the higher values of maximal oxygen uptake in trained individuals is correlated to an increase in muscle mitochondrial volume and to an increase in oxidative enzymes within the cell. One of the principal enzymes that is increased is the copper-containing protein, cytochrome oxidase (Terjung, Winder, Baldwin, & Holloszy, 1973). This would suggest that the copper requirement of the muscle cell is increased with exercise. It has been shown that ceruloplasmin copper can be incorporated into cytochrome oxidase, and cell receptor sites for ceruloplasmin have been identified (Stevens, Disilvestro, & Harris, 1984). Thus, it may be that the increased ceruloplasmin output in the athlete may be in part a response to increased extrahepatic copper requirements.

Whatever the mechanisms involved, both acute and chronic exercise affect copper metabolism. However, in contrast to zinc, where prolonged exercise tends to result in decreased serum levels of the element, copper levels increase significantly with prolonged exercise. The potential long-term effects of this distortion in serum copper and zinc levels are not known. An issue which needs to be resolved is whether the increased copper (ceruloplasmin) output from the liver seen with exercise results in a lowering of hepatic copper levels. If this is the case, then it could be argued that the highly trained athlete may have a higher requirement for dietary copper than do sedentary individuals. It should be stressed, however, that excessive dietary supplementation of copper is not warranted, and if dietary supplements are to be used, they need not exceed the current RDA level of 2 mg/day. Excess dietary copper can be quite toxic (Keen, Lonnerdal, & Hurley, 1982).

Iron Metabolism and Nutrition

Iron is the most abundant trace element in the body. The average 70 kg male contains between 2.5 and 4 grams of the element. The vast bulk of the body iron is found in the form of hemoglobin and myoglobin where it is involved in oxygen binding and transport. In contrast to zinc and copper, large amounts of storage iron are found in the form of ferritin and hemosiderin, which are principally localized in the liver, spleen, and bone marrow. Only a very small amount (< 300 mg) of the total body iron is associated with enzymes, the principal ones being the heme-containing cytochromes and iron-sulfur proteins of electron transport and oxidative phosphorylation, tryptophan oxygenase and catalase.

It is estimated that the typical iron intake in the United States is between 10 to 15 mg/day, compared to the RDA of 10 mg and 18 mg of iron/day for adult men and women, respectively. While the potential for zinc and copper deficiencies in the human population is not widely appreciated, most individuals are aware that iron deficiency can be a common problem. Iron deficiency can occur due to a relative lack of iron in the diet and/or as the result of extensive loss of iron from the body via bleeding or pregnancy. The usual symptoms associated with iron deficiency are a hypochronic anemia and loss of endurance. A detailed description of the causes and effects of iron deficiency is provided by Finch and Cook (1984).

Iron and Athletes

The concern of iron status in athletes stems from a series of reports that have documented the fact that iron-deficiency anemia can impair physical work performance (Andersen & Bankve, 1970; Dallman, 1982; Ohira et al., 1979; Veller & Hermansen, 1972; Wittenberg, 1970). The decrease in work performance associated with iron deficiency anemia is thought to be mainly the result of decreased oxygen transport to the muscle via hemoglobin, a reduction in muscle myoglobin levels that can result in a cellular deficiency of oxygen, and to a reduction in the activity of the cytochrome system (Andersen & Bankve, 1970; McDonald, Hegenauer, Sucec, & Saltman, 1984; Veller & Hermansen 1972; Wittenberg 1979). A reduction in muscle aerobic metabolism even with only moderate iron deficiency is suggested by the finding of Schoene et al. (1983) that blood lactate levels were significantly higher in female athletes with minimal iron-deficiency anemia following intense exercise than in iron-replete subjects.

Several papers have suggested that the athlete may be at particular risk with regard to developing iron deficiency anemia. A variety of facts including increased sweat loss of iron (Paulev, Jordal, & Pederson, 1983) and increased erythrocyte destruction with subsequent hemoglobinuria (Davidson, 1964; DuFaux, Hoedegrath, Streitbergen, Hollman, & Assman, 1981) may result in substantial iron loss. Gastrointestinal bleeding following long-distance running can also be a significant route of iron loss (Buckman, 1984). The incidence of iron deficiency in women athletes may be particularly high (Nickerson & Tripp, 1983; Parr, Bachman, & Moss, 1984). With the increased loss of iron due to intensive exercise, it could be predicted that an iron-deficiency anemia would be precipitated in those athletes consuming diets marginal in iron intake. This idea is supported by the observation of iron deficiency in a wide range of trained athletes (Ehn, Carlmark, & Hoglund, 1980; Hunding, Jordal, & Paulev, 1981; Stewart, Steel, Toyne, & Stewart, 1972; Wijn, Jongste, Mosterd, & Willebrand, 1971). Encouragingly, dietary iron supplementation can eliminate this anemia (Hunding et al., 1981). In those individuals who have iron deficiency anemia, it can be predicted that iron therapy would improve endurance athletic performance.

However, as with zinc, caution regarding the level of iron supplementation is warranted. Similar to the inhibitory effect of excess zinc on copper absorption, high levels of iron can inhibit the absorption of zinc (Aggett, Crofton, Khic, Gvozdanovic, & Gvozdanovic, 1983). Levels of iron supplementation as low as 50 mg can significantly inhibit intestinal uptake of zinc. Considering the fact that many athletes may already be marginal with regard to zinc status, the potential negative effects of excess iron supplementation should be clear. If iron supplements are to be used, it is suggested that they be on the order of 15 mg/day, and they should be taken preprandially to reduce a negative effect on zinc absorption.

Summary

This review has attempted to illustrate the fact that significant perturbations in trace mineral metabolism can occur in the trained athlete. Coupled with the marginal intake of trace minerals by some segments of the population, it is likely that the athletes may be at particular risk with regard to developing some trace mineral deficiencies. The degree and extent of such deficiencies in the athlete is an area of research needing attention. However, even at this early point in time, it must be emphasized that if mineral supplements are used to either correct a perceived deficiency or in the hopes of increasing athletic performance, the level of each supplement used should not be excessive. A reasonable level of supplementation that meets the U.S. RDA is recommended.

In this review, zinc, copper, and iron were discussed only as representative trace elements. The metabolism of other elements such as chromium (Beller, Maher, Hartley, Bass, & Wacker, 1975; Gupta & Srivastava, 1973; Lukaski et al., 1983; Refsum, Meen, & Stroome, 1973) may also be adversely affected by intensive exercise. Future studies on the mechanisms underlying the changes in mineral metabolism in the athlete and how these changes affect athletic abilities and health will undoubtedly provide exciting new information.

References

Aggett, P.J., Crofton, R.W., Khic, C., Gvozdanovic, S., & Govzdanovic, D. (1983). The mutual inhibitory effects on their bioavailability of inorganic zinc and iron. *Progress in Clinical Biological Research*, **129**, 117-124.

Andersen, H.T., & Bankve, H. (1970). Iron deficiency and muscular work performance: An evaluation of cardio-respiratory function of iron-deficient subjects with and without anemia. *Scandinavian Journal of Clinical Laboratory Investigation*, **144** (Suppl 25), 1-39.

Anderson, R.A., Polansky, M.M. Bryden, N.A., Roginski, E.D., Patterson, K.Y., & Reamer, D.C. (1982). Effect of exercise (running) on serum glucose, insulin, glucagon and chromium excretion. *Diabetes*, **31**, 212-216.

Beller, G.A., Maher, J.T., Hartley, L.H., Bass, D.E., & Wacker, W.E.C. (1975, May). Changes in serum and sweat magnesium levels during work in the heat. *Aviation, Space and Environmental Medicine*, pp. 709-712.

Brooks, S.M., Sanborn, C.F., Albrecht, B.H., & Wagner, W.W. (1984). Diet in athletic amenorrhea. *Lancet, i,* 559-560.

Buckman, M.T. (1984). Gastrointestinal bleeding in long-distance runners. *Annals of Internal Medicine*, **101**, 127-128.

Buzina, R., Jusci, M., Sapunar, J., & Milanovic, N. (1980). Zinc nutrition and taste acuity in school children with impaired growth. *American Journal of Clinical Nutrition*, **33**, 2262-2267.

Cartwright, G.E., & Wintrobe, M.M. (1964). Copper metabolism in normal subjects. *American Journal of Clinical Nutrition*, **14**, 224-232.

Consolazio, C.F., Nelson, R.A., Matoush, L.R., Hughes, R.C., & Urone, P. (1964). The trace mineral losses in sweat (Report No. 284). Denver, CO: U.S. Army Medical Research and Nutrition Laboratory.

Dallman, P.R. (1982). Manifestations of iron deficiency. *Seminars in Hematology,* **19,** 19-30.

Davidson, R.J.L. (1964). Exertional haemoglobinuria: a report on three cases with studies on the hemolytic mechanism. *Journal of Clinical Pathology,* **17,** 536-540.

Dowdy, R.P., & Burt, J. (1980). Effect of intensive, long-term training on copper and iron nutriture in man. *Federation Proceedings,* **39,** 786.

Dowdy, R.P., & Dohm, G.L. (1972). Effect of training and exercise on serum ceruloplasmin in rats. *Proceedings of the Society of Experimental Biology and Medicine,* **139,** 489-491.

Dressendorfer, R.H., & Sockolov, R. (1980). Hypozincemia in runners. *the Physician and sportsmedicine,***8,** 97-100.

Dressendorfer, R.H., Wade, C.E., Keen, C.L., & Scaff, J.H. (1982). Plasma mineral levels in marathon runners during a 20-day road race. *The Physician and sportsmedicine,* **10,** 113-118.

DuFaux, B., Hoedegrath, A., Streitbergen, I., Hollman, W., & Assman, G. (1981). Serum ferritin, transferrin, haptoglobin, and iron in middle- and long-distance runners, elite rowers, and professional racing cyclists. *International Journal of Sports Medicine,* **2,** 43-46.

Dunlap, W.M., James, G.W., & Hume, D.M. (1974). Anemia and neutropenia caused by copper deficiency. *Annals of Internal Medicine,* **80,** 470-476.

Ehn, L., Carlmark, B., & Hoglund, S. (1980). Iron status in athletes involved in intense physical activity. *Medicine and Science in Sports and Exercise,* **12,** 61-64.

Falchuk, K.H. (1977). Effect of acute disease and ACTH on serum zinc proteins. *New England Journal of Medicine,* **296,** 1129-1134.

Finch, C.A., & Cook, J.D. (1984). Iron deficiency. *American Journal of Clinical Nutrition,* **39,** 471-477.

Fisher, P.W.F., Giroux, A., & L'Abbe, M.R. (1984). Effect of zinc supplementation on copper status in adult man. *American Journal of Clincial Nutrition,* **40,** 743-746.

gupta, J.S., & Srivastava, K.K. (1973). Effect of potassium magnesium aspartat on endurance work in man. *Indian Journal of Experimental Biology,* **11,** 392-394.

Hackman, R.M., & Keen, C.L. (1983). Trace element assessment of runners. *Federation Proceedings,* **42** , 830.

Hackman, R.M., & Keen, C.L. (1984). Zinc supplementation in runners and nonrunners. *Federation Proceedings,* **43,** 870.

Halsted, J.A., Ronaghy, H.A., Abadi, P., Haghshenass, M., Amirhakima, G.H., Barakat, R.M., & Reinhold, J.G. (1972). Zinc deficiency in man: The Shiraz experiment. *American Journal of Medicine,* **53,** 277-284.

Halsted, J., Smith, J.C., & Irwin, I.M. (1974). A conspectus of research on zinc requirements of man. *Journal of Nutrition,* **104,** 345-378.

Haralambie, G. (1975). Changes in electrolytes and trace elements during exercise. In H. Howard & J.R. Poortmans (Eds.), *Metabolic adaptation to prolonged exercise* (pp. 340-351). Basel, Switzerland: Birkhausen Verlag.

Haralambie, G. (1981). Serum zinc in athletes in training. *International Journal of Sportsmedicine* **2,** 135-138.

Haralambie, G., & Keul, J. (1970). Das Verhalten von serum-coeruloplasmin und kupfer bei langdavernder korperbelastony. *Arzneimittel—Forsch,* **24,** 112-115.

Hetland, Ø., Brubak, E.A., Refsum, H.E., & Strømme, S.B. (1975). Serum and erythrocyte zinc concentrations after prolonged heavy exercise. In H. Howard & J.R. Poortmans (Eds.), *Metabolic adaptation to prolonged physical exercise.* (pp. 367-370). Basel, Switzerland: Birkhausen Verlag.

Hooper, P.L., Visconti, L., Garry, P.J., & Johnson, G.E. (1980). Zinc lowers high-density lipoprotein-cholesterol levels. *Journal of the American Medical Association,* **244,** 1960-1961.

Hunding, A., Jordal, R., & Paulev, P.-E. (1981). Runners anemia and iron deficiency. *Acta Medica Scandinavia,* **209,** 315-318.

Hurley, L.S. (1981). Teratogenic aspects of manganese, zinc and copper nutrition. *Physiologic Review,* **61,** 249-295.

Hurley, L.S., Gordon, P., Keen, C.L., & Mekhofer, L. (1982). Circadian variation in rat plasma zinc and rapid effect of dietary zinc deficiency. *Proceedings of the Society of Experimental Biology and Medicine,* **170,** 48-52.

Hurley, L.S., Keen, C.L., & Lonnerdal, B. (1983). Aspects of trace element interactions during development. *Federation Proceedings,* **42,** 1735-1739.

Jameson, S. (1983). Zinc nutrition and human pregnancy. *Progress in Clinical and Biological Research,* **129,** 53-69.

Karlson, J., Diamant, B., & Saltin, B. (1968). Lactic dehydrogenase activity in muscle after prolonged exercise in man. *Journal of Applied Physiology,* **25,** 88-91.

Keen, C.L., Feldman, B.F., Knight, J., O'Neill, S., Ferrell, F., & Hurley, L.S. (1982). The influence of high concentrations of dietary copper on vitamin K-dependent coagulation factors. *Proceedings of the Society of Experimental Biology and Medicine,* **170,** 471-475.

Keen, C.L., Lonnerdal, B., & Fisher, G.L. (1981). Seasonal variations and the effects of age on serum copper and zinc values in the dog. *American Journal of Veterinary Research,* **42,** 347-350.

Keen, C.L., Lonnerdal, B., & Hurley, L.S. (1982). Teratogenic effects of copper deficiency and excess. In J.R.S. Sorenson (Ed.), *Inflammatory diseases of copper* (pp. 109-121). New Jersey: Humana Press.

Klevay, L.M. (1980). Interactions of copper and zinc in cardiovascular disease. *Annals of New York Academy of Science,* **355,** 140-151.

Krotkiewski, M., Gudmundsson, M., Backstrom, P., & Mandroukas, K. (1982). Zinc and muscle strength. *Acta Physiologica Scandinavia,* **116,** 309-311.

Lichti, E., Turner, M., & Henzel, J. (1971). Changes in serum zinc following periods of increased metabolic activity in differences in arterial and venous zinc concentrations following surgically inflicted wounds. In D. Hemphill (Ed)., *Trace substances in environmental health, IV* (pp. 326-335). Columbia, MO: University Of Missouri Press.

Lichti, E., Turner, M., Deweese, M., & Henzel, J. (1970). Zinc concentration in venous plasma before and after exercise in dogs. *Missouri Medicine,* pp. 303-304.

Lonnerdal, B., Keen, C.L., Ohtake, M., & Tamura, T. (1983). Iron, zinc, copper and manganese in infant formulas. *American Journal of Diseases of Children,* **137,** 433-437.

Lukaski, H.C., Bolonchuk, W.W., Klevay, L.M., Milne, D.B., & Sandstead, H.H. (1983). Maximal oxygen consumption as related to magnesium, copper and zinc nutriture. *American Journal Clinical Nutrition,* **37,** 407-415.

Mason, K.E. (1979). A conspectus of research on copper metabolism and requirements of man. *Journal of Nutrition,* **109,** 1979-2066.

Masters, D.G., Keen, C.L., Lonnerdal, B., & Hurley, L.S. (1983). Zinc deficiency teratogenicity: The protective role of maternal tissue catabolism. *Journal of Nutrition,* **113,** 905-912.

McDonald, R., Hegenauer, J., Sucec, A., & Saltman, P. (1984). Effects of iron deficiency and exercise on myoglobin in rats. *European Journal of Applied Physiology,* **52,** 414-419.

Moynahan, E.J. (1974). Acrodermatitis enteropathica: A lethal inherited human zinc deficiency disorder. *Lancet,* i, 399-400.

Moynahan, E.J., & Barnes, P.M. (1973). Zinc deficiency and a synthetic diet for lactose intolerance. *Lancet, i,* 676-677.

Nickerson, H.J., & Tripp, A.D. (1983). Iron deficiency in adolescent cross-country runners. *The Physician and Sportsmedicine,* **11,** 60-68.

O'Dell, B. (1984). Copper. In *Nutrition reviews present knowledge in nutrition* (5th ed.) (pp. 506-518). Washington, DC: The Nutrition Foundation.

Oh, S.H., Deagen, J.T., Whanger, P.D., & Weswig, P.H. (1978). Biological function of metallothionein. V. Its inducation in rats by various stresses. *American Journal of Physiology, Endocrinology, Metabolism, and Gastrointestinal Physiology,* **3,** E282-E285.

Ohira, Y., Edgerton, V.R., Gardner, G.W., Senewirante, B., Barnard, R.J., & Simpson, D.R. (1979). Work capacity, heart rate, and blood lactate responses to iron treatment. *British Journal of Haematology,* **41,** 365-370.

Ohno, H., Hirata, F., Terayama, K., Kawarabayashi, T., Doi, R., Kondo, T., & Taniguchi, N. (1983). Effect of short physical exercise on the levels of zinc and carbonic anhydrase isoenzyme activities in human erythrocytes. *European Journal of Applied Physiology,* **51,** 257-268.

Olha, A.E., Klissouras, V., Sullivan, J.D., & Skoryna, S.C. (1982). Effects of exercise on concentration of elements in the serum. *Journal of Sports Medicine and Physical Fitness,* **22,** 414-424.

Parr, R.B., Bachman, L.A., & Moss, R.A. (1984). Iron deficiency in female athletes. *The Physician and Sportsmedicine,* **12,** 81-86.

Parr, R.B., Porter, M.A., & Hodgson, S.C. (1984). Nutrition knowledge and practice of coaches, trainers and athletes. *The Physician and SportsMedicine* **12,** 127-138.

Paulev, P.-K., Jordal, R., & Pederson, N.S. (1983). Dermal excretion of iron in intensely training athletes. *Clinica Chimica Acta,* **127,** 19-27.

Phillips, A.G. (1982). Zinc in total parenteral nutrition. In A.S. Prasad, I.E. Dreosti, & B.S. Hetzel (Eds.), *Current topics in nutrition and disease* (pp. 169-180). New York: Alan R. Liss.

Prasad, A.S. (1983). Zinc deficiency in human subjects. *Progress in Clinical and Biological Research,* **129,** 1-33.

Prasad, A.S., Brewer, G.J., Shoomaker, E.B., & Rabbani, P. (1978). Hypocupremia induced by zinc therapy in adults. *Journal of the American Medical Association,* **240,** 2166-2168.

Prasad, A.S., Miale, A., Farid, Z., Schulent, A., & Sandstead, H.H. (1963). Zinc metabolism in patients with syndrome of iron deficiency anemia, hypogonadism and dwarfism. *Journal of Laboratory Clinical Medicine,* **61,** 537-549.

Refsum, H.E., Meen, H.D., & Stromme, S.B. (1973). Whole blood, serum and erythrocyte magnesium concentrations after repeated heavy exercise of long duration. *Scandinavian Journal of Clinical Laboratory Investigation,* **32,** 123-127.

Reinstein, N.H., Lonnerdal, B., Keen, C.L., & Hurley, L.S. (1984). Zinc-copper interactions in the pregnant rat. Fetal outcome and maternal and fetal zinc, copper, and iron. *Journal of Nutrition,* **114,** 1266-1279.

Richardson, J.H., & Drake, P.D. (1979). The effects of zinc on fatigue of striated muscle. *Journal of Sports Medicine,* **19,** 133-134.

Schoene, R.B., Escourrou, P., Robertson, H.T., Nilson, K.L., Parsons, J.R., & Smith, N.J. (1983). Iron repletion decreases maximal exercise lactate concentrations in female athletes with minimal iron-deficiency anemia. *Journal of Laboratory Clinical Medicine,* **102,** 306-312.

Stevens, M.D., Disilvestro, R.A., & Harris, E.P. (1984). Specific receptor for ceruloplasmin in membrane fragments for aortic and heart tissue. *Biochemistry,* **23,** 261-266.

Stewart, G.A., Steel, J.E., Toyne, A.H., & Stewart, M.J. (1972). Observations on the hematology and the iron and protein intake of Australian Olympic athletes. *Medical Journal of Australia, 2,* 1339-1343.

Terjung, R.L., Winder, W.W., Baldwin, K.M., & Holloszy, J.O. (1973). Effect of exercise on the turnover of cytochrome C in skeletal muscle. *Journal of Biological Chemistry, 248,* 7404-7406.

Uhari, M., Pakarinen, A., Hietala, J., Nurmi, T., & Kouralainen, K. (1983). Serum iron, copper, zinc, ferritin, and ceruloplasmin after intense heat exposure. *European Journal of Applied Physiology, 51,* 331-335.

Vallerand, A.L., Cuerrier, J.-P., Shapcott, D., Vallerand, R.J., & Gardiner, P.F. (1984). Influence of exercise training on tissue chromium concentrations in the rat. *American Journal of Clinical Nutrition, 39,* 402-409.

Veller, O.D., & Hermansen, L. (1972). Physical performance and hematological parameters, with special reference to hemoglobin and maximal oxygen uptake. *Acta Medica Scandinavia,* 1(Suppl. 552), 1-40.

Wade, C.E., Dressendorfer, R.H., O'Brian, J.C., & Claybaugh, J.R. (1982). Overnight basal urinary findings during a 500 km race over 20 days. *Journal of Sports Medicine and Physical Fitness, 22,* 371-376.

Walravens, P.A., & Hambidge, K.M. (1977). Zinc metabolism. In G.J. Brewer & A.S. Prasad (Eds.), *Current aspects in health and disease* (p. 61). New York: Alan Press.

Widdowson, E.M., McCance, R.A., & Spray, C.M. (1951). The chemical composition of the human body. *Clinical Science, 10,* 113-125.

Wijn, J.F., Jongste, D.E., Mosterd, W., & Willebrand, D. (1971). Hemoglobin packed cell volume, serum iron and iron binding capacity of selected athletes during training. *Nutrition and Metabolism, 13,* 129-139.

Williams, D.M. (1982). Clinical significance of copper deficiency and toxicity in the world population. *Current Topics in Nutrition and Disease, 6,* 277-299.

Wittenberg, J. (1970). Myoglobin-facilitated oxygen diffusion: A role of myoglobin in oxygen entry into muscle. *Physiological Review, 50,* 559-635.

5

Loss of Electrolytes by Sweat in Sports

Dieter Böhmer
UNIVERSITY OF FRANKFURT-am-MAIN
FRANKFURT, WEST GERMANY

Optimal concentrations of electrolytes are a prerequisite for maximal performance in sport. Insufficient intake, malabsorption, or a high loss of electrolytes cause a reduction of muscular work. The kidneys mainly keep the water-salt-metabolism exactly in balance in the body. During intensive and long-lasting sport performance, an additional excretion of sweat occurs. In temperate climates the loss of sweat during sports is about 1L/hr. The humidity of the inhaled air can also affect the water-salt balance. However, the highest amounts of electrolytes are excreted by sweat.

With the help of a formula (Böhmer, 1981) the loss of fluid can be calculated by the determination of the body weight before and after training. The loss of electrolytes is much more difficult to estimate due to (a) the technical problem of collecting unadulterated sweat during exercise, and (b) the different individual electrolyte concentrations in sweat. Sweat production and composition depend upon the region of the body (eccrine and apocrine glands) from which it is being produced. Low levels in serum occur only in situations of heavy deficiency of electrolytes. We have tried to answer the following question with regard to the different influences of the electrolytes in sweat: What is the amount of the electrolyte loss by sweat during sport performance?

- Is there a correlation between the level of training and the electrolyte concentration in sweat?
- Is there a correlation between the electrolyte concentration in sweat and sex?
- Does the electrolyte concentration change during 1 hour of athletic activities?

Methods

Anus-praeter bags were used for collecting sweat. The opening was extended 4 x 6 cm. The advantage of these specific bags is the quick fixation without irritating the skin. Four bags were fixed onto the back of the sportsmen. Before and after the sportive exercise, the body weight was measured and a blood sample was taken. The temperature, pressure, and humidity of the atmosphere were recorded. Even under strenuous performance, only a few bags fell off.

Subjects

The physical characteristics of the subjects are shown in Table 1.

The athletes belonged to national teams and were well-trained in their sport-discipline. The cyclists were investigated before and after a preparatory training period for the world championship. The load took place on the bicycle ergometer with an increase every 3 minutes to the point of exhaustion. Yachtsmen reached this point after 18 min, rowers, and cyclists after 22 min. All plastic bags were fixed on their backs before they started the ergometer work. The skin was first cleaned with cotton soaked in alcohol before the experiment and afterwards with sterile water.

Electrolyte concentrations 10 minutes after the beginning of work are shown in Table 2 and electrolyte concentrations at the end of the test in Table 3. The total loss calculated indirectly by loss of weight is shown in Table 4.

In a second series of tests we examined male and female handball players. The subjects performed their normal 75-min training routine. Examinations were conducted according to the following plan outlined in Table 5.

Loss of body weight and pulse frequency at the end of the training show an intensive stress during the 75-min training. The selection of the groups and their biodata are shown in Table 6. Room temperature was about 20° C, humidity 55%, atmospheric pressure was 1,023 mbar. The results of the sweat analysis are listed in Table 7. Total losses are shown in Table 8. A female handball team was examined according to the same criteria before and after preparatory training of 4 months (Table 9).

Table 1. Physical characteristics of subjects

Group	N	Age	Height (cm)	Weight (kg)	Loss of weight (kg)
Yachtsmen	8	18	180	68	0.30
Rowers	8	21	189	85	0.65
Cyclists I	11	17	180	70	0.50
Cyclists II	11	17	177	7	0.55

Table 2. Electrolyte concentration (mmol/L) in sweat 10 min after beginning bicycle ergometer work

Group	NA	K	CA	MG	CL
Yachtsmen	67.4	7.47	1.30	0.49	51.8
Rower	24.5	7.00	1.00	0.27	15.8
Cyclists I	47.3	6.23	0.86	0.33	36.1
Cyclists II	26.7	7.31	0.80	0.25	21.8

Table 3. Electrolyte concentration (mmol/L) in sweat at the end of 18-22 min test on a bicycle ergometer

Group	NA	K	CA	MG	CL
Yachtsmen	77.1	5.27	0.59	0.27	61.8
Rower	42.7	5.19	0.50	0.11	33.9
Cyclists I	72.9	5.85	0.40	0.16	62.5
Cyclists II	50.3	5.16	0.29	0.10	40.0

Table 4. Total loss of electrolyte (mmol) following bicycle ergometer work

Group	NA	K	CA	MG	CL
Yachtsmen	23.1	1.58	0.18	0.08	18.5
Rower	27.7	3.38	0.32	0.07	22.0
Cyclists I	36.5	2.93	0.20	0.08	31.3
Cyclists II	27.7	2.84	0.16	0.06	22.0

Table 5. Data Collection Schedule

Phase of Activity	Minutes	Sample
Warm-up	5	Bloodsample
Training with ball	25	Sweatsample
Game	50	Sweatsample
Rest	75	Blood & Sweat
	90	Sweatsample

Table 6. Biodata of the handball players

Group		n	Age (Years)	Height (cm)	Weight (kg)	(g)	%
F	very well trained (+ + +)	9	24.7 ± 4.1	169 ± 3.6	64.8 ± 5.2	1111 ± 132	1.7 ± 0.2
F	well trained (+ +)	10	22.3 ± 3.7	167.9 ± 5.7	60.33 ± 4.69	960 ± 173	1.6 ± 0.3
M	well trained (+ +)	11	23.6 ± 3.8	183 ± 4.0	84.85 ± 6.72	1623 ± 458	1.9 ± 0.4
M	medium trained (+)	11	23.9 ± 5.4	180.3 ± 7.0	77.8 ± 5.9	1373 ± 174	1.8 ± 0.3

Table 7. Electrolyte concentration (mmol/L) in sweat during 75-min handball training

	Na⁺	25	50	75	90
			Time, Minutes		
F	+ + +	46.3 ± 13.7	47.8 ± 4.3	46.2 ± 20.8	40.0 ± 10.4
F	+ +	65.4 ± 14.9	57.4 ± 8.9	61.3 ± 11.3	61.4 ± 11.4
M	+ +	63.1 ± 15.6	69.0 ± 18.4	66.3 ± 18.2	60.6 ± 12.6
M	+	48.9 ± 6.8	52.3 ± 8.7	49.4 ± 11.3	44.5 ± 11.7

	Cl⁻	25	50	75	90
F	+ + +	44.8 ± 9.6	42.3 ± 2.9	44.8 ± 13.8	35.1 ± 6.1
F	+ +	56.1 ± 13.6	46.4 ± 8.5	49.7 ± 9.8	46.4 ± 11.7
M	+ +	54.4 ± 15.5	59.5 ± 18.0	56.7 ± 18.5	51.5 ± 14.6
M	+	36.6 ± 6.2	40.7 ± 8.1	39.7 ± 10.7	33.6 + 12.7

	K⁺	25	50	75	90
F	+ + +	4.60 ± 1.13	3.86 ± 0.99	4.41 ± 1.31	4.82 ± 1.32
F	+ +	5.42 ± 1.36	4.20 ± 0.73	3.83 ± 0.44	3.93 ± 0.44
M	+ +	4.87 ± 1.43	3.81 ± 0.98	3.66 ± 1.07	3.40 ± 0.96
M	+	6.86 ± 1.67	5.64 ± 1.30	4.53 ± 1.26	3.96 ± 1.12

	Ca⁺⁺	25	50	75	90
F	+ + +	0.35 ± 0.16	0.22 ± 0.10	0.37 ± 0.24	0.31 ± 0.11
F	+ +	0.44 ± 0.20	0.26 ± 0.08	0.22 ± 0.03	0.23 ± 0.03
M	+ +	0.20 ± 0.12	0.04 ± 0.06	0.06 ± 0.09	0.05 ± 0.10
M	+	0.64 ± 0.24	0.38 ± 0.14	0.22 ± 0.22	0.17 + 0.10

	Mg	25	50	75	90
F	+ + +	-	-	-	-
F	+ +	0.12 ± 0.05	0.08 ± 0.03	0.07 ± 0.02	0.06 ± 0.03
M	+ +	0.08 ± 0.03	0.07 ± 0.03	0.05 ± 0.01	0.05 ± 0.01
M	+	0.12 ± 0.03	0.09 ± 0.03	0.08 ± 0.02	0.08 ± 0.02

+ = medium training.
+ + = well trained.
+ + + = very well trained.

Table 8. Handball players, 75-min training

mmol/l	Na⁺	K⁺	Ca⁺⁺	Mg⁺⁺	Cl⁻
Female (N = 9) very well trained (+ + +) a 0.88 l/sweat					
S.C.	45.1	4.4	0.31	–	41.7
T.L.	39.7	3.9	0.27	–	36.7
Female (N = 10) well trained (+ +) a 0.79 l/sweat					
S.C.	61.4	4.4	0.29	0.08	49.7
T.L.	48.5	3.5	0.23	0.06	39.3
Male (N = 11) well trained (+ +) a 1.3 l/sweat					
S.C.	64.8	4.0	0.09	0.06	55.6
T.L.	84.2	5.1	0.12	0.08	72.3
Male (N = 11) medium trained (+) a 1.1 l/sweat					
S.C.	48.8	5.3	0.35	0.09	37.7
T.L.	53.7	5.8	0.39	0.10	41.5
Medium daily intake					
	150	100	25	15	150

S.C. = Sweat concentration of electrolytes.
T.L. = Total loss.
a 1/sweat = average loss of sweat.

Discussion

Standard Values for Electrolyte Concentrations in Sweat

The initial values for electrolyte concentration in sweat in our group depend on (a) the type of sport, (b) the level of training, and (c) the duration of performance. Significantly higher values were found in yachtsmen who were only moderately trained in endurance sports compared with athletes who show very high-endurance capability (race cyclists and regatta rowers). In order to generalize, other sport disciplines must be included in the investigation.

Within the groups of handball players and cyclists, we could observe a certain influence training as on the electrolyte concentrations. An intensive training of 6 weeks of the already well-trained race cyclists led to a further reduction of electrolyte concentration in sweat.

No difference was found between male and female athletes in the initial values or in the reduction of salt content in sweat after training. It is possible that the type of sport influences the composition of sweat. The rapid increase of stress intensity on the bicycle ergometer caused a considerable increase of electrolytes in serum. Among the group of yachtsmen, rowers, and cyclists, the potassium level rose to an average of 5.5 mmol/l (in individual cases to 7.5 mmol/l). This is caused by a marked acidity in the blood. The lactate level rose to an average of 11.5 mmol/l. These extreme values are not reached during handball training. The electrolytes in serum did not increase significantly

Table 9. Biodata and electrolyte concentration before and after a preparation training period of a female handball team

Date	N	age, yr.	Height cm	Weight kg	Weight kg	Na$^+$	Cl$^-$	K$^+$	Mg^{++}	Ca^{++}
May 83	10	22.3 ± 3.7	168 ± 0.06	60.3 ± 4.7	0.96 ± 0.17	65.4	56.1	5.4	0.44	0.120
Sept. 83	8	23.4 ± 4.1	170 ± 0.05	63.6 ± 3.3	1.28 ± 0.24	44.1	37.4	3.9	0.39	0.085

at the end of training. The first sweat samples could be gained 10 min after the beginning of performance on the bicycle ergometer but only after 25 min during handball training.

Sex Differences

No difference was apparent in the behavior of electrolytes in sweat between female and male handball players. According to the level of training, the values of female athletes were between average and well-trained handball players. The total amount of sweat during training was significantly lower than in male athletes. Correlated to body weight, loss in weight was nearly equal. Hence, it seems likely that there is no fundamental difference in the secretion and composition of sweat between female and male athletes. A possible influence of age was not examined.

Variations of Electrolyte Concentration During Athletic Performance

The content of electrolytes in sweat has its peak after the start of athletic performance. Under strenuous exercise the sodium and chloride concentration increased to 50% from the initial values. Similar findings were described by Kobayashi, Ando, Hosoi, and Takeuchi (1976) and Costill (1977). Potassium, magnesium, and calcium decreased in sweat slightly during 1 hour of sport and decreased significantly after an hour. This reaction was found in all examinations. At the beginning of the athletic performance all four bags were fixed to the back of the athlete and then subsequently removed. For this reason, all details of total losses are only approximate values.

The amount of loss of electrolytes depends not only on condition and type of training, but also on climate, mental condition, and nutrition. Former examinations with a determination of total body potassium K^{40} (Böhmer & Böhlau, 1976) showed that a considerable amount of potassium was still excreted in the urine 24 hours after strenuous endurance performance. Loss of electrolytes in sweat is relatively small under normal athletic conditions. Only sodium and chloride ions which are easily replaceable are excreted distinctively. However, this is only the case in temperate climates during performances that last about 1 hour and with a loss of about 1 liter of sweat. Further losses of salt should be prevented. The normal diet is sufficient for the replacement of salt losses caused by standard activities. Only after unusual strenuous and long-lasting exercises do athletes need extra substitution of electrolytes.

Summary

Concentrations of electrolytes in sweat were measured during and after performance on the bicycle ergometer and during handball games. The results showed a dependence of the concentration of electrolytes on conditions of training, type of sport, and duration of performance. Also, no difference was apparent between male and female athletes. A distinctive loss of sodium and chloride ions was observed during 1 hour of sport performance in a temperate climate. The loss of K^+, Mg^{++}, and Ca^{++} by sweat has a mean value at the same duration.

References

Böhmer, D. (1981). Der einfluss des hochleistungssportes auf den wasser-salz-haushalt. In H. Rieckert (Ed.), *Sport an der grenze menschlicher leistungsfähigkeit* (pp. 188-192). Berlin-Hiedelberg-New York: Springer.

Böhmer, D., Böhlau, R. (1976). Loss of potassium and sodium by athletes after long lasting performance and the experiment of substituting it. *3rd International Symposium on Biochemistry of Exercise,* Quebec. Miami: Symposia Specialists.

Costill, D.L. (1977). Sweating: Its compositions and effects on body fluids. *Annals of the New York Academy of Science,* **301,** 160-173.

Kobayashi, Y., Ando, Y., Hosoi, T., Takeuchi, T. (1976). Therminal adaptation in highly trained athletes in hot environment. *Japanese Journal of Physical Education,* **1,** 39-45.

6

High- and Low-Dosage Iron-Supplementation in Iron-Deficient, Endurance Trained Females

Douglas B. Clement, Jack E. Taunton, Donald C. McKenzie, Lynne L. Sawchuk, and J. Preston Wiley
UNIVERSITY OF BRITISH COLUMBIA
VANCOUVER, BRITISH COLUMBIA, CANADA

Iron deficiency remains the most commonly recognized of the nutritional deficiencies. Although it reaches its greatest prevalence and severity in developing countries, it is also frequently encountered in affluent societies. According to the Nutrition Canada Survey (1973), large numbers of Canadians of all ages are affected by iron deficiency. Furthermore, iron deficiency is becoming increasingly common among those involved in regular exercise (Clement & Asmundson, 1982; Nickerson & Tripp, 1983; Wishnitzer, Vorst, & Berrebi, 1983).

Because females are already at special risk due to the increased iron requirement related to menstruation, the possibility of an increased iron demand associated with exercise is of particular concern to female athletes involved in regular, strenuous training. As a result, close monitoring of the dietary iron intake of female athletes has been recommended and the regular use of iron supplements considered (de Wijn, deJongste, Mosterd, & Willebrand 1973; Haymes, 1973). However, despite these attempts to alleviate the problem, there is still a lack of documentation regarding the extent to which dietary iron supplementation is beneficial in the prevention and treatment of iron deficiency in female athletes.

Cooter and Mowbray (1978) concluded that iron supplementation of 18 mg a day for a 4-month period had no effect on the iron status of female college basketball players. Similarly, Pate, Maguire, and Van Wyke (1979) found that administration of iron supplements of 50 mg a day for 5 to 9 weeks had no statistically significant impact on hemoglobin or iron status. However, in both cases, the conclusions were based on data collected from normal nonanemic subjects. Furthermore, an assessment of body iron stores from serum ferritin levels was absent in these investigations which included only hemoglobin, hematocrit, serum iron, total iron-binding capacity, and percent saturation values.

In contrast, Plowman and McSwegin (1981) found a significant increase in hemoglobin with dietary iron supplementation in nonanemic female cross-country runners. The subjects received a considerably higher dosage of iron than the previous studies (234 mg/day) for a minimum of 12 weeks. Ascorbic acid (450 mg/day) was taken in combination with the iron to enhance bioavailability. However, there was no determination of serum ferritin and, consequently, any changes in body iron stores could not be detected.

The following study was undertaken to further clarify the responses to oral iron therapy in iron-deficient female athletes and to help devise appropriate supplementation recommendations.

Methods

Female subjects engaged in endurance exercise were screened for iron deficiency by blood test. Iron deficiency was defined as a serum ferritin value at or below 20 ng/ml. Twelve females who met this criteria volunteered to participate in the study after giving informed consent. Blood tests done at a commercial biomedical laboratory included serum ferritin and hemoglobin to determine iron status.

Following the blood tests, the subjects were arbitrarily assigned to either a low-dosage or high-dosage iron supplementation regime. Subjects on the low-dosage schedule were instructed to take 300 mg ferrous gluconate (34.8 mg iron) three times a day (104.4 mg elemental iron/day). Those on the high-dosage schedule were instructed to take 600 mg ferrous gluconate (69.6 mg iron) three times a day (208.8 mg elemental iron/day). Both dosages are within the safety guidelines of the Compendium of Pharmaceuticals and Specialties (1983). After a period of iron supplementation ranging from 3 to 12 weeks, the subjects underwent another blood test to determine the response to therapy.

Nutritional information was obtained from 10 of the 12 subjects. Dietary intake was recorded for 7 days and analyzed to provide mean daily intakes of iron, energy, protein, carbohydrate, and fat (Action B.C. Nutrition Evaluation Computer Program).

The average changes in hemoglobin, serum ferritin, and total body iron following the supplementation period were compared to detect any differences between the two groups. These changes were determined from the difference between the presupplementation and postsupplementation values. Total body iron was estimated from the hemoglobin and serum ferritin levels. Each gram of hemoglobin contains 3.4 mg iron, and the serum ferritin level has been shown to correspond with the amount of storage iron in the ratio of 8 mg iron for every 1 ng/ml of serum ferritin (Bothwell, Charlton, Cook, & Finch, 1979). Total body hemoglobin calculations were based on the assumption that blood volume is equal to 79 ml/kg of body weight (Guyton, 1981).

Results

All but 1 of the subjects were engaged in endurance running. The one exception was a basketball player who practiced daily. The average weekly distance in training was 73 km and 56 km for the high-and low-dosage groups, respectively. The age of the subjects ranged from 19 to 30 years with a mean age of 23 years for the high-dosage group and 26 years for the low-dosage group. None of the subjects had a history of excessive blood loss, and none had donated blood within the past 3 months. Menstrual flow was light to average in all but 1 subject who reported greater than average blood loss. One subject had noted blood-tinged stool after running a marathon. Individual profiles are shown in Table 1.

All subjects demonstrated iron deficiency with serum ferritin levels at or below 20 ng/ml. The mean ferritin level presupplementation was 7.6 ng/ml for the high-dosage group and 13.3 ng/ml for the low-dosage group. Some subjects had progressed to the more advanced stage of iron deficiency indicated by hemoglobin levels less than 12 gm/dl. Presupplementation hemoglobin values averaged 11.7 gm/dl and 13.2 gm/dl for the high-dosage group and low-dosage group, respectively.

Following a supplementation period of approximately 8 weeks, the subjects in the high-dosage group showed greater changes than those in the low-dosage

Table 1. Subject profiles

Group	Subject	Age (yrs)	Height (cm)	Weight (kg)	Activity*
High	1	19	173	59.5	Running (48)
Dosage	2	20	158	45	Running (64)
	3	28	170	52	Running (96)
	4	25	168	56	Running (40)
	5	29	156	50	Running (96)
	6	22	165	54	Running (96)
	7	19	168	56	Running (72)
Low	1	28	165	59	Running (48)
Dosage	2	24	168	52	Running (80)
	3	26	168	68	Running (32)
	4	21	175	68	Basketball
	5	30	173	61	Running (64)

*Kilometers of running per week indicated in parentheses.

group for all levels including serum ferritin, hemoglobin, and total body iron. However, due to the large variability within the groups, the change in hemoglobin was the only significant difference at $p = 0.05$. The difference between the changes in total body iron for the two groups was significant at $p < 0.06$. Individual values are shown in Table 2 and mean values are shown in Table 3. Although the initial presupplementation mean values differed between groups, following supplementation serum ferritin and hemoglobin were increased to much the same levels for both groups.

All but 2 of the subjects who participated in the nutritional evaluation had dietary intakes below the recommended daily intake of 18 mg (Committee on Dietary Allowances, 1980). The average daily iron intakes for the high-dosage group were 14.6 mg and 12.5 mg, respectively. Mean daily protein, carbohydrate, fat, and energy intakes are shown in Table 4.

Discussion

Therapeutic trials with oral iron usually consist of doses between 36 and 74 mg elemental iron as a ferrous iron salt administered three times a day (Bothwell et al., 1979). In the present study, similar dosages of 34.8 and 69.6 mg elemental iron as ferrous gluconate were prescribed three times a day for a total of 104 to 209 mg a day. It has been suggested that the maximal safe toler-

Table 2. Individual changes in iron status pre and post supplementation with corresponding weeks of therapy

Group	Subject	Serum ferritin (ng/ml)		Hemoglobin (gm/dl)		△Total body iron (mg)	Weeks of therapy
		Pre	Post	Pre	Post		
High	1	4.0	13.0	10.1	14.4	759.1	8
Dosage	2	3.0	12.0	10.2	12.3	325.8	7
	3	8.5	23.0	13.8	13.9	130.0	10
	4	14.0	50.0	13.2	13.4	318.1	8.5
	5	4.8	14.9	10.0	13.8	591.1	9.75
	6	4.7	28.5	12.2	13.2	335.4	6
	7	14.0	20.0	12.1	13.4	243.5	3
Mean		7.6	23.1	11.7	13.5	386.1	7.5
± S.D.		4.7	13.3	1.6	0.7	215.2	2.4
Low	1	20.0	21.6	12.8	12.1	-98.1	10
Dosage	2	12.0	38.0	12.6	13.1	277.8	11
	3	5.8	25.8	13.5	14.4	324.4	9.5
	4	12.5	21.1	13.3	13.9	178.4	7.5
	5	16.0	22.0	13.9	13.8	31.7	2
Mean		13.3	25.7	13.2	13.4	142.8	8
± S.D.		5.3	7.1	0.5	0.9	175.2	3.5

Table 3. Changes in mean hemoglobin, ferritin, and total body iron pre and post supplementation

Group	Hemoglobin (gm/dl)			Serum ferritin (ng/ml)			Total body iron (mg)
	Pre	Post	Δ[a]	Pre	Post	Δ	Δ[b]
High Dosage (n = 7)	11.7	13.5	1.8 ± 1.7	7.6	23.1	15.5 ± 10.8	386.1 ± 215.2
Low Dosage (n = 5)	13.2	13.4	0.2 ± 0.6	13.3	25.7	12.4 ± 10.2	142.8 ± 175.2

[a]Significant difference between groups (P = .05).
[b]Significant difference between groups (P = .057).

Table 4. Nutritional evaluation*

Group	Subject	Iron (mg)	Protein (gm)	Carbohydrate (gm)	Fat (kcal)	Calories
High	1	18.3	64.5	296	79	2087
Dosage	3	10.4	65.2	343	104	2541
	4	12.3	66.2	278	94	2190
	6	12.3	83.2	269	102	2337
	7	19.6	113.0	427	127	3275
Mean		14.6	78.4	323	101	2486
± S.D.		4.1	20.8	65	18	473
Low	1	11.9	69.1	224	62	1705
Dosage	2	10.5	69.2	264	78	1974
	3	11.2	90.7	207	83	1918
	4	12.0	85.0	277	92	2221
	5	17.1	80.6	358	110	2793
Mean		12.5	79.0	266	85	2122
± S.D.		2.6	9.6	59	18	418

*Per day intakes averaged for 7 days.

ance level of highly ionized iron is approximately 250 mg a day (Bogert, Briggs, & Calloway, 1973). Most previous studies of iron supplementation in female athletes used considerably lower dosages, and these investigations generally used nonanemic female athletes and failed to assess body iron stores (Cooter & Mowbray, 1978; Pate et al., 1981; Plowman & McSwegin, 1981). Consequently, the results were inconclusive and the need for further research was emphasized.

In the present investigation, oral iron supplementation for approximately 8 weeks resulted in higher mean values for hemoglobin, serum ferritin, and total body iron for both supplementation groups. These changes were more marked in the group of iron-deficient female athletes that were instructed to take the higher dosage of iron (Table 3). However, this group was also more iron deficient than the group instructed to take the lower dosage of iron. Due to the three individuals in the higher dosage group with frank anemia, the average hemoglobin value for this group was less than 12 gm/dl (indicative of anemia). In contrast, the lower dosage group had an average hemoglobin value of 13.2 gm/dl and a greater average serum ferritin value suggestive of larger iron stores. Although the similar postsupplementation values for the two groups imply a better response in the higher dosage group, the absorption capacity of this group would be greater due to their relatively more depressed iron status (Bothwell et al., 1979). Consequently, this initial presupplementation difference in the iron status of the two groups confounds the interpretation of the results and makes it difficult to make any conclusive statements.

Furthermore, differences in the administration of the iron therapy could have affected the response. In particular, iron absorption can be influenced by taking the supplements on an empty stomach, with meals, or with ascorbic acid (Bothwell et al., 1979). Patient compliance was not monitored and could have affected the results. The present experimental design mirrored the true-life situation involving the initial prescription of the iron supplements by the physician, the ensuing patient compliance, and the resultant response to the therapy. It was assumed that the subjects maintained the same presupplementation level of activity throughout the study. Because exercise may impose an iron demand on the athlete (Clement & Asmundson, 1982; Nickerson & Tripp, 1983; Wishnitzer et al., 1983) changes in physical activity could mask the response to iron therapy and complicate interpretation of the data.

Nutritional intake was evaluated in the present study because the nature of the diet is an important consideration in iron deficiency. The average iron intakes for both groups were inadequate when compared to the recommended daily intake of 18 mg (Committee on Dietary Allowances, 1980). Considering the amount of iron supplied by the low-dose iron therapy was approximately 15 times their dietary intake, it appears safe to assume this minimal contribution was not of major concern in the response to therapy. All subjects had protein intakes greater than 1 gm/kg body weight, and the mean values for both groups were almost identical. Thus, protein intake was considerably higher than the recommended daily intake of 0.8 gm/kg (Committee on Dietary Allowances, 1980) and probably did not contribute to the observed iron deficiency in these females.

Summary

The responses to high-and low-dosage iron supplementation were compared in iron-deficient female athletes. Following approximately 8 weeks of oral iron therapy, both groups showed increased hemoglobin, serum ferritin, and estimated total body iron values. The group instructed to take the higher dosage (209 mg elemental iron/day) showed greater changes in serum ferritin, hemoglobin, and estimated total body iron when compared to the mean values for the group instructed to take the lower dosage (104 mg elemental iron/day).

Due to the large variability within the groups and the relatively small sample size, the change in hemoglobin was the only significant difference between the groups. Conclusive statements regarding the better dosage are not possible from the present study because the groups proved to be at different stages of iron deficiency at the outset. Because iron status affects iron absorption and the associated response to therapy, this initial difference between the two groups confounded the interpretation of the results and prevented any valid conclusions from being drawn. However, the present enquiry serves to stimulate further research on optimal iron therapy for iron-deficient athletes and will be valuable for future reference concerning the design of such investigations.

References

Bogert, L.J., Briggs, G.M., & Calloway, D.H. (1973). *Nutrition and physical fitness.* Philadelphia: W.B. Saunders.

Bothwell, T.H., Charlton, R.W., Cook, J.D., & Finch, C.A. (1979). *Iron metabolism in man.* Oxford: Blackwell Scientific Publications.

Clement, D.B., & Asmundson, R.C. (1982). Nutritional intake and hematological parameters in endurance runners. *The Physician and Sportsmedicine, 10,* 37-43.

Committee on Dietary Allowances, Food and Nutrition Board, National Research Council. (1980). Recommended dietary allowances. (9th ed.) Washington: National Academy of Sciences.

Cooter, G.R., & Mowbray, K.W. (1978). Effects of iron supplementation and activity on serum iron depletion and hemoglobin levels in female athletes. *Research Quarterly, 49,* 114-117.

deWijn, J.F., deJongste, J.L., Mosterd, W., & Willebrand, D. (1971). Hemoglobin, packed cell volume, serum iron and iron binding capacity of selected athletes during training. *Nutrition and Metabolism, 13,* 129-139.

Guyton, A. (1981). *Textbook of medical physiology* (6th ed.). Philadelpia: W.B. Saunders.

Haymes, E.M. (1973). Iron deficiency and the active woman. In D.V. Harris (Ed.), *DGWS Research Reports: Women in Sports* Vol. II, pp. 91-97). Washington: AAHPER Press.

Nickerson, H.J., & Tripp, A. (1983). Iron deficiency in adolescent cross-country runners. *The Physician and Sportsmedicine, 11,* 60-66.

Nutrition Canada. (1973). *Nutrition: A national priority.* Ottawa: Health and Welfare.

Pate, R.R., Maguire, M., & Van Wyke, J. (1979). Dietary iron supplementation in women athletes. *The Physician and Sportsmedicine, 7,* 81-88.

Plowman, S.A., & McSwegin, P.C. (1981). The effects of iron supplementation on female cross country runners. *The Journal of Sports Medicine, 21,* 407-416.

Wishnitzer, R., Vorst, E. & Berrebi, A. (1983). Bone marrow iron depression in competitive distance runners. *The International Journal of Sports Medicine, 4,* 27-30.

7

Strenuous Exercise May Increase Dietary Needs for Chromium and Zinc

Richard A. Anderson, Marilyn M. Polansky, Noella A. Bryden, and Helene N. Guttman
BELTSVILLE HUMAN NUTRITION RESEARCH CENTER
BELTSVILLE, MARYLAND, USA

Since the early times of athletic competition, athletes have been searching for elusive dietary substances to improve their performance. Numerous dietary modifications have been attempted; however, no evidence exists that supplementation with any specific nutrient influences athletic performance above that obtained with a well-balanced diet. The exception to this may be iron, which in certain groups, especially young women who exercise often and strenuously, may be required in amounts not met by normal dietary intakes. The effects of strenuous exercise on trace elements other than iron such as chromium (Cr) and zinc (Zn) have not been thoroughly investigated, nor have the effects of supplementation with these elements on overall performance been evaluated.

Chromium and zinc are trace minerals required for normal carbohydrate and lipid metabolism. Even in sedentary individuals dietary intakes of these nutrients are usually less than the amount suggested for optimal health (Anderson, 1981; Smith, Morris, & Ellis, 1983). Marginal intake of Cr is associated with glucose intolerance, elevated circulating insulin, elevated cholesterol and triglycerides, and increased incidence of aortic plaques (Anderson, 1981). Marginal Zn nutritive intake is associated with decreased growth, appetite, taste and smell, sexual maturation, wound healing, and increased risks of atherosclerosis (Smith et al., 1983). The consequences of the increased nutrient requirements associated with exercise with Cr and Zn intake need to be established.

Methods

Experimental Design

Nine male runners ranging in age from 23 to 46 years were selected. All runners appeared healthy and were taking no medications except for 1 subject who was taking isoniazid. Details of subjects and their selection have been reported (Anderson, Polansky, & Bryden, 1984). The study was approved by the Human Nutrition Study Committee, United States Department of Agriculture. All subjects were informed of the purpose of the experiment and signed an informed consent form. Subjects were examined by a physician prior to the run with special attention given to cardiovascular problems but none were detected. Subjects were asked to fast from 12 midnight until 2 hours after running; no foods or drinks other than water and black coffee were permitted until the 2-hour postrun when blood and urine samples were collected. Subjects were instructed to run a 6-mile course at or near their maximal running capacity. Running commenced at 10:00 a.m., and all subjects were able to eat their usual lunches at approximately 12:45 p.m., following the 2-hour sampling period.

Collection of Urine and Blood Samples

The runners collected separate urine collections from (a) midnight the day of the run until the run, (b) within 5 minutes of completing the run, (c) 2 hours after the run, and (d) until midnight. A 24-hour urine sample was then collected beginning at midnight. Blood was drawn before the run, immediately after, and 2 hours following the run, using a Minicath-21 infusion set and a 25 ml Sarstedt Safety-Monovette. All containers and blood collection apparatus have been shown to contribute negligible amounts of contaminating trace elements. Serum values obtained from samples collected immediately following running were corrected for hemoconcentration using hemoglobin and hematocrit values. Analytical determinations were made as described (Anderson et al., 1982, 1984). Statistical analysis were performed using repeated measure analysis of variance and Duncan's Multiple Range Test.

Results

Serum glucose of all runners tested was elevated immediately following running 6 miles. Prerun serum glucose values ranged from 86 to 97 mg/dl, mean 90 ± 1 (see Table 1) and increased following running to a high in 1 runner of 300 mg/dl. Mean for all runners was 185 ± 19 mg/dl. Maximal increases in serum glucose could not be correlated with degree of training, running speed, or any of the other parameters tested. Increases in blood glucose are usually accompanied by increases in circulating insulin; however, in this study, running did not alter insulin levels (see Table 1). Simultaneous increases in serum glucagon paralleled those observed for serum glucose (see Table 1). Because serum insulin remained relatively constant, serum glucagon concentration was not related to serum insulin. Serum cortisol concentration followed the same

Table 1. Effects of running 6 miles on serum glucose, insulin, glucagon, and cortisol

Variable	Prerun	Postrun	2 hr postrun
Glucose (mg/dl)	90 ± 1[b]	185 ± 19[a]	77 ± 2[b]
Insulin (µU/ml)	7.1 ± 1.2[a]	9.6 ± 1[a]	5.9 ± 0.4[a]
Glucagon (µg/ml)	0.46 ± 0.02[b]	0.58 ± 0.03[a]	0.47 ± 0.02[b]
Cortisol (µg/dl)	31 ± 2[b]	41 ± 7[a]	31 ± 3[b]

Mean ± SEM.
[a]Postrun sample was taken immediately after running. Values in the same row with [b] superscripts are significantly different ($P < 0.05$).

pattern as that of glucose and glucagon, namely, a significant increase in samples collected immediately after the run and a return to prerun levels 2 hours following the run.

The trace elements, chromium, zinc, and copper (Cu), are also involved in glucose metabolism. Therefore, factors such as exercise that affect glucose metabolism may also alter the concentration and relative distribution of these nutrients. Serum Cr increased immediately following running and remained elevated 2 hours following the run (see Table 2). Increased serum Cr was accompanied by increased urinary Cr losses. Chromium concentrations of urine samples taken 2 hours following running ranged from 1.5-to 8.6-fold higher with a mean Cr concentration nearly 5-fold higher than that of the prerun samples (Anderson et al., 1982). Daily urinary Cr losses were approximately 2-fold higher on a run versus a nonrun day (see Table 3).

Serum zinc measured following running was similar to prerun values but decreased significantly in the ensuing 2 hours (see Table 2). Daily urinary Zn losses were elevated approximately 1.6-fold on a run versus a nonrun day (see Table 3).

Table 2. Effects of running 6 miles on serum Cr, Zn, Cu, Ca, K, and Na.

Element	Prerun	Postrun	2 hr postrun
Cr (ng/dl)	12 ± 2[b]	17 ± 3[a]	19 ± 3[a]
Zn (µg/dl)	81 ± 4[a]	85 ± 4[a]	75 ± 4[b]
Cu (µg/dl)	93 ± 5[a]	95 ± 4[a]	94 ± 4[a]
Ca[a] (mg/dl)	9.3 ± 0.1[a]	9.3 ± 0.1[a]	9.6 ± 0.1[a]
Na[a] (meq/l)	123 ± 2[a]	122 ± 1[a]	125 ± 1[a]
K (meq/l)	4.6 ± 0.1[b]	5.0 ± 0.2[a]	4.7 ± 0.1[ab]

Mean ± SEM.
[a]Postrun sample was taken immediately after running. Values in the same row with [b] superscripts are significantly different ($p < 0.05$).

Table 3. Daily urinary excretion of Cr and Zn on a day of running 6 miles and a nonrun day

Element	Run	Nonrun
Cr (μg/day)	0.37 $\pm$ 0.08[a]	0.20 $\pm$ 0.04[b]
Zn (μg/day)	711 $\pm$ 496[a]	489 $\pm$ 342[b]

Mean $\pm$ SEM.
[a]Values in same row with [b] superscripts are significantly different ($p < 0.05$).

Serum values for Cu, calcium (Ca), and sodium (Na) were not altered significantly following running (see Table 2). Serum potassium (K) increased following runing but returned to prerun levels within 2 hours. Urinary losses of Ca, Na, and K were not altered by running (data not shown).

Strenuous running also leads to transitory increases in serum high-density lipoproteins, triglycerides, and inorganic phosphate, but these all returned to prerun levels within 2 hours of completing the run. Serum creatinine, bilirubin, uric acid, and alkaline phosphatase were also elevated following running and remained elevated 2 hours following the run. Total serum protein and blood urea nitrogen concentrations were not altered due to strenuous running.

Discussion

Although it is generally accepted that optimal nutrition is one of the basic conditions necessary for peak physical and mental performance, it is not universal as to what constitutes optimal nutrition. Attention to proper nutrition is essential for athletes because deficiencies in calories, nutrients, and/or water often lower athletic performance (Fox & Mathews, 1981). Proper nutrition for the athlete is usually focused on obtaining adequate calories from the basic four food groups. Caloric requirements of athletes vary depending upon size, age, type of competition, and level of training, with many athletes consuming between 3,000 and 6,000 calories per day (American Dietetic Association, 1980).

These high-caloric requirements may be required not only to assure sufficient energy supply, but also to obtain the minimum required amount of Cr. Additional Cr may be required to correct for the increased losses due to strenuous exercise. Recent studies indicate that there are approximately 15 μg of Cr per 1,000 calories. The suggested daily safe and adequate intake range for chromium is 50-200 μg. Therefore, a daily intake of 3,000 to 6,000 calories by athletes eating their usual training diets would only provide 45 to 90 μg of Cr. Because this level of Cr would be near the minimum required for sedentary adults, and unless there are unknown mechanisms to compensate for the increased losses due to exercise, strenuously exercising individuals on such diets probably have a marginal Cr intake. Increased losses of Cr due to strenuous exercise appear to be partially offset by increased caloric intake of exercising individuals. However, individuals who are exercising strenuously as a means to control or lose weight would not be consciously increasing caloric intake but may actually be consuming less calories and, therefore, less Cr, which may exacerbate marginal Cr deficiency.

Caloric intake and trace-element balance are especially important for athletes during the off-season and in postcompetitive years. Many athletes develop weight problems at these times because they fail to compensate for the decreased energy output with a decreased caloric intake. There is a decreased insulin sensitivity (Lipman et al., 1972) that accompanies the weight problem, often necessitating higher insulin levels and increased needs for Cr.

Urinary zinc losses were also elevated following strenuous exercise and like Cr, Zn is also marginal in most diets (Smith et al., 1983). Normal U.S. diets appear to contain approximately 1 mg of Zn per 220 calories; therefore, approximately 3400 calories would be required to obtain the RDA for Zn of 15 mg. Whether individuals who exercise regularly can compensate for increased Cr and Zn losses by increased efficiencies in Cr and Zn absorption and/or metabolism needs to be documented. Increased trace-element losses appear well-established; however, it is still unclear whether there is compensation for those losses.

Serum glucose was elevated dramatically following running, reaching 200 mg/dl in several runners and was 300 mg/dl in 1 subject (see Table 1) (Anderson et al., 1982). Elevated levels of glucose immediately following running appear to be a normal response and not related to impaired glucose tolerance. None of the subjects passed sugar in their urine following running and all had normal glucose tolerance. The consequences of such dramatic increases in blood glucose of runners unable to utilize glucose efficiently requires further study. For example, the effects of increases in blood glucose to 200-300 mg/dl due to exercise in individuals with impaired glucose homeostasis need to be ascertained (Anderson et al., 1982). Individuals prone to glucose intolerance may need to take additional precautions when exercising strenuously. Elevated glucose was not accompanied by elevated insulin. This represents another example: Following exercise, other endogenous mechanisms in addition to blood glucose regulate insulin response. However, increased glucose was accompanied by changes in glucagon, cortisol, Cr, and Zn (see Table 1), which may be involved in glucose homeostasis.

Strenuous exercise also leads to acute changes in numerous metabolites found in serum, most of which returned to prerun values within 2 hours of running. Acute changes in blood and urine are often dramatic, and anemia, liver disease, myocardial ischemia, or renal disease might erroneously be diagnosed unless the physician is aware of the exercise habits of the patient (Bunch, 1980).

In summary, strenuous exercise leads to significant urinary losses of essential nutrients, Cr and Zn. Normal diets usually are low in both Cr and Zn, and diets containing more than 3,000 calories are required to meet the minimum suggested amount of Cr and the recommended daily allowance for Zn; increased losses due to strenuous exercise are not necessarily met at these intakes. Increased Cr and Zn losses, coupled with marginal dietary intakes of these nutrients, may be associated with impaired health. Long-term marginal dietary intakes of Cr and Zn are linked to impaired carbohydrate metabolism, which is associated with increased risk of maturity-onset diabetes (Type II) and cardiovascular disease.

References

American Dietetic Association. (1980). Nutrition and physical fitness. *Journal of the American Dietetic Association.* **76**, 437-443.

Anderson, R.A. (1981). Nutritional role of chromium. *Science Total Environment.*, **17**, 13-29.

Anderson, R.A., Polansky, M.M., Bryden, N.A., Roginski, E.E., Patterson, K.Y. & Reamer, D.C. (1982). Effect of exercise (running) on serum glucose, insulin, glucagon and chromium excretion. *Diabetes,* **31**, 212-216.

Anderson, R.A., Polansky, M. M. & Bryden, N.A. (1984). Strenuous running: Acute effects on chromium, copper, zinc and selected clinical variables in urine and serum of male runners. *Journal of Biological Trace Element Research,* **6**, 327-335.

Bunch, T.W. (1980). Blood test abnormalities in runners. *Mayo Clinic Proceedings,* **55**, 113-117.

Fox, E., & Mathews, D. (1981). *The physiological basis of physical education and athletics.* Philadelphia: Saunders College Publishing.

Lipman, R.L., Raskin, P., Love, T., Triebwasser, J., Lecocq, F.R., & Snure, J.J. (1972). Glucose intolerance during decreased physical activity in man. *Diabetes,* **21**, 101-107.

Smith, J.C. Jr., Morris, E.R., & Ellis, R. (1983). Zinc requirements, bioavailabilities and recommended dietary allowances. *Zinc Deficiency in Human Subjects* (147-169). New York: Alan R. Liss.

8

Changes in Serum Zinc and Copper Levels After Zinc Supplementation in Running and Nonrunning Men

Robert M. Hackman
UNIVERSITY OF OREGON
EUGENE, OREGON, USA
Carl L. Keen
UNIVERSITY OF CALIFORNIA
DAVIS, CALIFORNIA, USA

Mounting evidence indicates that physical activity is a variable that can affect nutritional requirements. While this association is best demonstrated for kilocalories, there are suggestions that micronutrient requirements may also be influenced by physical activity. Belko et al. (1983) have demonstrated that riboflavin requirements are increased in women when they run for 20 to 50 minutes a day, compared to when the same individuals are sedentary. Trace element status may also be compromised by exercise. For example, serum zinc concentrations in runners have been found to vary inversely as a function of the number of miles per week engaged in training, with zinc levels roughly 25 to 30% below clinically accepted normal values in some runners (Dressendorfer & Sockolov, 1980). Low serum zinc values have also been found in runners in Honolulu and Eugene (Hackman & Keen, 1983). Because low serum zinc values are associated with a compromised zinc status, we investigated the effect of a zinc supplement on serum zinc levels in both runners and nonrunners.

There is a well-documented interaction between zinc and copper and some suggestion of a zinc-iron interaction as well (Hackman & Keen, 1985). High concentrations of zinc are known to inhibit the absorption or transport of copper.

Dietary zinc intake of over 60 mg per day is implicated in reducing the absorption of dietary iron. Thus, in a study of zinc supplementation, the levels of serum copper and iron were also monitored for possible deleterious effects due to antagonism.

Methods

The research protocol was approved by the University of Oregon Committee for the Protection of Human Subjects. The subjects were 21 nonsmoking men from the Eugene area between the ages of 21 and 35 years who ran between 30 and 45 miles per week for the past month and who continued to train at the same distance. Fifteen men in the same age range, also nonsmokers, and not running or engaging in more than 60 min of aerobic activity per week, were recruited for the nonrunning group. The runners and nonrunners were randomly assigned in a double-blind manner to either a zinc-supplementation group that received 22.5 mg of zinc as zinc sulphate in combination with a moderate dose of B-vitamins, vitamin E, and vitamin C (Z-BEC, A.H. Robins Co., Richmond, VA) or to a group that received only a placebo. A placebo was formulated in the identical size and shape of the zinc supplement and contained riboflavin to ensure similar urinary color.

Prior to supplementation, resting preprandial blood samples were obtained in the morning by venipuncture with whole blood collected in a silicon-coated vacutainer tube. Runners did not run on the day they gave the blood sample. The blood was clotted at room temperature and centrifuged at 5,000 rpm for 15 min. Serum was aspirated and stored individually in acid-washed polypropylene vials and frozen until time of assay. After the initial blood sample, all subjects received their first week's supply of tablets; they were instructed to take one tablet daily with their morning meal. Subjects returned every 7 days after the initial blood sample for the next 4 weeks, at which time a resting preprandial blood sample was taken and processed as described previously. Compliance was monitored, and any subject whose compliance rate was below 85% was dropped from the study.

Three-day food records were collected from each subject upon entry and during the last 3 days of the study. The records were analyzed for dietary zinc content from standard reference tables.

The serum was analyzed for zinc, copper, and iron levels. After an acid digestion and dilution in double-distilled deionized water, trace element concentrations were determined using a Perkin-Elmer model 370 atomic absorption spectrophotometer (Clegg, Keen, Lonnerdal, & Hurley, 1981). Values were expressed in parts per million (ppm or ug/100 ml).

Data were analyzed using statistical programs for analysis of variance with repeated measurements (Dixon, 1983).

Results

The mean age of the study population was 25.4 years. The runners averaged 300 min per week in aerobic activity, while the nonrunners averaged 44 min weekly. Dietary analysis showed that the runner groups averaged 7.4 mg of dietary zinc intake per day, with a range from 3.1 to 19.4. Nineteen (90%) of the runners consumed less than 15 mg of zinc per day, the current RDA value; and 17 (81%) consumed 10 mg or less of zinc per day (less than two thirds of the RDA). For the nonrunners, the mean dietary zinc intake was 5.7 mg per day. All of the nonrunners consumed less than 10 mg of zinc per day. Thus, 94% of the total study population ate less than the daily recommended dietary allowance for zinc.

The distribution of baseline serum zinc values for runners is shown in Figure 1. Eight of the 21 runners had serum zinc values below 0.8 ppm; three had values below 0.7 ppm. Thirteen of the runners had serum zinc values above 0.8 ppm, with three subjects having serum zinc values above 1.1 ppm. In the nonrunners, 5 of the 11 subjects had serum zinc values below 0.8 ppm, while 6 of the 11 had serum zinc levels above 0.8 ppm. Four subjects had serum zinc levels below 0.7 ppm, and none had serum zinc levels above 1.1 ppm.

Mean serum zinc levels in runners following zinc supplementation is shown in Figure 3. The mean serum zinc level increased over the supplementation period with the value at Week 4 significantly greater than that at Week 0. Runners consuming the placebo showed a nonsignificant change in serum zinc levels. Serum zinc levels in nonrunners are shown in Figure 4. Subjects who received zinc showed marked increases in their serum zinc levels, with the highest mean level found at Week 2. Final mean zinc levels were significantly greater than initial group zinc levels in the zinc supplemented nonrunners. Nonrunners receiving the placebo showed a nonsignificant change in serum zinc values over the course of the study.

The serum copper levels in runners are shown in Figure 5. Runners taking zinc showed mean serum copper levels of 0.89 ppm at Week 0 and 0.78 ppm by Week 4, with a slight mean decrease for each of the weeks in between. Runners receiving the placebo showed no changes in their serum copper lev-

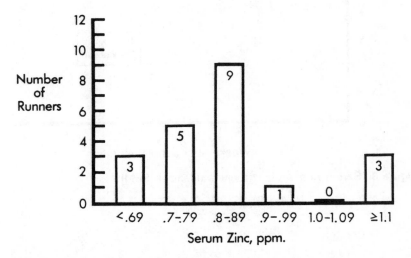

Figure 1. Distribution of baseline serum zinc levels in runners

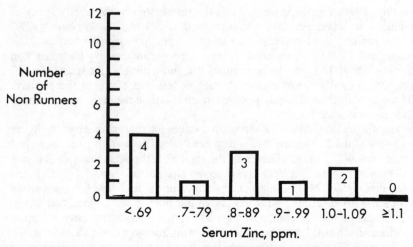

Figure 2. Distribution of baseline serum zinc levels in nonrunners

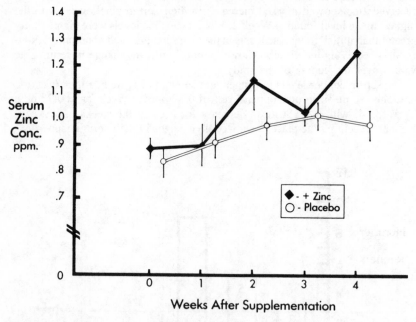

Figure 3. Serum zinc levels in runners (Mean ± SEM)

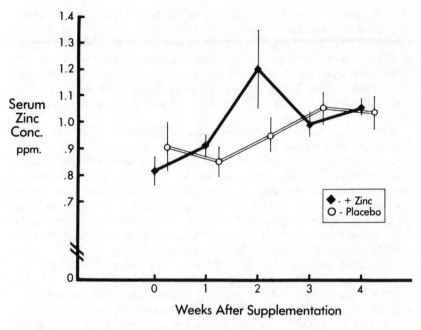

Figure 4. Serum zinc levels in nonrunners (Mean ± SEM)

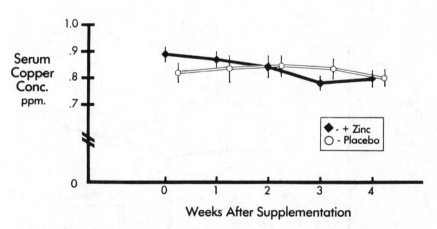

Figure 5. Serum copper levels in runners (Mean ± SEM)

els, with values averaging around 0.8 ppm. Serum copper levels in nonrunners are shown in Figure 6. Nonrunners taking zinc had serum copper levels between 0.68 and 0.78 ppm throughout the study, with a slight mean increase in serum copper after Week 2 of the supplementation. Nonrunners taking the placebo had significantly higher mean copper levels than the nonrunners taking the zinc during Weeks 1 and 2 of the supplementation phase, but these levels decreased to a range similar to those found in the zinc supplemented group by Week 3.

Serum iron levels for runners are shown in Figure 7. There was a slight increase in the mean serum iron level for runners who took zinc, although this increase was not significant. There were no apparent changes in serum iron levels in the runners taking the placebo. The variance around the mean for the iron values were substantially greater than the variance found for the zinc and copper levels. Serum iron levels in nonrunners are shown in Figure 8. Again, there are no apparent differences between the nonrunners consuming zinc and those assigned to the placebo group in terms of serum iron concentration, with wide variance around the mean.

Analysis of variance for serum zinc levels as a function of zinc supplementation, running activity, and weeks involved in the program revealed a significant effect for the number of weeks in the study ($p < .01$). There was also a significant interaction between the week and running factors ($p < .05$).

Analysis of variance for serum copper values showed there was a significant effect of running on serum copper levels ($p < .05$). There was also a significant week by running interaction ($p < .05$). A three-way interaction between week, zinc, and running was also significant ($p < .05$).

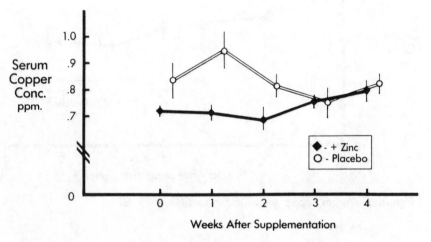

Figure 6. Serum copper levels in nonrunners (Mean ± SEM)

Discussion

The present results show that a substantial number of men surveyed in this study had serum zinc levels below 0.80 ppm, the clinically accepted "normal" value for serum zinc for a normal adult. Previous studies have found a range of serum zinc values, with mean levels between 0.90 and 1.00 ppm. For example, Hackley et al. (1968) found mean serum zinc concentration of 0.96 ± 0.13 ppm (mean ± SD) in 96 men and 97 women surveyed. Other studies (Davies, 1972; Meret & Henken, 1971) also report mean serum zinc values of approximately 0.95 ppm. In the latter two studies, serum zinc values did range as low as 0.63 and 0.72 ppm, respectively, for a small number of individuals.

A study of zinc status in runners who entered a 20-day road race in Hawaii found prerace mean serum zinc values for men of 0.76 ± 0.13 ppm (mean ± SD), with a range of 53 to 116 ppm (Dressendorfer & Sockolov, 1980). These investigators found a mean serum zinc concentration of 94 ± 12 ppm in male nonrunners, with a range for 78 to 121 ppm. Low serum zinc levels in trained athletes have also been reported in other surveys (Dressendorfer et al., 1982; Hackman & Keen, 1983). Thus, it may be that runners are compromised in their zinc status or at least display a different metabolic profile for zinc.

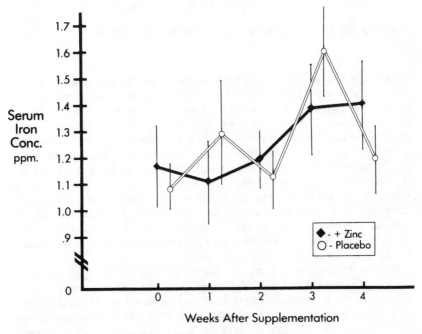

Figure 7. Serum iron levels in runners (Mean ± SEM)

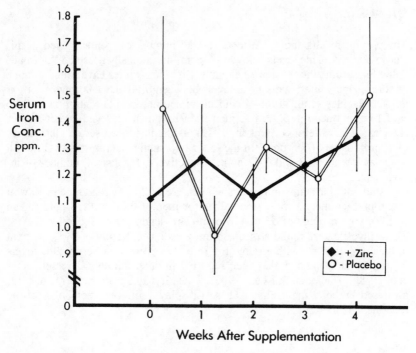

Figure 8. Serum iron levels in nonrunners (Mean ± SEM)

Other studies also indicate that exercise may compromise zinc status. Lichti, Turner, and Henzel (1971) reported that brief, intense exercise in humans who ran up four flights of stairs resulted in large increases in plasma zinc levels. Hetland, Brubak, Refsum, and Stromme (1975) followed serum and erythrocyte zinc concentration in humans after long-term physical activity of men participating in a 5 hour, 70 km cross-country skiing competition. Postrace serum zinc levels were significantly higher (approximately 19%) than prerace levels. One day after the race, serum zinc levels were back to prerace values. Two days after the race, serum zinc levels were generally increased over prerace values. In contrast to serum, erythrocyte zinc levels did not change with exercise. Hematocrits were measured during each sampling period, and values varied no more than 4%, thus excluding hemoconcentration as an explanation for the fluctuations in serum zinc levels.

Results of the analysis of variance for serum zinc found a significant effect between the interaction of zinc supplementation and duration in the study. This effect occurred because the serum zinc level increased over time in the subjects taking the zinc supplements over the 4 week study compared to those taking the placebo. The changes in serum zinc values for the runners and nonrunners are not apparent until the third and fourth weeks of supplementation. One possible explanation is that the first 2 weeks of the supplementation period were used to normalize a partially depleted zinc store in the subjects, and not until the third week was there a discernable mean increase in serum zinc.

Results of the analysis of variance of serum copper values found no effect of the zinc supplement on serum copper values, but there was a significant effect of running on serum copper. Runners had lower serum copper levels than nonrunners during the first 2 weeks of the study, which accounted for this effect independent of taking the zinc supplement. This influence during the early part of the study also accounts for the significant two and three-way interactions.

There were no apparent deleterious effects of the zinc supplementation on the serum copper or iron levels in either the runners or nonrunners. While antagonism of copper or iron by zinc has been reported when levels of dietary zinc exceed 50 mg per day, we could find no such effects when the levels were 22.5 mg per day. While it is still too early to make a firm statement, it appears that the level of zinc used in this study caused no harm in the course of the 1-month supplementation period.

Zinc is an essential element in the function of more than 90 enzymes. These enzymes involve the metabolism of carbohydrates, lipids, proteins, and nucleic acids. Examples of such metalloenzymes include: carboxypeptidase, alkaline phosphatase, alcohol dehydrogenase, superoxide dismutase, thymidine kinase, and carbonic anhydrase. Because the involvement of zinc is so widespread, it seems reasonable that a deficiency of this element could have major metabolic significance. Prasad, Miale, Farid, Schulent, and Sandstead (1963) first demonstrated zinc deficiency in humans in the Middle East, with symptoms of delayed sexual maturation, skin lesions, and growth retardation in malnourished men. This syndrome of zinc deficiency improved significantly with supplementation of dietary zinc (Halsteàd et al., 1972). Other examples of severe zinc deficiency have also been documented in humans (Prasad, 1983) as well as marginal zinc deficiency. Hambidge, Hambidge, Jacobs, and Baum (1972) reported a marginal zinc deficiency in young children for middle-class families living in Denver. These children exhibited symptoms of reduced taste acuity, poor appetite, and growth retardation. Zinc supplementation ameliorated these symptoms. Other reports have also found impaired growth in children who demonstrated low hair and plasma zinc levels (Buzina, Jusic, Sapunar, & Milanovic, 1980).

There is some debate as to whether serum is the best tissue to measure regarding assessment of zinc status. The previously cited studies clearly find that low serum zinc is associated with physiological symptoms attributable to zinc deficiency. It is not known whether the same association is applicable to relatively healthy men who may be marginally deficient. Other parameters in addition to serum zinc have been suggested as possible indicators of zinc status. One parameter is the enzyme nucleoside phosphorylase, a zinc metalloenzyme (Anonymous, 1984). Corroborative measurements of this enzyme in runners and nonrunners would be useful.

Subjects in this study demonstrated initial plasma zinc levels lower than the clinically accepted normal range of 0.8 ug/dl in both the running and nonrunning groups. The dietary zinc intake of the study population averaged less than 15 mg per day (the RDA standard), suggesting that one reason to explain the serum zinc values is an inadequate intake of dietary zinc.

It is still difficult to make a firm statement regarding the direct influence of running on serum zinc and copper levels, and the analyses suggest that a complex array of factors contribute to these changes. Additional research with a larger number of subjects will help to delineate the factors that influence serum trace element concentrations.

References

Anonymous (1984). Nucleoside phosphorylase: A zinc metalloenzyme and a marker of zinc deficiency. *Nutrition Reviews, 42*, 279-281.

Belko, A.Z., Obarzanek, E., Kalkwarf, H.J., Rotter, M.A., Bogusz, S., Miller, D., Haas, J.D., & Roe, D.A. (1983). Effects of exercise on riboflavin requirements of young women. *American Journal of Clinical Nutrition, 37*, 509-517.

Buzina, R., Jusic, M., Sapunar, J., & Milanovic, N. (1980). Zinc nutrition and taste acuity in school children with impaired growth. *American Journal of Clinical Nutrition, 33*, 2262-2267.

Clegg, M.S., Keen, C.L., Lonnerdal, B., & Hurley, L.S. (1981). Influence of ashing techniques on the analysis of trace elements in animal tissue. I. Wet ashing. *Biological Trace Element Research, 3*, 107-115.

Davies I.J. (1972). Plasma zinc concentration in patients with bronchogenic carcinoma. *Lancet, 1*, 149.

Dixon, W.J. (Ed.), (1983). *BMDP statistical software.* Berkeley: University of California Press.

Dressendorfer, R.H., & Sockolov, R. (1980). Hypozincemia in runners. *Physician and Sportsmedicine, 8*, 97-100.

Dressendorfer, R.H., Wade, C.E., Keen, C.L., & Scatf, J.H. (1982). Plasma mineral levels in marathon runners during a 20-day road race. *The Physician and Sportsmedicine, 8*, 97-100.

Hackley, B.M., Smith, J.C., & Halsted, J.A. (1968). A simplified method for plasma zinc determination by atomic absorption spectrophotometry. *Clinical Chemistry, 14*, 1-5.

Hackman, R.M., & Keen, C.L. (1983). Trace element assessment of runners. *Federation Proceedings, 42*, 830.

Hackman, R.M., Keen, C.L., (1986). Trace elements in athletic performance. In F. Katch (Ed.), *Sport, Health, and Nutrition.* Champaign, IL: Human Kinetics.

Halstead, J.A., Ronaghy, H.A., Abadi, P., Haghshenass, M., Amirhakima, G.H., Barakat, R.M., & Reinhold, J.G. (1972). Zinc deficiency in man: The Shiraz experiment. *American Journal of Medicine, 53*, 277-284.

Hambidge, K.M., Hambidge, C., Jacobs, M., & Baum, J.D. (1972). Low levels of zinc in hair, anorexia, poor growth and hypogeusia in children. *Pediatric Research, 60*, 868-874.

Hetland, O. Brubak, E.A., Refsum, H.E., & Stramme, S.B. (1975). Serum and erythrocyte concentrations after prolonged heavy exercise. In H. Howard & I.R. Poortmans, (Eds.), *Metabolic adaptation to prolonged physical exercise* (pp. 367-370). Basel, Switzerland: Berkhausen Verlag.

Lichti, E., Turner, M., & Henzel, J. (1971). Changes in serum zinc following periods of increased metabolic activity in differences in arterial and venous zinc concentrations following surgically inflicted wounds. In D. Hemphill (Ed.), *Trace Substances in Environmental Health, IV* (pp. 326-335), Columbia, MO: University of Missouri Press.

Meret, S. & Henkin, R.I. (1971). Simultaneous direct estimation by atomic absorption spectrophotometry of copper and zinc in serum, urine, and cerebrospinal fluid. *Clinical Chemistry,* **17**, 369-373.

Prasad, A.S. (1983). Zinc deficiency in human subjects. *Progress in Clinical and Biological Research,* **129**, 1-33.

Prasad, A.S., Miale, A., Farid, Z., Schulent, A., & Sandstead, H.H. (1963). Zinc metabolism in patients with the syndrome of iron deficiency anemia, hypogonadism and dwarfism. *Journal of Laboratory and Clinical Medicine,* **61**, 537-549.

9

Iron Storage in Female Distance Runners

Russell R. Pate
UNIVERSITY OF SOUTH CAROLINA
COLUMBIA, SOUTH CAROLINA, USA

Pu Jun-Zong
BEIJING MEDICAL COLLEGE
BEIJING, PEOPLE'S REPUBLIC OF CHINA

Victoria Dover
BALL STATE UNIVERSITY
MUNCIE, INDIANA, USA

Michael Lambert
UNIVERSITY OF SOUTH CAROLINA
COLUMBIA, SOUTH CAROLINA, USA

Laurie Goodyear
NIKE SPORT RESEARCH LABORATORY
EXETER, NEW HAMPSHIRE, USA

Iron deficiency is generally recognized as the most common nutritional deficiency in the United States and is particularly common among menstruating females (Monsen, Kuhn, & Finch, 1967; Scott & Pritchard, 1967). Several authors have reported relatively low levels of iron storage in various athletic groups (Clement & Asmundson, 1982; Hunding, Jordal, & Paulev, 1981); this has led to speculation that exercise training may contribute to depletion of body iron stores. In recent years running has become one of the most prevalent forms of fitness-inducing exercise, and competitive road races have become exceptionally popular. Despite the popularity of distance running and the apparent risk of iron depletion in young females, little is known about iron-storage levels in female runners. The purposes of the present study were to quantify iron-storage and hematological status in recreation female-distance runners and to compare the runners with a sedentary reference group.

Methods

Subjects were young adult females who had recently participated in a 5 kilometer (5K) road race (N = 17) or a marathon (42K) road race (N = 18). Subjects were not highly competitive but had been running regularly for an average of 4.5 years. The marathoners averaged 53 miles of running per week over the 3-month period preceding data collection; the 5K runners had averaged 16 miles per week over that same period. Twenty inactive women served as a reference group. Descriptive data on the three groups are provided in Table 1.

A single 10 ml blood sample was collected from each subject. Venesection at an antecubital vein was completed in the morning with the subject in the postabsorptive state and at least 14 hours following the subject's last vigorous exercise bout. Whole blood samples were assayed for hemoglobin concentration (Hb) and hematocrit (Hct) using the cyanmethemoglobin (Drabkin & Austin, 1935) and microhematocrit techniques, respectively.

Plasma ferritin concentration (PF) was taken as a marker for total body iron storage (Jacobs & Worwood, 1975) and was measured using a double antibody radioimmune assay kit (New England Nuclear Co.). All blood chemistry parameters were assayed in duplicate with the average taken as the criterion value for data analyses.

Relative dietary iron intake was estimated from food-frequency reports. Subjects completed a questionnaire that provided a report of typical weekly frequency of intake of 42 common foods known to contain significant amounts of iron. Relative iron intake was quantified simply as the reported typical weekly frequency of intake of the listed food items. No attempt was made to estimate daily iron intake in absolute terms (e.g., mg per day).

The following criteria were adopted for the purpose of categorizing subjects as iron deficient and/or anemic: Iron depletion was indicated by a PF lower than 10 ng/ml; Anemia was defined as a hemoglobin concentration less than 11 g/dl.

Intergroup differences were examined by analysis of variance (ANOVA). In addition, associations among variables were studied by correlational procedures.

Table 1. Characteristics of subjects

Variable	Marathon runners ($n = 18$)		5K runners ($n = 17$)		Reference group ($n = 20$)	
Age (years)	28.1	± 5.9	27.5	± 7.0	25.0	± 5.1
Height (cm)	163.9	± 5.3	163.5	± 4.7	162.2	± 4.3
Weight (kg)	56.2	± 4.4	54.5	± 5.6	58.5	± 6.7
Number of menstrual periods in the past year	10.8	± 3.2	9.9	± 4.6	10.5	± 2.9
Years of regular running	5.3	± 3.4	3.7	± 3.6	Not Applicable	
Weekly running mileage over previous 3 months	53.1	± 17.2	15.6	± 10.2	Not Applicable	

Values are $\bar{X} \pm$ SD.

Results

The results of the study are summarized in Table 2. ANOVA comparisons of group means indicated that there were no statistically significant differences between the groups for Hb, Hct, or PF ($p > .05$). Group means for these three hematological variables were within the normal clinical range for young adult females. The group means for PF, although within the clinically normal range (12-100 ng/ml), were toward the low end of that range for all three groups. Also, the three groups did not differ significantly in reported weekly frequency of intake of iron-containing foods.

Using the categorization criteria previously cited, the percentages of iron-deficient and anemic subjects in each group were determined. Results indicated that approximately 20% of subjects in each group were iron deficient (PF < 10 ng/ml). Only 1 subject was identified as anemic (Hb < 11 g/dl), and she was a member of the 5K group.

Zero-order correlations were computed among the following four variables: Hb, Hct, PF, and reported frequency of intake of iron-containing foods. These analyses, summarized in Table 3, indicated that reported frequency of intake of iron-containing foods did not correlate significantly with any of the three hematological variables. As expected, Hb and Hct were highly correlated with one another ($r = 0.75$, $p < .001$). However, PF was not signficantly correlated with Hb and Hct ($p > .50$).

Discussion

The principal finding of this study was that recreational female-distance runners did not differ significantly from sedentary controls on measures of iron-storage and hematological status. Previous studies of iron status in females runners have not included sedentary reference groups (Clement & Asmundson, 1982; Hunding et al., 1981). Thus, those studies did not address the central purpose

Table 2. Plasma ferritin (PF), hemoglobin concentration (Hb), and hematocrit (Hct) in marathon runners, 5K runners, and reference subjects ($\bar{X} \pm$ SD).

Variable	Marathon runners ($n = 18$)	5K runners ($n = 17$)	Reference group ($n = 20$)	F	P
PF (ng/ml)	20.3 $\pm$ 12.7	27.5 $\pm$ 24.8	22.4 $\pm$ 18.1	1.35	0.24
Hb (g/dl)	14.7 $\pm$ 1.4	12.8 $\pm$ 1.2	13.1 $\pm$ 0.9	0.84	0.69
Hct (%)	42.4 $\pm$ 2.6	39.6 $\pm$ 2.4	40.9 $\pm$ 1.7	1.05	0.45

Table 3. Matrix of zero-order correlations among plasma ferritin (PF), hemoglobin concentration (Hb), hematocrit (Hct), and reported weekly frequency of intake of iron-containing foods (IFF).

Variables		PF	Hct	Hb
	r	0.08	-0.15	-0.21
IFF	P	.60	0.28	0.13
	N	50	55	53
	r		0.06	0.02
PF	P		0.65	0.88
	N		52	52
	r			0.75
Hct	P			0.01
	N			56

of this study. Our findings suggest that recreational female-distance runners are not systematically different than less active young women in terms of iron-storage levels.

The data collected on the runners in the present study are very similar to those reported by Clement and Asmundson (1982) who studied highly competitive female runners. They reported mean values of 13.3 g/dl for Hb, 37.6% for Hct, and 27.9 ng/ml for PF. Of particular interest are the plasma ferritin (PF) data. In both the present study and that of Clement and Asmundson (1982), mean PF was near the low end of the clinically observed range. Also, a substantial percentage of subjects in both studies were patently iron deficient based on PF measures. These data suggest that the typical female runner may be iron deficient or at risk for development of this condition. However, it is not at all clear that this state is unique to female *runners*. Our findings that young female controls were as likely to be iron deficient as the runners suggests that the runners are simply representative of young, menstruating females who have a tendency toward iron deficiency. Normative data for PF in young women indicate that this may be the case (Cook, Finch, & Smith, 1976), but confirmation must await studies of iron status in large groups of female runners and age-matched sedentary controls.

There were no signficant correlations between reported weekly frequency of intake of iron-containing foods and the hematological variables. While dietary iron intake in female athletes has been studied previously (Barry et al., 1981; Clement & Asmundson, 1982; Steel, 1970), correlations between iron intake and hematological variables have not been reported by other investigators. Clement and Asmundson (1982) reported that iron intake was lower than the recommended level in female runners, but other studies of nutrition practices of female athletes have found iron intake to be adequate (Steel, 1970). The findings of the present study suggest that iron intake per se is not a strong predictor of iron or hematological status. However, it should be noted that the measure of iron intake employed in the present study was not precise. It is, of course, possible that other factors associated with iron metabolism are as or more important than dietary iron intake in determining iron-storage levels. Possible important factors are iron absorption (Ehn, Carlmark, & Hoglund, 1980), sweat loss (Vellar, 1968), hemoglobinuria (Dressendorfer, Wade, & Amsterdam, 1981) and menstrual blood loss. Thus, in correlational analyses the importance of dietary iron intake may be obscured by the combined influence of other factors.

Our observation that PF was not significantly correlated with Hb or Hct is consistent with the current understanding of body iron metabolism (Hillman & Finch, 1974). Tissue iron stores constitute a reservoir of iron that can be used in syntheses of hemoglobin and other iron-containing proteins. In cases of dietary iron deficiency or excessive iron loss, the body reservoir tends to be reduced to maintain circulating Hb at a normal level. Iron-deficiency anemia results only after tissue iron stores are virtually depleted. Thus, it was not surprising that PF, which is a marker for tissue iron storage, was not significantly correlated wih Hb or Hct. Although Clement and Asmundson (1982) did not report correlations among PF, Hb, and Hct, they did observe normal Hb and Hct in female runners who were low in PF. A very similar pattern was observed in the present study.

In summary, the recreational female-distance runners observed in this study did not differ significantly from sedentary controls on measures of iron-storage or hematological status. Iron stores were low and incidence of iron deficiency was substantial in both runners and controls. This suggests that chronic participation in running does not lower body iron stores below the low levels typically observed in young menstruating females. We recommend that future studies of iron status of active women be studied in larger groups and that well-matched reference groups be included for comparison.

References

Barry, A., Cantwell, T., Doherty, F., Folan, J.C., Ingoldsby, M., Kevany, J.P., O'Broin, J.D., O'Connor, H., O'Shea, B., Ryan, B.A., & Vaugh, J. (1981). A nutritional study of Irish athletes. *British Journal of Sports Medicine, 15*, 99-109.

Clement, D.B., & Asmundson, R.C. (1982, March). Nutritional intake and hemalotogical parameters in endurance runners. *Physician and Sportsmedicine, 10*, 37-43.

Cook, J.D., Finch, C.A., & Smith, N. (1976). Evaluation of the iron status of a population. *Blood, 48*, 449-455.

Drabkin, D.L., & Austin, J.H. (1935). Spectrophotometric studies. II. Preparations from washed cells; nitric oxide, hemoglobin and sulfhemoglobin. *Journal of Biological Chemistry, 112*, 51.

Dressendorfer, R.H., Wade, C.E., & Amsterdam, E.A. (1981). Development of pseudoanemia in marathon runners during a 20-day road race. *Journal of The American Medical Association. 246*, 1215-1218.

Ehn, L., Carlmark, B., & Hoglund, S. (1980). Iron status in athletes involved in intense physical activity. *Medicine and Science in Sports and Exercise, 12*, 61-64.

Hillman, R.S., & Finch, C.A. (1974). *Red cell manual* (4th ed.). Philadelphia: F.A. Davis Company.

Hunding, A. Jordal, R., & Paulev, P.E. (1981). Runner's anemia and iron deficiency. *Acta Medica Scandinavica* **209**, 315-318.

Jacobs, A., & Worwood, M. (1975). The clinical use of serum ferritin estimation. *British Journal of Haematology* **31**, 1-3.

Monsen, E.R., Kuhn, I.N., & Finch, C.A. (1967). Iron status of menstruating women. *American Journal of Clinical Nutrition,* **20**, 842-849.

Scott, D.E., & Pritchard, J.A. (1967). Iron deficiency in healthy young college women. *Journal of the American Medical Association,* **199**, 147-150.

Steel, J.E. (1970). A nutritional study of Australian Olympic athletes. *Medical Journal of Australia,* **2**, 119-123.

Vellar, O.D. (1968). Studies on sweat losses of nutrients, I: Iron content of whole body sweat and its association with other sweat constituents, serum iron levels, hematological indices, body surface area and sweat rate. *Scandinavian Journal of Clinical and Laboratory Investigation,* **21**, 157-167.

10

Nutritional Practices of Women Cyclists, Including Recreational Riders and Elite Racers

Joanne L. Slavin and Elizabeth A. McNamara
UNIVERSITY OF MINNESOTA
ST. PAUL, MINNESOTA, USA

Judy M. Lutter
MELPOMENE INSTITUTE FOR WOMEN'S HEALTH RESEARCH
ST. PAUL, MINNESOTA, USA

Little is known about the nutritional practices of elite women athletes. It is generally agreed that athletes need advice on nutrition, but athletes are seldom in contact with nutrition professionals. Most often diet advice is provided by coaches or other athletes, so the advice is not always nutritionally sound (Wolf, Wirth, & Lohman, 1979). Recent data show that exercise can affect the menstrual cycle of women athletes (Shangold, 1980). Most published data concern the effects of running on menstrual function (Lutter & Cushman, 1982). The importance of diet in determining whether a women athlete is amenorrheic has only been recently reported; there is a higher incidence of amenorrhea in women who consume vegetarian diets compared to meat-containing diets (Brooks, Sanborn, Albrecht, & Wagner, 1984). Thus this paper's purpose is to examine nutritional habits and menstrual regularity of recreational riders and elite racers. The role of exercise intensity and diet composition in determining menstrual regularity is also examined.

Methods

In the study 112 women cyclists were surveyed about their nutritional habits and menstrual histories. Of the respondents 36 participated in the 1982 Coors Classic, which is an annual world-class stage bicycle race held in Colorado; and 76 respondents were tourists who participated in several organized rides in Minnesota in 1983. All the women filled out a detailed, 12-page questionnaire including sections on cycling history, menstrual history, contraceptive data, data on cycling while pregnant, and nutritional information. The nutrition and menstrual data are presented in this paper. The Coors cyclists were also asked to submit 3-day diet records, which only 8 of the women completed. The results of a computerized nutrient analysis were returned to the women.

Results

The average Coors Classic participant was 27 years old, weighed 123 lbs, and was 66 in. tall. An average week for the racers was more than 200 miles of cycling, 80% of it at race pace. In contrast, the average tourist was 32 years old, weighed 130 lbs, and was 65 in. tall. About 30% of the 60 miles biked by tourists weekly was commuting and approximately 70% was touring.

About 30% of the racers described themselves as overweight. The racers felt they ate more, 72% estimating their average caloric intake as greater than 2,000 calories. However, an objective assessment of the self-reported height-weight data show that few of the racers were overweight. Of the tourists, 45% thought they were overweight, but only 46% described their calorie intake as 2,000 calories or greater. Although some tourists were overweight, objective estimates for overweight in the tourists would be less than 45%.

About one-third of each group described their diet as "modified vegetarian"; this diet included milk, eggs, fish, and poultry (see Table 1). Another third of the tourists described their diets as "typical American" (high protein, high fat), whereas only 17% of the elite racers chose this category. More tourists (38%) than racers (25%) reported carbohydrate loading; however, most described it as "just eating more carbohydrates." The racers were heavy users of nutritional supplements (see Table 2), reporting to consume megadoses of

Table 1. Diet Description

Diet	Number Reporting	
	Racers	Tourists
Modified vegetarian (includes poultry and fish)	11	25
Fast food, junk food	---	2
Typical American	6	20
Unrefined	6	3
Other*	13	25

*Generally were unrefined, more vegetarian diets.

Table 2. Reported supplement usage by women cyclists

Supplement	Racers	Tourists
	(% reporting)	
Vitamin C	58	32
Multivitamin	64	20
Iron	47	21
Calcium	11	13
B-complex	56	18
Protein supplement	6	1
Electrolyte drink	17	0

many vitamins, especially vitamin C and B-complex. Almost half of the women racers consumed an iron supplement in contrast to only 20% of the tourists. Half of both groups described their preferred prebiking meal as "high in complex carbohydrates." And more than 60% of the racers and 35% of the tourists preferred to wait at least 3 hours after eating before starting to exercise.

The 8 racers who completed the diet histories had excellent nutrient intakes. Most consumed a modified vegetarian diet, including a wide variety of fruits and vegetables. (It is quite possible that only the cyclists with the best diets returned the food records.)

The racers and tourists reported they received most of their nutrition information from magazines, other cyclists, and coaches. Tourists also received nutrition advice from friends and fellow cyclists. Ten percent of the tourists and 8% of the racers consulted a nutritionist or dietitian.

Racers tended to have more problems with amenorrhea than did tourists (see Table 3). (Amenorrhea was defined as less than three menstrual cycles during the previous year.) About 33% of the racers and 12% of the tourists were amenorrheic. All 12 amenorrheic racers were also vegetarians, excluding red meat from their diets, and 20 of the women racers with normal menstrual cycles also consumed vegetarian diets. About half of the amenorrheic tourists were vegetarians.

Furthermore, approximately 46% of the racers and 27% of the tourists thought cycling affected their menstrual cycles. The major change was less cramping.

Table 3. Frequency of menstrual cycles

Frequency	Racers (n = 36)	Tourists (n = 76)
Less than 27 days	10	28
28-35 days	14	35
36-50 days	0	4
Every 4 months	2	1
Never	4	5
Sporadic, difficult to say	6	3

Discussion

The diets of women tourists and racers were similar, but the racers reported consuming more calories. The diet histories for the racers confirmed that they usually ate more than 2,000 calories daily. Depending upon the sport and the participant, caloric intakes of athletes vary greatly, from 400 calories for gymnasts to 10,000 calories for football players (Short & Short, 1983). Women generally consume fewer calories than men yet are much more concerned about their body weight. In our study, 30% of the racers thought they were overweight, while it may be that none were "overfat."

About one-third of both the tourists and the racers described their diet as modified vegetarian. In most cases, this meant a diet that excluded red meat only. The consequences of a low-calorie vegetarian diet can be a low-iron intake. Iron deficiency has been described in various groups of women athletes (Frederickson, Puhl, & Runyan, 1983; Parr, Bachman, & Moss, 1984). Iron was the only nutrient that was marginally low in the women racer's diets. A study of male runners, rowers, and cyclists showed that only the runners had low stores of iron; thus cyclists may not be at risk for iron deficiency as much as are runners (Dufaux, Hoederath, Streitberger, Hollman, & Assman, 1981).

Recently, consumption of a vegetarian diet has been related to amenorrhea in women athletes (Brooks, et al, 1984). In this study a vegetarian was classified as anyone who ate less than 200 grams of meat (either poultry or red meat) per week. The vegetarian diet was also lower in fat than the meat-containing diet. Although all of our amenorrheic racers were vegetarians, many of the racers with normal menstrual cycles were also vegetarians. Only 8 of the 76 tourists were amenorrheic, and 4 were vegetarians. When the surveys completed by 197 members of the Melpomene Institute in 1983 were examined, 31% of the vegetarians had secondary amenorrhea, whereas only 4% of the members who ate a "balanced, four food group" diet had amenorrhea (Slavin, Lutter, & Cushman, 1984). Other aspects of diet such as trace elements or plant hormones may affect menstruation, and these factors deserve further study.

In addition the racers were more likely than tourists to use nutrient supplements, although both groups reported using a wide variety of vitamin, mineral, and other nutritional ergogenic aids. A recent survey of world-class amateur and professional athletes found that 92% of the athletes took vitamin/mineral supplements (Grandjean, 1983). Many of these athletes reported consuming several times the recommended dietary allowance (RDA) for certain vitamins and minerals. It was encouraging to see that so many of the women racers took iron supplements. More of the tourists should be consuming supplemental iron because many of these women are on low-calorie diets and are probably not ingesting adequate iron.

Few women reported carbohydrate loading, except for "just eating more carbohydrates." Recent data show that a severe carbohydrate depletion phase is not needed, if an athlete is depleting glycogen stores daily (Sherman, Costill & Fink, 1981). Most women racers were consuming vegetarian diets high in carbohydrates.

Eating disorders may be prevalent in woman athletes (Calabrese, 1983), and it is unfortunate that elite athletes do not seek nutritional guidance. Athletes receive nutrition information mainly from coaches and sporting journals; we believe that nutrition educators should familiarize themselves with these avenues if they wish to provide nutrition counseling to athletes.

References

Brooks, S.M., Sanborn, C.F., Albrecht, B.H., & Wagner, W.W. (1984). Diet in athletic amenorrhea. *Lancet,* 1, 559-560.

Calabrese, L.H. (1983). Menstrual abnormalities, nutritional patterns, and body composition in female classical ballet dancers. *The Physician and Sportsmedicine,* 11, 86-96.

Dufaux, B., Hoederath, A., Streitberger, I., Hollman, W., & Assman, G. (1981). Serum ferritin, transferrin, haptoglobin, and iron in middle- and long- distance runners, elite rowers, and professional racing cyclists. *International Journal of Sports Medicine,* 2, 43-46.

Frederickson, L.A., Puhl, J.L., & Runyan, W.S. (1983). Effects of training on indices of iron status of young female cross-country runners. *Medicine and Science in Sports and Exercise,* 15, 271-276.

Grandjean, A.C. (1983). Vitamins, diet, and the athlete. *Clinics in Sports Medicine,* 2, 105-114.

Lutter, J.M., & Cushman, S. (1982). Menstrual patterns in female runners. *The Physician and Sportsmedicine,* 10, 60-72.

Parr, R.B., Bachman, L.A., & Moss, R.A. (1984). Iron deficiency in female athletes. *The Physician and Sportsmedicine,* 12, 81-88.

Shangold, M.M. (1980). Sports and menstrual function. *Physician and Sportsmedicine,* 8, 66-78.

Sherman, W.M., Costill, D.L., & Fink, W.J. (1981). Effect of exercise-diet manipulation on muscle glycogen and its subsequent utilization during performance. *International Journal of Sports Medicine,* 2, 114-117.

Short, S.H., & Short, W.R. (1983). Four-year study of university athletes' dietary intake. *Journal of The American Dietetic Association,* 82, 632-645.

Slavin, J., Lutter, J., & Cushman, S. (1984). Amenorrhea in vegetarian athletes. *Lancet,* 1, 1474-1475.

Wolf, E.M., Wirth, J.C., & Lohman, T.G. (1979). Nutritional practices of coaches in the Big Ten. *The Physician and Sportsmedicine,* 7, 113-118.

PART II

Nutrition, Health, and Health Behaviors

11

Exercise, Postexercise Metabolic Rate, and Appetite

William E. Reger and Thomas G. Allison
WHEELING HOSPITAL
WHEELING, WEST VIRGINIA, USA

Robert L. Kurucz
WEST VIRGINIA UNIVERSITY
MORGANTOWN, WEST VIRGINIA, USA

A casual reading of popular periodical literature will reveal the intense concern of contemporary American society with body weight and dieting. Exercise is frequently recommended as a means of maintaining or losing weight. Indeed, numerous scientific investigations have reported weight loss as a primary or secondary outcome of physical training (Altekrese & Wilmore, 1973; Woo, Garrow, & Pi-Sunyer, 1981); however, not every study has shown that exercising subjects will necessarily lose weight (Allison, Iammarino, Metz, Skrinar, Kuller, & Robertson, 1981). To date little investigation has been made into the pattern of exercise best suited for weight control.

A homeostatic model of weight control implies that energy expenditures are ideally balanced by caloric intake through a set of regulatory mechanisms labeled "appetite." Appetite has obviously both a physiologic and cognitive basis. Losing weight by increasing caloric expenditure through exercise without consciously restricting food intake implies a suppression of the appetite. Animal studies have suggested that exercise suppresses food intake. In laboratory rats and mice, exercise up to a certain duration suppresses food intake, whereas food intake increases with exercise duration beyond that point (Mayer, Marshall, Vitale, Christensen, Mashayekhi, & Stare, 1954). Appetite suppression with exercise is observed to be less significant in female rats (Nance, Bromley, Barnard, & Gorski, 1977). Human epidemiologic studies suggest that activity level may be more important than food intake in maintaining body weight (Brown, 1970; Johnson, Burke, & Mayer, 1956).

In human studies, the accurate quantification of food intake and appetite is difficult to study without intruding on the natural response patterns of subjects. Physiologic measures of appetite previously employed include the measurement of the rate of salivation (Wooley & Wooley, 1981), the assessment of arterial-venous glucose differences (Mayer, 1955), and the monitoring of insulin and growth hormone levels (Woods, Decke, & Vasselli, 1974). Food intake has been determined through electronically controlled feeding devices (Campbell, Hashim, & Van Itallie, 1971), the unobstructive monitoring of standardized and precalculated food items (Southgate & Durnin, 1979), the use of self-reports of food intake, and the calculation of the speed of eating (Hodgson & Green 1980). Psychophysical assessments have included hunger, appetite (Durrant & Royston, 1979), and food appeal scales (Wooley, Wooley, & Woods, 1975).

A parametric study of the effects of exercise on appetite is necessary to better develop exercise prescriptions for weight control. The present investigation was initiated to determine (a) if exercise served to suppress appetite and food intake, (b) how the duration and intensity of exercise were related to the suppressant effect, and (c) the time-course postexercise for the appetite-suppression effect.

Methods

Subjects:

The subjects were 11 normal weight, ostensibly healthy, untrained female volunteers aged 27 (± 3) years. All subjects were within 10% of the weight norms from the 1982 Metropolitan Life Tables with a mean weight of 56 kg (± 8) and height of 162 cm (± 8). Maximal oxygen uptake ($\dot{V}O_2$ max) averaged 40 ml$\cdot$kg^{-1} $\cdot$min^{-1}($\pm$ 8).

Experimental Design:

Subjects underwent four orientation sessions in small groups and subsequently completed four experimental trials spaced 1 week apart ($\pm$ 2 days). Orientation sessions familiarized subjects with all procedures. Maximal oxygen uptake was assessed during a treadmill test (Naughton protocol) on the final session. Subjects were requested not to follow a weight-reduction diet or exercise program during the 4 weeks of the study and to avoid unusual activities on the testing day and the 1 day preceding and following.

The four experimental trials were presented by random assignment:

1. Trial 60C: 60 min of continuous treadmill exercise at 50% of $\dot{V}O_2$max.
2. Trial 30C: 30 min of continuous treadmill exercise at 50% of $\dot{V}O_2$max.
3. Trial 30I: 30 min of intermittent treadmill exercise 1 min at 70% $\dot{V}O_2$max. alternating with 3 min at 40% $\dot{V}O_2$max.
4. Trial N: No exercise.

Procedures:

Each subject reported to the laboratory on the morning of an experimental trail after a 12-hour fast. The subject underwent an appetite assessment battery consisting of the following sequence:

1. Baseline salivation and subjective hunger rating.
2. Food-stimulated salivation and appetite rating.
3. Heart rate and blood pressure determination.
4. Collection of 3-minute expired gas sample.

Following the preexercise battery, the subject performed the assigned exercise trial or sat quietly for 30 minutes. During exercise, heart rate was monitored continuously (Avionics Model 3000 Exerstress System or IMC Viagraph I) and was used to regulate the speed on the treadmill (Avionics Model 14-1 or IMC Model 200). For all trials, a grade of 5% was employed. For the 60C and 30C trials, a 1-minute expired gas sample was collected at midexercise. On the 30I trial, two 1-minute samples were collected at midexercise during the 1st min at 70% $\dot{V}O_2$max; and during the 3rd min at 40% $\dot{V}O_2$max. The subject was kept well-hydrated during exercise and recovery.

Immediately after the final battery, the subject was given a preweighed test meal consisting of one tray of 16 open-faced chicken, tuna, or egg salad hors d'oeuvres and another tray of fruit slices. Every attempt was made to keep the subject unaware that her consumption was being monitored. Uneaten food was weighed, and the length of time it took to eat was measured unobtrusively. Finally, the subject was given a 36-hour food intake record and dismissed.

Appetite Assessments

Food intake records (Short Report) were analyzed by computer. The *baseline and food-stimulated saliva collection* procedures were based on a system discussed by Wooley and Wooley (1981). The subject inserted a Johnson and Johnson No. 3 cotton dental roll cross-wise beneath the tongue for 3 minutes. The dental roll was placed in a zip-lock plastic bag and weighed in grams to 2 decimal places. During the baseline collection, the subject listened to a distracting tape devoid of food cues but was presented a highly palatable food stimulus during the food-stimulated collection. *Hunger*, defined as physiologic sensations felt with one's body, was rated at the 2 1/2-minute mark of the 3-min baseline collection. *Appetite,* measuring the subject's desire to eat the specific food stimulus, was rated during the food-stimulated collection. *Expired gas samples* were collected in plastic Douglas bags and analyzed according to standard procedures (Consolazio, Johnson, & Pecora, 1963) using a mass-spectrometer (Perkin-Elmer MGA 1100) and a tissot tank (Collins 120-liter Gasometer). Data analysis was performed on all appetite assessment variables using a three-way ANOVA (treatment × subject × time). Test meal calories, speed of eating the test meal, food intake record calories, and total calories (test meal and food recorded) were analyzed using a two-way ANOVA (treatment × subject).

Results

Analysis of the hunger and appetite ratings provide some evidence of a transitory appetite suppressant effect. Hunger rating was depressed immediately postexercise for trial 30I relative to N, while appetite ratings were significantly lower than N immediately postexercise for both 30I and 30C (Figure 1). By 1 hour postexercise, no differences were seen in subjective ratings among trials.

No significant differences in baseline or food-stimulated salivation rates were noted (see Figure 1), although salivation increased over time for all four trials. Calories consumed for the test meal, food intake record, or total calories failed to vary significantly across the four experimental trials (Table 1). However, a very strong trend ($p < .06$) toward an increase in total caloric consumption was noted for the 30I trial. Speed of eating was not significantly different for any of the trials.

Discussion

The primary focus of this study was the identification of a possible suppressant effect on various appetite and food intake measures due to different patterns of exercise. To this end, a transitory suppressant effect was noted after the 30I and 30C trials on subjective rating of appetite and after the 30I only on hunger. Though limited in magnitude and of short duration, this lowered subjective report of appetite following exercise supports previous observations by Mayer, Roy, and Mitra (1956) and Epstein, Masek, and Marshall (1978).

Hemeostatic theory would imply that exercise should increase food intake. The food intake values for 2 days following the research trials and the net energy expenditure of exercise, however, suggest a relative food intake suppression following 60C and 30C. Subjects ate 128 fewer kcalories on the average following the 60C treatment. The net cost of exercise averaged 218 kcal. By subtracting the net cost of exercise from the total kcalories for 2 days after the 60C research trial, the following net kcalorie values were observed: 2,902 for 60C; 3,187 for 30C; 3,981 for 30I; and 3,227 for N. A two-way ANOVA was not significant ($p < .10$). It is noteworthy that a 325 kcal difference existed between 60C and N. The cost of recovery was estimated at 72 kcal. Although the biphasic nature of the $\dot{V}O_2$ recovery curve (see Figure 2) and the lack of measurements in the first 11 minutes postexercise prevented exact calculations, total excess postexercise $\dot{V}O_2$ was roughly estimated by using immediate recovery data from 4 additional subjects and by using a total recovery time value obtained by projecting heart rate postexercise (see Figure 2) back to baseline. This would increase the total deficit of 397 kcal. By extrapolation, this caloric deficit could account for 0.75 kg of fat-weight loss per month if subjects exercised for 60 min every other day.

The situation was different following 30I. Food intake was 878 kcal greater than N. This represents an ample replacement of the cost of exercise and recovery, although the intake excess decreased to 761 kcal by subtracting the 117 kcal net cost of exercise. Paradoxically, hunger and appetite seemed most suppressed immediately following the 30I bout. Only 558 kcal were eaten for the

Table 1. Food intake in kcalories of the 11 subjects for the four research trials

Food Intake Measures	60C	30C	30I	N
Speed of eating				
kcal per minute	41.2 (± 13.9)	45.1 (± 18.5)	43.3 (14.8)	46.5 (±15.0)
Test meal				
total kcal consumed	588 (± 211)	604 (± 214)	558 (± 146)	615 (± 263)
36 hour food intake				
total kcal consumed	2,511 (±1,097)	2,708 (± 764)	3,547 (± 2,127)	2,611 (± 1,236)
Total kcalories				
2 days	3,099 (± 1,203)	3,132 (± 849)	4,105 (± 2,195)	3,227 (± 1,368)
Protein kcal. (%)*	490 (16)	550 (17)	599 (15)	505 (16)
CHO kcal. (%)*	1,328 (43)	1,316 (40)	1,731 (42)	1,230 (38)
Fat kcal. (%)*	964 (31)	1,293 (39)	1,406 (34)	1,178 (37)

*Percentage of total 48-hour caloric intake from each major food component. Balance of calories are from alcohol.
Note. No significant differences were observed in any of the food intake measures for any of the four research trials.

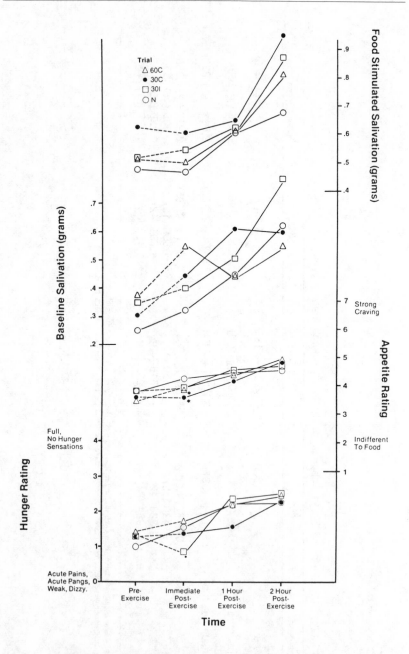

Figure 1. Food stimulated and baseline salivation in grams as well as the mean hunger and appetite ratings pre- and postexercise for four research trials. Hunger was significantly depressed (*p* < .01) for 30I, compared to N, whereas appetite was significantly depressed (*p* < .05) immediately postexercise for 30C and 30I. The solid line represents a period of quiet reading. Time spent exercising is represented by the broken line

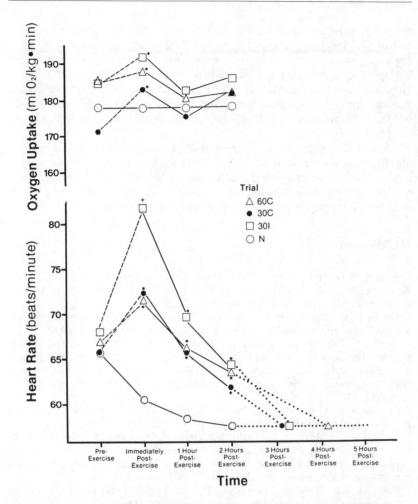

Figure 2. Pre- and post-exercise oxygen uptake and heart rate response curves. $\dot{V}O_2$ was elevated immediately post-exercise only, as indicated by the asterisks. The immediately post-exercise heart rate for 30I (+) was significantly higher ($p < .05$) than for 30C (*) and 60C (*) which were significantly higher ($p < .05$) than N. The heart rates (*) at one and two hours post-exercise for the three exercise trials were higher ($p < .05$) than for N. The dotted line is the projection of the observed heart rate back to baseline. Exercise is represented by the broken line. The solid line represents quite reading by the subjects.

test meal after 30I versus 588 for 60C, 604 for 30C and 615 for N. The physical trauma of the more intense exercise period may have accounted for these differences.

The increase in food intake after 30I may be a glucostatic response. The weighted respiratory quotient (RQ) for 30I was .94 versus .87 for 60C and 30C and .81 for N, suggesting that more glucose was being used as fuel for the 30I exercise trial than for the other trials. Perhaps, the glucose depletion was of sufficient magnitude that a physiologic threshold was crossed, stimulating a compensatory increase in food intake. That compensation which exceeded the spent kcalories may indicate a lack of precise short-term regulation. However, it is possible that the reason for the increase in food intake after 30I was primarily cognitive; that is, subjects perceived that they had worked harder and consequently felt that they could eat more food without gaining weight.

In conclusion, exercise induced a short-term suppression of subjective appetite in young, normal-weight females. Food intake following 60 min of continuous exercise actually decreased compared to no exercise. This suggests that low intensity, long-duration exercise may be best for weight control. More intensive, intermittent exercise may actually increase food intake.

References

Allison, T.G., Iammarino, R.M., Metz, K.F., Skrinar, G.S., Kuller, L.H., Robertson, R.J. (1981). Failure to exercise to increase high density lipoprotein cholesterol. *Journal of Cardiac Rehabilitation, 2*(4), 257-265.

Altekrése, E.B., & Wilmore, J.H. (1973). Changes in blood chemistries following a controlled exercise program. *Journal of Occupational Medicine, 15,* 110-113.

Brown, J. (1970). Nutritional and epidemiological factors related to heart disease. In *World Review of Nutrition and Dietetics Vol. 12* (pp. 102-125). Basel, Switzerland.

Campbell, R.D., Hashim, S.A., & Van Itallie, T.B. (1971). Responses to variations in nutritive density in lean and obese subjects. *The New England Journal of Medicine, 285,* 1402-1407.

Consolazio, F., Johnson, R., & Pecora, L. (1963). *Physiological measurements of metabolic methods in man.* New York: McGraw Hill.

Durrant, M., & Royston, P. (1979). Short term effects of energy density on salivation, hunger and appetite in obese subjects. *International Journal of Obesity, 3*, 335-347.

Epstein, L.H., Masek, B.J., & Marshall, W.R. (1978) Prelunch exercise and lunch time calorie intake. *Behavioral Therapist, 1*, 15-18.

Hodgson, R.J., & Green, J.G. (1980). The saliva priming effect, eating speed and the measurement of hunger. *Behavioral Research and Therapy, 18*, 243-247.

Johnson, M.L., Burke, B.S., & Mayer, J. (1956). Relative importance of inactivity and overeating in the energy balance of obese high school girls. *American Journal of Clincial Psychology, 4*, 37-44.

Mayer, J. (1955). Regulation of energy intake and body weight: The glucostatic theory and the lipostatic hypothesis. *Annnals of the New York Academy of Science, 63*, 15-43.

Mayer, J., Marshall, N.B., Vitale, J.J., Christensen, J.H., Mashayekhi, M.B., & Stare, F.J. (1954). Exercise, food intake and body weight in normal rats and genetically obese mice. *American Journal of Physiology, 177*.

Mayer, J., Roy, P., & Mitra, K.P. (1956). Relation between calories intake, body weight and physical work: Studies in an industrial male population in West Bengal. *American Journal of Clincial Nutrition, 4*, 169-175.

Nance, D.M., Bromley, B., Barnard, B.J. & Gorski, R.A. (1977). Sexually dimorphic effects of forced exercise on food intake and body weight in the rat. *Physiology and Behavior, 19*, 155-158.

Southgate, D.A.T., & Durnin, J.V.G.A. (1979). Caloric conversion factor: An experimental reassessment of the factors used in the calculation of the energy value of humans. *British Journal of Nutrition,* **24**, 517-535.

Woo, R., Garrow, J.S., & Pi-Sunyer, F.X. (1981). Effects of exercise on spontaneous calorie intake in obesity. *American Journal of Clinical Nutrition,* **36**, 470-477.

Woods, S.C., Decke, E., Vasselli, J.R. (1974). Metabolic hormones and regulation of body weight. *Psychological Review,* **81**, 26-43.

Wooley, O.W., & Wooley, S.C. (1981). Relationship of salivation in humans to deprivation, inhibition and the encephalization of hunger. *Appetite: Journal of Intake Research,* **2**, 331-350.

Wooley, O.W., Wooley, S.C., & Woods, W.A. (1975). Effect of calories on appetite and palatable food in obese and nonobese humans. *Journal of Comparative and Physiological Psychology,* **89**, 619-625.

12

Changes in Clinical Risk Factors in a Health Promotion Program in the Workplace

Robert M. Hackman, Elizabeth L. Wagner, J. Douglas Seelbach, and Lorraine G. Davis
UNIVERSITY OF OREGON
EUGENE, OREGON, USA

Medical insurance expenses are rising, and organizations are seeking various methods to contain these costs. One attempt at reducing expenses has been through the implementation of health promotion programs at the worksite. A variety of health promotion programs have been instituted in some of the largest corporations in America (Parkinson, 1982). Success is reported in terms of improved employee health and morale, but such subjective measurements provide little objective data for determining the effectiveness of worksite health programs (Berry, 1981). Because of a need for a well-controlled study, a 6-month pilot program was conducted to assess the effects of a health promotion program on state employees. This report details some of the clinical assessments and changes in risk factors associated with the study.

Methods

Seven state agencies in Salem, Oregon, agreed to participate in the program. A 1-month recruitment program identified those individuals in six of the agen-

Partial support of this project was provided by the State of Oregon, Bargaining Units Benefits Board. Additional funds came from the College of Human Development and Performance, University of Oregon.

cies that participated in the study. Employees of the seventh agency served as the no-intervention control group. In early January, 1983, 487 people from the seven agencies were screened for a variety of clinical risk factors. After an overnight fast, each person reported to a centralized facility, signed an informed consent form, completed a health assessment questionnaire, was weighed, and had his or her blood pressure recorded. A blood sample was taken by venipuncture, clotted at room temperature and centrifuged at 5,000 rpm for 20 min. The serum was removed, stored individually, and frozen until time of assay.

The serum was analyzed for total cholesterol, HDL cholesterol, triglycerides, and glucose. Total cholesterol was determined enzymatically (Allain, Poon, Chan, Richmond, & Fu, 1974). HDL cholesterol was measured in a similar manner after the precipitation and removal of both very low-density and low-density lipoproteins from serum. Serum triglycerides were also determined enzymatically (Bucolo & David, 1973).

The participants were primarily young middle-aged (mean age = 41.3 yrs.) females (65%) involved mainly in desk/organizational work rather than heavy physical labor. Individuals were prescreened for the clinical study parameters, and those persons with elevated blood pressure, total cholesterol, triglycerides, or glucose were contacted and requested to check with their physicians regarding participation in the study.

The intervention consisted of a 5.5-month program of two 40-min aerobic fitness classes and one 30-min health education class each week. Employees were provided release time for attending half of each class; the remaining time came from the person's lunch break or from staying after work. Attendance at all classes was monitored. The fitness sessions consisted of walk-jog, jogging, or aerobics classes, all of which emphasized strengthening and flexibility as well as cardiovascular conditioning. Among the topics included in the education curriculum were nutrition, drugs, safety, medical compliance, insurance cost containment, and fitness. Physical and health education graduate students who received special training for this study conducted the classes.

At the end of the intervention, a second assessment of the clinical risk factors for cardiovascular disease was conducted. Data were entered into a computer file for processing and analysis. Statistical tests were performed using the Statistical Package for the Social Sciences (SPSS, Inc., 1983).

Results

Attendance at the fitness classes is shown in Table 1. Approximately 17% of the people attended no fitness classes, 26% came to less than 6% of the fitness classes, 50% came to 31% or less of the classes, and 25% came to over half of the fitness classes.

Attendance in the health education classes is shown in Table 2. Approximately 35% of the people attended no health education classes, 53% attended less than 25% of the classes, and 23% came to over half of the health education classes.

Table 1. Attendance at fitness classes by the experimental group ($N = 408$)

Percentage of attendance	Percent of group
0% (never attended)	17.4%
1-6%	8.3%
7-31%	24.5%
32-56%	24.6%
57-97%	25.2%

Table 2. Attendance at health education classes by the experiment group ($N = 408$)

Percentage of attendace	Percentage of group
0% (never attended)	35.3%
1-25%	17.9%
26-50%	19.8%
51-100%	27.0%

The mean preprogram and postprogram values for nine clinical parameters for the intervention and control groups are shown in Tables 3 and 4, respectively. The values reflect measurements from those people who attended the biomedical screening and are not partitioned by attendance in the program.

The mean values for the biomedical parameters show that four of the nine values reduced from preprogram to postprogram testing times for both the experimental and control group. The actual values are within similar ranges for both groups with the means falling in the "normal" expected values for healthy individuals. Total cholesterol and the ratio of total to HDL cholesterol were the parameters which decreased the most in terms of actual values.

The number of people in the study with clinical risk factors identified from the preprogram screening is shown in Table 4.

For the intervention group, stepwise regression analyses were performed to determine which clinical measurements changed as a function of attendance in the program or as a function of age or sex after accounting for seasonal differences and correcting for pretest variability. These data are shown in Table 5.

Attendance at the fitness classes was significantly and inversely associated with both systolic and diastolic blood pressure and triglyceride levels. Health education class attendance was significantly associated with body weight: The most attendance in these classes, the higher the person's body weight. Systolic blood pressure and total serum cholesterol levels were associated with the person's age. HDL cholesterol and the ratio of total to HDL cholesterol were influenced by the sex of the person, with HDL cholesterol being higher and the ratio being lower in females.

Table 3. Biomedical values for intervention and control groups

Parameter (units)	Preprogram Mean Values (# of people)	Postprogram Mean Values (# of people)
Intervention group		
Weight	158.1	155.0
(lbs)	(408)	(187)
Resting heart rate	74.3	73.0
(beats/minute)	(401)	(187)
Systolic blood pressure	121.1	125.3
(mm Hg)	(398)	(187)
Diastolic blood pressure	79.1	80.2
(mg Hg)	(397)	(187)
Total cholesterol	205.2	177.0
(mg/dl)	(364)	(161)
HDL cholesterol	45.9	50.4
(mg/dl)	(357)	(180)
Ratio, total: HDL	4.8	3.8
cholesterol	(350)	(168)
Triglycerides	104.0	107.0
(mg/dl)	(367)	(179)
Glucose	77.5	82.6
(mg/dl)	(357)	(181)
Control group		
Weight	160.2	155.1
(lbs)	(79)	(35)
Resting heart rate	73.3	72.5
(beats/minute)	(79)	(32)
Systolic blood pressure	119.8	127.5
(mm Hg)	(77)	(35)
Diastolic blood pressure	81.0	82.4
(mm Hg)	(76)	(35)
Total cholesterol	204.3	174.7
(mg/dl)	(74)	(31)
HDL cholesterol	44.8	48.8
(mg/dl)	(75)	(32)
Ratio, Total: HDL	4.8	3.6
cholesterol	(73)	(31)
Triglycerides	98.8	107.6
(mg/dl)	(73)	(33)
Glucose	73.3	82.5
(mg/dl)	(73)	(33)

Table 4. Number of people with elevated clinical risk factors in the intervention group identified from the preprogram biomedical screening

Parameter	# of people	Percent of total
Total size of intervention group	408	100
Elevated systolic blood pressure (above 150 mm Hg)	14	3.4
Elevated diastolic blood pressure (above 90 mm Hg)	45	11.0
Elevated total cholesterol (above 250 mg/dl)	42	10.3
Elevated ratio, total: HDL cholesterol (5 or above)	124	30.4
Elevated triglycerides (above 200 mg/dl)	57	14.0
Elevated glucose (above 130 mg/dl)	9	2.2

Table 5. Residuals using stepwise regression

Independent variable	Dependent variable	F	P
Fitness attendance	Diastolic blood pressure	5.55	.02
Age	Systolic blood pressure	10.13	.00
Fitness attendance	Systolic blood pressure	10.13	.00
Health education attendance	Body weight	4.31	.04
Age	Total cholesterol	16.52	.00
Sex	HDL cholesterol	5.68	.02
Age	Blood glucose	2.10	.15
Fitness attendance	Triglycerides	5.72	.02
Sex	Total cholesterol	6.78	.02

Discussion

Ideally, full participation in a research program is desirable for a well-controlled study. If a laboratory setting were employed, such figures might be obtained. However, for reasons ranging from lack of motivation, changes in time schedules, poor facilities, and lack of management support, many people chose to discontinue attending this health promotion program over the 6-month period. Certainly, the results of this intervention are less clear than a controlled laboratory setting but may represent a typical voluntary health and fitness program. Approximately 25% of the original participants came to over half of the sessions.

The data presented in Table 3 shows gross changes in the mean values of the risk factors assessed but are not corrected for program attendance. The preprogram values are similar for the intervention and control groups, indicating that employees in the no-intervention agency had a similar clinical health profile as those entering the 6-month study. Both the intervention and control groups showed mean drops in total cholesterol and increases in HDL cholesterol, suggesting that either seasonal variations were occurring, that diet and exercise changes ensued in the control group over the 6 months, or that laboratory analysis of pre- and postprogram samples was variable. The later case was not found to be true, however, as some samples from the pretest were analyzed a second time with the reagents used for the posttest analysis with a variability of approximately 5%.

A further examination of the intervention group reveals a substantial number of people presenting with one or more elevated clinical risk factor (Table 4). Although some subjects are counted more than once in the tabulations (i.e., more than one risk factor), there are, nonetheless, approximately 30% of the group with at least one clinical factor increasing their risk of cardiovascular disease. This is an alarming percentage of individuals who display compromised health status, and the implications for the employer could be enormous health-related expenditures.

Correction of the data for attendance in the program provides another picture. As reported in Table 6, there was a significant effect of lowered triglyceride levels and decreased systolic and diastolic blood pressure as a function of the number of fitness classes attended. These results clearly show the benefits of regular physical activity. A direct relationship was evident between attendance in the health education classes and a person's body weight. This interpretation is not clear; people who weighed more came more frequently to the education classes compared to those who weighed less. Other significant associations were due to age and sex, which were apparently stronger predictors of some clinical chemistry changes than was the intervention.

References

Allain, C.C., Poon, L.S., Chan, C.G.S., Richmond, W., & Fu, P.C. (1974). Enzymatic determination of total serum cholesterol. *Clinical Chemistry, 20*, 470-475.

Berry, C.A. (1981). *Good health for employees and reduced health care costs for industry*. Washington, DC: Health Insurance Association of America.

Bucolo, G., & David, H. (1973). Quantitative determination of serum triglycerides by the use of enzymes. *Clinical Chemistry, 19*, 476-482.

Parkinson, R.B. (Ed.). (1982). *Managing health promotion in the workplace*. Palo Alto, CA: Mayfield.

SPSS, Inc. (1983). SPSS-X. New York: McGraw-Hill.

13

FITCOMP Computerized Assessment System to Evaluate Body Composition, Nutrition, and Exercise

Frank I. Katch
UNIVERSITY OF MASSACHUSETTS
AMHERST, MASSACHUSETTS, USA

FITCOMP (acronym for fitness by computer) grew from the need to provide a rapid system of data analysis for various professional sport teams measured in the early 1970s. FITCOMP is an interactive computer system for input, analysis, and output to provide individualized reports on a timely basis. The computerized approach enables one to assemble and compile a vast amount of anthropometric data for later quantitative analysis of basic relationships. What was evident was the need to integrate information about body composition (chiefly recommendations concerning weight loss and an optimal playing-weight range) with nutritional recommendations and various parameters of physical fitness (muscular strength and endurance, cardiovascular capacity, and flexibility).

Early on, a decision was made against assessment of nutrient intake from daily recall of foods consumed or 3- to 7-day food diaries; instead the position was taken that a computer could be programed to plan daily menus based on food preferences selected by the individual. It was a firm belief then, and still is, that individuals respond more favorably with regard to weight loss when they are allowed to make choices about food consumption and exercise. Instead of selecting specific calorie menus from cookbooks, a computer program was devised that constructs nutritionally balanced breakfasts, lunches,

---

For further information on FITCOMP questionnaire processing write to: Computer Diet, P.O. Box 431, Amherst, MA 01004.

and dinners from a basic list of foods selected by the individual. Preselection of foods is the major distinguishing characteristic between the FITCOMP meal plan and all other computer-based food-record-type nutrition programs.

The food list in the FITCOMP program is essentially that devised by the American Dietetic Association and incorporated into its food exchange plan. The essence of the FITCOMP approach is to combine body composition, nutrition, and exercise into one computer program, either separately or in combination so the individual receives a comprehensive plan to achieve an ideal body fat percentage and to improve aerobic fitness.

Body Composition Computer Report

Table 1 lists three different approaches currently in use as part of the body composition report, depending on the level of sophistication required for the analysis.

In the simplest form, a desired weight loss is requested by the individual, and the output is adjusted so body weight can be reduced by at least 1.2 lbs/week but no more than 2.4 lbs, depending on the option selected for exercise. Figure 1 shows an actual example of a weight loss curve for a 35.0-lb decrease in weight for a middle-aged executive. The algorithm takes into account the magnitude of weight loss, an estimate of changes in resting metabolic rate, change

Table 1. Three different ways to generate the body composition report.

Method	User Input	Computer Output
1	Current body weight and projected "ideal" weight. No criterion for projected weight; entirely self-selected.	Weight loss curve if request is for weight loss. No weight curve for maintenance or weight gain.
2	Body density from underwater weighing or % body fat computed from density or some other method such as K^{40}, deuterium oxide, or tritiated water.	% fat (relative fat), fat, kg (absolute), lean body weight, lean to fat ratio, optimal body weight range based on desirable body fat depending on age, race, and gender.
3	3 to 5 fatfolds or 6 to 11 girths.	Prediction of % body fat, kg fat, and lean body weight based on multiple regression analysis that uses % fat (density) as the criterion dependent variable and the fatfolds or girths as independent variables. The current data base for $N = 7,900$ subjects has been cross-validated on large subsamples of the data base where the minimum $N = 100$, depending on the specific athletic team or sport, race, age, and gender.

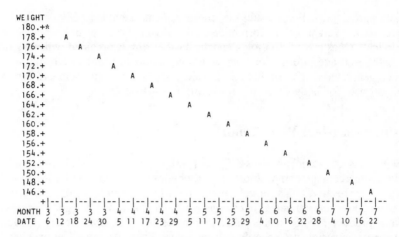

Figure 1. Computer-generated 35-lb weight-loss curve to accompany a 1,418-cal meal plan. It is possible to draw up to three weight-loss curves on the same printout, each geared for a different rate of weight loss depending on caloric level and intensity of the exercise prescription

in status of physical activity (e.g., inactive to vigorous), as well as duration and intensity of exercise participation. If the individual adheres to the dietary and exercise prescription, then the theoretical endpoint or target "goal" weight can reasonably be expected to occur during a given week and month. A specific date is assigned as a target so individuals can work toward their goals realistically.

Note that in this particular example, there is a weight loss of 35 lbs, from an initial weight of 180 lbs to a target weight of 145 lbs. The duration of the weight loss is 136 days (about 20 weeks), a weight loss of about 1.8 lbs/week. Note also that the curve of weight loss is not linear but curvilinear to account for changes in metabolism and the new pattern of physical activity that includes a progressive increase in exercise intensity.

If body density data are available, then the individual's current level of body fat, independent of weight, is used to generate the weight-loss curve. Data from the world literature are used to provide guidelines for theoretical versus expected alterations in body composition. Because dietary plans in the FIT-COMP program are never generated without concomitant exercise regimens, weight loss by diet restriction alone is not allowed. In this way, the initial weight loss, chiefly by dehydration, is avoided and lean mass is spared. Preservation of lean mass is a common occurrence when diet is accompanied by exercise—preferably large muscle exercise performed at an intensity that elevates pulse rate to between 60 and 85% of maximum.

If fatfolds or girths are available, then age-, sex-, or fitness-specific regression equations can be used to predict percentage body fat. The data base includes mean values from the pertinent literature and unpublished data on approximately 7,900 individuals, including several thousand "high caliber" football, baseball, basketball, volleyball, and soccer players, as well as body builders, weight lifters, gymnasts, rowers, and combat sport and track and field participants. For all subjects, measurements included body density by hydrostatic weighing with correction for residual air volume and duplicate or triplicate measures of 5 fatfolds and 11 basic girths. Combined with height, weight, and age information, regression equations to predict body fat have been generated that yield multiple R values above 0.90 with standard errors of estimate for body fat in the range of $\pm$ 1.4 to 2.4.

Nutrition Meal Plan Report

Figure 2 is an example of days 3-5 of a 1,418-calorie food plan. In this example, the percentage composition for carbohydrate, protein, and fat is 54, 23, and 23 respectively. The usual procedure is to generate a 14-day plan; because foods are arranged as exchanges within a given food category (breads, dairy products, fruits, meats, fats, vegetables, alcohol, and "treats"), each exchange is assigned a specific calorie value. Therefore, one can exchange any one food within a food category with any other food in that category. One-half cup of cooked grits (70 cal), for example, can be exchanged for one-half cup of cooked cereal, bran flakes, cooked barley or spaghetti, lima beans, or one ear of corn-on-the-cob, one small baked potato, and so on. In addition, any one complete breakfast, lunch, or dinner can be interchanged for any other breakfast, lunch, or dinner. This makes the number of food combinations for a given day equal to 14 factorial. There is also an override function, so hundreds of consecutive meal plans could be generated, even for low-fat meals (e.g. 20-25% of total calories.)

In practice, up to 35 consecutive days of meals have been generated for individuals enrolled in supervised university-based weight-loss experiments; thereafter, individual food items are reviewed and new menus generated. The basic food list includes 11 food choices from the milk category, 35 each from breads and fruits, 42 from meats, 17 from fats, 28 from vegetables, seven from low-calorie vegetables, 12 from treats, and a choice from seven common alcoholic beverages. The current list of 194 foods was based on those most frequently chosen by approximately 13,000 individuals throughout the United States who responded to a questionnaire which included 234 food items. Examples of foods not included are goat's milk, powdered milk, bratwurst, wheat germ, and apricot juice.

Aerobic Exercise Report

The FITCOMP aerobic exercise program is designed so individuals will eventually expend approximately 300 to 500kcal per exercise session. The three basic exercise plans are geared for the beginner, intermediate, or advanced participant. The appropriate level is assigned based on age, sex, and on the response to questions concerning physical activity from the questionnaire.

The three main activities are walking, jogging or running, and swimming or cycling. A person can also select activities from nine other popular choices: racquetball, circuit training, squash, badminton, basketball, downhill skiing, tennis, golf, and aerobic dancing. Figure 3 outlines steps 6 and 7 of a 21-step exercise program for a sedentary housewife who selected eight activities for her exercise program.

```
---+-----------------------+-----------------------+-----------------------+
   |      BREAKFAST        |        LUNCH          |       DINNER          |
---+-----------------------+-----------------------+-----------------------+
DAY|English Muffin         |Graham crackers        |Popcorn (popped)       |
 3 |     1                 |     4                 |     3  CUP            |
   |Milk - 2%              |Yogurt-fruit           |Cooked spaghetti       |
   |     2/3  CUP          |     1/2  CUP          |     1  CUP            |
   |Egg                    |Chicken                |Milk - 2%             |
   |     1                 |     1  OUNCE          |     2/3  CUP         |
   |Prune juice            |Diet Margarine         |Pork Chops            |
   |     1/4  CUP          |     2  TSP            |     3  OUNCE         |
   |                       |Oranges                |Spinach               |
   |                       |     2  SMALL          |     1 1/2  CUP       |
   |                       |                       |Lettuce               |
   |                       |                       |          NO LIMIT    |
   |                       |                       |Diet Margarine        |
   |                       |                       |     2/3  TSP         |
   |                       |                       |Apple sauce           |
   |                       |                       |     1/2  CUP         |
---+-----------------------+-----------------------+-----------------------+
   |      BREAKFAST        |        LUNCH          |       DINNER          |
---+-----------------------+-----------------------+-----------------------+
DAY|Bagel                  |Graham crackers        |Wine red/white        |
 4 |     1                 |     4                 |     3 1/2  OUNCE     |
   |Milk - 2%              |Milk - 2%             |Baked potato          |
   |     2/3  CUP          |     2/3  CUP          |     1  SMALL         |
   |Cottage cheese         |Cottage cheese         |Milk - 2%             |
   |     1/4  CUP          |     1/4  CUP          |     2/3  CUP         |
   |Diet Margarine         |Diet Margarine         |Ground beef           |
   |     2/3  TSP          |     2 2/3  TSP        |     3  OUNCE         |
   |Orange juice           |Apple                  |Cauliflower           |
   |     1/2  CUP          |     2  SMALL          |     1 1/2  CUP       |
   |                       |                       |Radishes              |
   |                       |                       |          NO LIMIT    |
   |                       |                       |Tangarines            |
   |                       |                       |     1  MEDIUM        |
---+-----------------------+-----------------------+-----------------------+
   |      BREAKFAST        |        LUNCH          |       DINNER          |
---+-----------------------+-----------------------+-----------------------+
DAY|Raisin bread           |Graham crackers        |Candy bar, choc       |
 5 |     2  SLICE          |     4                 |     1  SMALL         |
   |Milk - 2%              |Yogurt-fruit           |Lima beans            |
   |     2/3  CUP          |     1/2  CUP          |     1/2  CUP         |
   |Swiss cheese           |Tuna                   |Milk - 2%             |
   |     1  OUNCE          |     1/4  CUP          |     2/3  CUP         |
   |Grapefruit juice       |Diet Margarine         |Fish-fresh/frzn       |
   |     1/2  CUP          |     2  TSP            |     3  OUNCE         |
   |                       |Oranges                |Green pepper          |
   |                       |     2  SMALL          |     1 1/2  CUP       |
   |                       |                       |Lettuce               |
   |                       |                       |          NO LIMIT    |
   |                       |                       |Diet Margarine        |
   |                       |                       |     2/3  TSP         |
   |                       |                       |Grapes  MEDIUM        |
   |                       |                       |     12               |
```

Figure 2. Reproductions of 3 days of actual breakfast, lunch, and dinner computer-generated menus. In the normal mode, 14 daily menus are produced; an override function allows the user to specify the desired number of meal plans, the daily calorie intake, or the percentage composition of carbohydrate, protein, or fat

In this example, all activities are listed together to show the approximate equivalency in terms of caloric expenditure for either a beginner, intermediate, or advanced level of participation. This kind of computer-generated output gives the person freedom to exchange activites for any given workout; it offers flexibility and variety in planning workouts to meet individual preferences. The major advantage, however, is the relative maintenance of caloric equivalency between the different activities that is linked with caloric input from the menus. If inclement weather prohibits jogging or cycling, then swimming or racquetball, for example, can be substituted without altering either the required calorie output (activity) or the required calorie input (food) side of the energy balance equation. In this way, the individual stays in phase with his or her tailor-made weight loss curve. The exercise prescription is sensitive to individual differences because it considers age, sex, current level of physical activity (relative fitness status), body size (height and weight), and body composition (percentage fat and lean body weight).

Practicality of Computer-Generated Reports

The most obvious advantage of computer-generated reports is that exercise and menu planning are based on individual preferences rather than on requiring

```
-----------------------------------------------------------------------
STEP    JOG FOR 1 3/4 MILES IN 19 MINUTES 52 SECONDS (11 MIN 21 SEC/MILE)
6       THIS EXERCISE BURNS 159 CALORIES.

        CYCLE 3 MILES IN 11 MINUTES 58 SECONDS (15.04 MILES/HOUR)
        THIS EXERCISE BURNS 96 CALORIES.

        SWIM 100 YARDS IN 2 MINUTES 59 SECONDS (33.51 YARDS/MIN)
        REPEAT THIS 7 TIMES. THIS EXERCISE BURNS 167 CALORIES.
        The following alternate activites will expend approximately the
        same number of calories as the aerobic activities above expend.
                    Basketball        for     11. minutes
                    Badminton         for     29. minutes
                    Squash            for     12. minutes
                    Circuit Training for      7. minutes
                    Racquetball       for     16. minutes
-----------------------------------------------------------------------
STEP    JOG FOR 2 MILES IN 20 MINUTES 38 SECONDS (10 MIN 19 SEC/MILE)
7       THIS EXERCISE BURNS 181 CALORIES.

        CYCLE 3 1/4 MILES IN 12 MINUTES 7 SECONDS (16.09 MILES/HOUR)
        THIS EXERCISE BURNS 106 CALORIES.

        SWIM 100 YARDS IN 2 MINUTES 49 SECONDS (35.50 YARDS/MIN)
        REPEAT THIS 8 TIMES. THIS EXERCISE BURNS 198 CALORIES.
        The following alternate activites will expend approximately the
        same number of calories as the aerobic activities above expend.
                    Basketball        for     12. minutes
                    Badminton         for     34. minutes
                    Squash            for     14. minutes
                    Circuit Training for      8. minutes
                    Racquetball       for     19. minutes
-----------------------------------------------------------------------
```

Figure 3. Computer-generated exercise prescription. This example shows the approximate caloric equivalency for three main activities—jogging, cycling, and swimming—and five of nine possible activities

adherence to the standard workouts and set meal plans typically outlined in popular books on exercise or diet. Spending time performing tedious calculations and trying to individualize a particular exercise and nutrition plan is unnecessary; the speed with which the final report can be obtained is only limited by the speed of the output device (printer) because the computations can be done in fractions of a second.

At present, the FITCOMP program is used in one of three ways:

1. Interactively with a large main-frame computer with a high-speed laser page printer. (A typical 14 to 16 page computer report is printed within 10 sec.)
2. At the user's workplace via tape access of the program through a lease arrangement.
3. Interactively with the new generation of powerful minicomputers that support full screen "touch" graphics and editing as well as data entry by "mouse cursor" or optical scanning. (A high-speed laser printer is used with an output of approximately 8 pages a minute.)

In summary, interactive computer-based technology can provide individualized reports that take into account body size, body composition, age, sex, current fitness status, and activity preference. Such reports can greatly enhance the quality of health services.

14

Free Radical Pathology: Rationale and Toxicology of Antioxidants and Other Supplements in Sports Medicine and Exercise Science

Harry B. Demopoulos, James P. Santomier, Myron L. Seligman, and Dennis D. Pietronigro
NEW YORK UNIVERSITY MEDICAL CENTER
NEW YORK, NEW YORK, USA

Patricia I. Hogan
NEW YORK UNIVERSITY
NEW YORK, NEW YORK, USA

As sports activities and vigorous exercise programs expand, the shortage of experts for supervisory training raises the probability of mishaps and disabilities (Jokl, 1984). Paralleling the expansion of sports and exercise with their increasing risk of adverse effects is a growing use of various supplements—some as medical agents and others as nutrient supplements—in an attempt to add strength, speed, and endurance. In some instances, as in the use of oral steroids for enhanced muscular development or the use of single amino acids, glandulars, trace metals, and other substances, additional pathology may be induced (American College of Sports Medicine, 1984).

Rationale

There is a scientific rationale for the safe use of carefully selected medical and nutrient supplements aside from water and balanced electrolytes. If used judiciously, the carefully selected supplements may help to minimize some of the adverse effects of sports and exercise.

The present studies deal with the rationale behind these supplementary substances as well as their safety and toxicities. Part of the rationale involves free radical reactions and the antioxidant supplements that can control them (Demopoulos, Pietronigro, Flamm, & Seligman, 1980; Demopoulos, Pietronigro, & Seligman, 1983). Another part of the rationale relates to the endogenous opioids released by stress, and the use of antioxidants to block the pathologic effects on the immune system and nervous system (Shavit, Lewis, Terman, Gale, & Liebeskind, 1984; Free & Sanders, 1979). Most antioxidants can be self-administered in a preventive manner (Pearson & Shaw, 1982). However, some are more complex and must be medically administered, as in the case of acute injuries to the central nervous system that may occur in skiing, boxing, and bobsleding (Demopoulos, Flamm, Seligman, Pietronigro, Tomasula, & DeCrescito, 1982).

Pathologic free radical reactions have been well demonstrated in traumatic injuries to the spinal cord and brain, perhaps the most serious nonfatal pathologic sequelae of sports (Demopoulos, Flamm, Pietronigro, & Seligman, 1980). The antioxidants required in these situations take the form of the emergency use (within 1 to 2 hours) of extraordinarily high antioxidant doses of *injected* gluco-corticosteroids such as methyl prednisolone (e.g. 2,000 mg/day) divided into three doses and given for 4 to 5 days, with the dose totaling 8,000 to 10,000 mg. This may reduce the consequent paralyses (Demopoulos, Seligman, Schwartz, Tomasula, & Flamm, 1984).

At a less debilitating level, some of the known physiologic changes occurring during sports and extensive exercise also may result in the production of pathologic free radicals and in the release of excessive quantities of endogenous opiates. However, these reactions occur at lower rates than in acute injuries to the central nervous system and, therefore, less powerful, safe antioxidants taken orally on an ongoing basis may suffice.

The basic rationale for the use of certain antioxidants rests on the production of pathologic free radicals and the release of excessive endogenous opioids during the sport and vigorous exercise. This paper will examine the substances that counter these pathogenic factors as well as other nutrient supplements such as single amino acids, glandulars, trace metals, oils, and neurotransmitter precursors.

Background

Free Radicals

A free radical is any chemical substance that has a lone, unpaired electron in an outer orbital (Singh, 1982). Some chemicals have this electron configuration normally, such as the air pollutant NO_2, while in others the free radical state must be induced, as by light, x-rays, or other chemicals (Pryor, 1976). Free radicals are unstable because of their lone electron. The unbalanced magnetic field created by the unpaired electron's spin adversely affects molecular structure and chemical reactivities (Pryor, 1976). Normal molecules generally are not magnetic.

The chemistry of free radicals differs from the chemistry of other organic molecules because of the lone spinning electron and its magnetic field. Most free radicals attempt to aquire another electron or lose their odd electron in order to return to a more stable configuration. The resulting reactions therefore become chain reactions and may actually branch and spread geometrically (Pryor, 1976). Termination of such spreading chain reactions requires the intercession of large numbers of chain-breaking antioxidants (Demopoulos, Flamm, Seligman, Pietronigro, Tomasula, & DeCrescito, 1982; Pryor, 1976). Substances that can easily donate hydrogen and then acquire a stable form afterward serve as excellent antioxidants (Mitamura, Seligman, Solomon, Flamm, Demopoulos, & Ranshoff, 1981). For example, thiol (-SH·) containing compounds readily donate their hydrogen, and the resulting sulfur free radical (-S) joins another sulfer radical (-S·) to form a stable disulfide (-S-S). Another example is the ready donation of hydrogen from the hydroxyl groups (-OH) of ascorbic acid (vitamin C) or alpha tocopherol (vitamin E), with the resulting formation of stable quinoid groups (=O) (King & Burns, 1975; McCay & King, 1980). These types of steps are summarized below, where X· represents a free radical:

$$(2) \ X \cdot \ + \ (2) \ \text{-SH} \ \rightarrow \ (2) \ XH \ + \ (2)\text{-S} \cdot$$
$$\text{-S} \cdot \ + \ \cdot \text{S-} \ \rightarrow \ \text{-S-S-}$$
$$\text{or}$$
$$X \cdot \ + \ \text{-OH} \ \rightarrow \ XH \ + \ =O$$

The aim is to provide hydrogen to terminate the free radicals. Hyperbaric hydrogen is an excellent antioxidant system but it is extremely dangerous because of its explosive flammability.

Free radical reactions occur normally and are responsible for a number of key biochemical events in virtually all life forms, except perhaps for anaerobic bacteria (e.g., Clostridium tetani, which causes tetanus). Table 1 lists the normal processes that are actually driven by free radical reactions in animal cells (Babior, 1982; Boveris, Cadenas, & Stoppani, 1976; Boveris, 1977; Hemler & Lands, 1980). There are additional free radical reactions in nature, as when light impinges on chlorophyl and when UV light interacts with oxygen molecules (O_2) in the topmost layers of the stratosphere to form ozone (O_3), which in turn absorbs 98% of the sun's UV and thereby prevents the destruc-

Table 1. Normally occurring, physiologic free radical reactions

- Mitochondrial electron transport, including coenzyme Q semiquinone and flavin free radical.
- Endoplasmic reticulum hydroxylation reactions that involve detoxification of chemicals, activation of carcinogens, synthesis of major biomolecules.
- Prostaglandin synthesis; in the initial formation of the first endoperoxide, PGG_2, ·OH radicals are required, while in the conversion of PGG_2 to PGH_2, an oxygen free radical is liberated (·Ox).

- Phagocytosis by macrophages and polymorphonuclear leucocytes results in the production of superoxide, $\cdot O_2^-$, and subsequently H_2O_2, $\cdot OH$, and singlet oxygen, $^1O_2$.
- Action of xanthine oxidase; in producing uric acid, $\cdot O_2^-$ and related radicals are formed.
- Normal metabolic degradation of catecholamines yields $\cdot O_2^-$ and other radicals.
- Normal oxidation of ascorbic acid, as in dopamine beta heydroxylase, produces $\cdot O_2^-$ and related radicals.
- Melanin synthesis produces a number of oxygen free radicals and the final polymerization occurs via free radical addition products; neuro-melanin as found in the substantia nigra and adenal medulla are somewhat similar polymerization products.

---

tion of life on earth. Free radicals, when they occur normally and under controlled circumstances, are therefore central to our existence. However, as research has demonstrated over the past 10 years, free radicals when uncontrolled are also central to many degenerative disease processes (Demopoulos, Pietronigro, & Seligman, 1983; Demopoulos, et al., 1984; Babior, 1982; Hemler & Lands, 1980; McCord & Roy, 1982; Hess, Manson, & Okabe, 1982; Singal, Kapur, Dhillon, Beamish, & Dhella, 1982; Bulkley, 1983; Parks, Bulkley, & Granger, 1983; Gardner, Stewart, Casole, Downey, & Chambers, 1983; Taylor, Martin, & Parker, 1983; Jenkins, Friedland, & Howald, 1984). There is a careful balance between free radical mediated aerobic life, as we know it, and free radical mediated pathology that may account for certain sport and exercise problems, and several of the degenerative diseases.

Antioxidants

The wide spectrum of antioxidants that evolution has progressively added to aerobic life forms is what makes the difference between aerobic life and free radical pathology (Singh, 1982; Demopoulos, 1973; King & Burns, 1975; McCay & King, 1980; McCord & Roy, 1982; Gardner et al., 1983; Jenkins et al., 1984; Retkau, 1982; Burton & Ingold, 1984). Table 2 lists these antioxidants.

Most of the chemical substances in Table 2 are simple and react one-on-one with free radicals (Demopoulos, 1973; Burton & Ingold, 1984). In such reactions, termed stochiometric, one antioxidant molecule is consumed for every free radical scavenged. Ascorbic acid (Vitamin C) can scavenge two free radicals since it has two hydroxyl (-OH) groups (King & Burns, 1975). The three enzymes listed at the bottom of Table 2 are different (Singh, 1982; Jenkins, et al., 1984; Petkau, 1982). One enzyme molecule can handle several thousand free radicals before the protein structure of the enzyme loses its functional configuration. Clearly, as these antioxidants and enzymes are used up, they must be replaced, or else the normally occurring free radicals that spill over from the aerobic metabolic pathways (Babior, 1982; Boveris et al., 1976; Boveris, 1977; Hemler & Lands, 1980; McCord & Roy, 1982; Singal et al.,

Table 2. Spectrum of endogenous cellular antioxidants and free radical controlling enzymes

Antioxidants
  carotenoids
  alpha-tocopherol
  ascorbic acid in high concentrations and in the absence of iron and copper
  thiol amino acids, e.g., cysteine, and $_{\beta,\beta}{}^1$-dimethylcysteine (D-penicil-
  lamine)
  phenolic amino acids, e.g., tyrosine
  catecholic amino acids, e.g., 3,4-dihydroxyphenylalanine (DOPA)
  selenium, independently of its prosthetic role in glutathione peroxidase
  corticosteroids
  dehydroepiandrosterone
  estriol, estrone, estradiol

Enzymes
  Superoxide dismutases in mitochondria and cytosol
  Catalase
  Glutathione peroxidase system

1982) listed in Table 1 will destroy the cell. Anaerobic bacteria, for example, lack sufficient antioxidant controls and die immediately upon exposure to plain oxygen (O_2), which is a diradical. This is why hyperbaric oxygen is some-times used in the treating anaerobic bacterial infections such as gas gangrene caused by *Clostridium welchii*. The increased oxygen levels kill these bacteria by free radical mechanisms.

There are many antioxidants that we must obtain from botanic life forms: ascorbic acid (vitamin C) from citrus fruits; beta carotene and allied carote-noids for carrots, squash, and oranges; alpha tocopherol (vitamin E) from grains; phenols and catechols (which have hydroxyl groups, -OH) from ap-ples, bananas, and potatoes. These are the most abundant antioxidants in our tissues, and some, like ascorbic acid, are actually concentrated 50 to 70 times in the brain and spinal cord to yield the highest tissue levels of this antioxidant (Spector, 1977). Botanic foods, such as fresh fruit and vegetables, are there-fore, the best natural sources to replenish the key antioxidants (Ames, 1983). From an evolutionary point of view, botanic life forms generally have more antioxidants compared to zootic forms because botanic life has had far more experience, by millions of years, with oxygen, which is diradical. In order to survive and evolve in an oxygen atmosphere, antioxidants are absolutely essential since O_2 is a very toxic gas to organisms lacking sufficient antiox-idants. The free radical based oxidative power of oxygen derives from the lone electron on each of the two atoms in a molecule of oxygen (O_2) (Masterton & Slowinski, 1977). A moment's reflection recalls that virtually every metal in the earth's crust has been attacked by O_2 and exists as the oxide. Iron and many other substances, unless treated, will crumble under the free radical at-tack of oxygen. The fact that we survive in this oxygen atmosphere, even with molecules that are far more easily attacked than iron, is a tribute to the evolu-tionary addition of a spectrum of abundant antioxidants in our tissues.

Free radicals are diverse in form and may require specific antioxidants to neutralize them. One basis for specificity is whether the free radical is in an aqueous or lipoidal environment. The cytoplasm of cells is generally an aqueous dispersion, but the molecular midzone of cell membranes is lipoidal. Ascorbic acid (vitamin C) does well in scavenging hydroxyl radicals ($\cdot$OH) in water, whereas alpha tocopherol (vitamin E) destroys free radicals (such as peroxyl radicals) in lipoidal areas. Table 3 summarizes the actions of the different types of antioxidants and free radical controlling enzymes.

Table 3. Specificity of antioxidants and enzymes

- Carotenoids such as beta carotene, and beta carotene 4-4[1]-dione function to *prevent* free radical reactions by specifically scavenging singlet oxygen ($^1O_2$), which otherwise initiates lipid peroxidation. The carotenes also act as *chain-breaking* antioxidants, but only at the low pO_2 levels present in tissues; the peroxyl radical (ROO$\cdot$) can then be specifically scavenged by the beta carotenes, which are lipoidal.

- Retinoids can also scavenge peroxyl radicals (ROO$\cdot$), as do the beta carotenes. They are lipoidal.

- Alpha tocopherol scavenges peroxyl (ROO$\cdot$) and hydroxyl ($\cdot$OH) radicals, and is a lipoidal chain-breaking antioxidant.

- Ascorbic acid is an aqueous antioxidant and can scavenge hydroxyl radicals ($\cdot$OH), as well as regenerate oxidized vitamin E (from tocopheryl quinone, back to tocopherol). Ascorbic acid, after it has been oxidized, becomes dehydro ascorbic acid, which can be recycled back to active ascorbic acid by NADH and other hydrogen carriers.

- Thiol amino acids, and the tripeptide, glutathione, are active in aqueous and lipoidal melieux; they donate the H of the -SH group and transiently form a radical center on the sulfur atom, S$\cdot$; generally, two such free radicals form and join to quench one another by forming a disulfide, -S-S-; in this way the thiols also stop free radical chain reactions.

- Phenolic and catecholic compounds react in much the same way as alpha tocopherol and are hydrophobic, lipoidal antioxidants, e.g., tyrosine, and 3,4-dihydroxyphenylalanine.

- The steroids such as the corticosteroids, dehyroepiandrosterone, and the estrogens are excellent lipoidal antioxidants based partially on the types of reactions seen with alpha tocopherol.

- Superoxide dismutases (SOD) are chain-breaking antioxidant enzymes. They are dependent on Mn or Cu/Zn; Mn-SOD is found in mitochondria, while Cu/Zn SOD is in the cytosol; SODs are the fifth most abundant protein in mammals (collagen, hemoglobin, albumin, globulin, SODs) and are essential for aerobic existence because 3-10% of O_2 utilized by mitochondria escapes four-electron reduction by cytochrome oxidase and is partially reduced by one electron to superoxide, $\cdot O_2{}^-$. This is converted to H_2O_2 by the SOD's. In the face of increased oxygen consumption, as during physical exertion or other stress that increases respiration, the total amount of $\cdot O_2\cdot$ produced rises; therefore, there is a need for a considerable reserve of SOD. If more $\cdot O_2{}^-$ is produced than can be handled by the local SOD levels, then

(Cont.)

Table 3 (Cont.)

$\cdot O_2^-$ will disproportionate to H_2O_2 and simultaneously produce singlet oxygen, $^1O_2$, a very dangerous species that causes lipid peroxidation. The H_2O_2 produced by SOD must under any circumstances be quickly converted to H_2O and O_2 by catalase.

- Catalase is plentiful and converts H_2O_2 to H_2O and O_2. Without some factor to handle the H_2O_2 two damaging events could occur: 1) H_2O_2 will split into two $\cdot OH$ radicals, as happens in the presence of iron and copper and 2) H_2O_2 can react with $\cdot O_2^-$ to produce $\cdot OH$.

- Glutathione peroxidase is part of an enzyme system that mutes already formed lipid peroxides (LOOH) *before* they can break down to propagate free radical chain reactions. Glutathione (GSH) is used in a reaction wherein OH is removed from LOOH, and H is removed from two GSH molecules, to form LOH and H_2. The GSH → GS-SG and then is recycled back to GSH from other H donors. Selenium acts as the essential prosthetic group in this enzyme and the essentiality of Se probably derives from this enzyme.

- Factors in intermediary metabolism and bioenergetics that aid in the flow of reducing equivalents help in the reduction of the oxidized main antioxidants. Substances such as pyridoxine, thiamine, pantothenic acid, cyanobalamine, niacin, and riboflavin can be considered as co-antioxidants because they foster a rapid rate of production of NADH and NADPH and other H carriers that recycle oxidized antioxidants such as dehydro ascorbic acid back to ascorbic acid, which in turn helps to recycle oxidized alpha tocopherol.

Free Radical Pathology

It is well known that oxygen-related free radicals can develop from the incomplete reduction of O_2 (Boveris, 1977; McCord & Roy, 1982; Bulkley, 1983; Jenkins, et al., 1984).

Normally, cytochrome oxidase in the mitochondrial electron transport chain gives four e's to one molecule of O_2, together with 4 H's to produce two molecules of H_2O:

$$O_2 + 4H^+ + 4e \rightarrow 2\ H_2O$$

If less than four e's are provided, then O_2 will be partially reduced by one, two, or three electrons.

$$O_2 + 1e \rightarrow \cdot O_2^- \text{ (Superoxide radical)}$$
$$O_2 + 2e + 2H^+ \rightarrow H_2O_2 \text{ (hydrogen peroxide)}$$
$$O_2 + 3e + 3H^+ \rightarrow H_2O + \cdot OH \text{ (hydroxyl radical)}$$

In mitochondria, approximately 3-10% of O_2 is incompletely reduced by one, two, or three electrons. The free radicals produced are scavenged by superoxide dismutase (destroys $\cdot O_2^-$), catalase (destroys H_2O_2), and ascorbic acid or vitamin E (destroy $\cdot OH$ and $\cdot OOH$, respectively). If the rate of O_2 is μl/minute passing through the mitochondria is normal, then the 3-10% "leakage" of

O_2 into free radicals is inconsequential and can be handled by the available free radical control systems (Burton & Ingold, 1984). However, if more O_2 is supplied per minute, as in hyperoxia from breathing pure O_2 (Taylor et al., 1983) the supply of antioxidants may be overwhelmed, since the 3-10% leakage is now a percent of a much larger number. A similar situation may occur in sports and exercise because the rate of O_2 consumption may rise dramatically and be analogous to a hyperoxic state. This may be one reason that superoixde dismutase and catalase levels climb in humans and laboratory animals undergoing physical training (Jenkins et al., 1984).

Pathologic free radicals may be produced in quantities that are beyond the amounts of available antioxidants, as in hyperoxia, or the free radicals formed may be of a type that cannot be destroyed by the available antioxidants such as nitrogen dioxide, NO_2. Free radical pathology is initiated when abnormal types or quantities of radicals attack the normal, susceptible biomolecules comprising key cellular structures.

Among biomolecules, the polyunsaturated fatty acids in membrane phospholipids and the cholesterol in membranes are highly susceptible to free radical reactions for three reasons:

1. Polyunsaturated fatty acids have an inherent normal structure of unconjugated double bonds that create alpha methylenic carbons between the carbons with the double bonds; the hydrogen atoms on such methylenic carbons are allylic and readily enter into free radical reactions; cholesterol is readily attacked for similar reasons (see Figures 1, 2 and 3).
2. Molecular oxygen is approximately 700% more soluble within lipids than within water (Lawerence, Loomis, Tobias & Turpin, 1946); membrane lipid molecules create an appropriate hydrophobic milieu that fosters enhanced O_2 solubility. This is like bringing "the fox into the chicken coop."
3. Molecular oxygen has outer orbitals that have unpaired electrons, thereby conferring upon oxygen certain properties of free radicals such as magnetic susceptibility and the ability to initiate free radical chain reactions among susceptible biomolecules that are not protected by sufficient antioxidants (Demopoulos, Flamm, Seligman, & Pietronigro, 1982). Molecular oxygen, when liquified, will accumulate between the pole pieces of a sufficiently chilled (to maintain O_2 as a liquid) electromagnet in much the same way as iron fillings will (Masterton & Slowinski, 1977). This magnetic susceptibility has helped to demonstrate the free radical nature of moleculer O_2 and has likewise fostered the development of molecular orbital theory (see Figure 4).

Because of the physical properties of cell membranes and molecular oxygen, the membranes are often the site of many free radical reactions, both physiologic and pathologic. Among the physiologic and pathologic free radical reactions are the synthesis of prostaglandins (PGs) and other free radical oxygenated products of arachidonic acid[1], a highly polyunsaturated fatty acid that has four

---

[1]Footnote: Oxy-arachidonic acid products include the PGs, hydroxyeicosatetraenoic acids (HETEs), the hydroperoxyeicosatetraenoic acids (HPETEs) and the leucotrienes (Samuelsson & Paoletti, 1982).

I. Initiation and formation of metastable intermediary products

$$X\cdot \quad + \quad -CH_2-CH=CH-CH_2-CH=CH-CH_2- \tag{1}$$

$$\downarrow -H$$

alkyl radical
$$XH \quad + \quad -CH_2-CH=CH-CH-CH=CH-CH_2- \tag{2a}$$

alkyl radical, isomer   alkyl radical, isomer
$$-CH_2-CH=CH-CH=CH-CH-CH_2- \quad \text{and} \quad -CH_2-CH-CH=CH-CH=CH-CH_2- \tag{2b}$$

$$\downarrow +O_2 \qquad\qquad\qquad\qquad \downarrow +O_2$$

$$-CH_2-CH=CH-CH=CH-CH-CH_2- \quad \text{and} \quad -CH_2-CH-CH=CH-CH=CH-CH_2- \tag{3}$$
$$\underset{+RH}{\overset{|}{O-O\cdot}} \qquad\qquad\qquad \underset{}{\overset{|}{O-O\cdot}} \ +RH$$

$$R\cdot \ + \ -CH_2-CH=CH-CH=CH-CH-CH_2- \quad \text{and} \quad -CH_2-CH-CH=CH-CH=CH-CH_2- \ + \ R\cdot \tag{4}$$
$$\qquad\qquad\qquad\qquad \overset{|}{O-OH} \qquad\qquad\qquad\qquad\quad \overset{|}{O-OH}$$

Eq. 1. Part of a fatty acid chain with two unsaturated bonds; however, identical reactions occur in fatty acids with one unsaturation and in cholesterol; X is a free radical (a substance with a lone electron) and most often represents molecular O_2 (a diradical) or the hydroxyl radical ($\cdot OH$).

Eq. 2a. A radical center is located on the carbon that is adjacent to carbons with double bonds, and is now referred to as an alkyl radical; the original free radical ($X\cdot$) has abstracted a hydrogen to initiate radical damage to this lipid and is now no longer a radical (XH).

Eq. 2b. Several configurational changes occur almost immediately; there are massive electron shifts which (a) result in the lone electron being shifted to other carbon atoms, (b) cause the double bonds to move closer together and thus form conjugated unsaturations which can be detected spectrophotometrically as an index of early radical damage, (c) cause some of the double bonds to change from the bent (-*cis*) configuration that characterizes normal unsaturated fatty acids to the straight (-*trans*) configuration.

Eq. 3. Oxygen adds by free radical reactions to form peroxy radicals.

Eq. 4. The peroxy radicals have abstracted hydrogen from nearby molecules (other unsaturated lipids, proteins, antioxidants, nucleic acids, represented as RH) and have become metastable lipid hydroperoxides; metastable means that the product is only transiently stable.

II. Catalysis and propagation

$$-CH_2-CH=CH-CH=CH-CH-CH_2- \quad + \quad \text{spontaneously or metal catalyzed} \tag{5}$$
$$\overset{|}{O-OH}$$

alkoxy radical
$$-CH_2-CH=CH-CH=CH-CH-CH_2 \quad + \quad \cdot OH \tag{6}$$
$$\overset{|}{O\cdot}$$
$$\downarrow +RH \qquad\qquad\qquad \downarrow +RH$$

$$-CH_2-CH=CH-CH=CH-CH_2+R\cdot \qquad HOH + R\cdot \tag{7}$$
$$\overset{|}{OH}$$

Eqs. 5 & 6. A hydroperoxide can break up spontaneously to form hydroxyl radicals and oxygen-centered radicals on the lipid which are termed alkoxy radicals; metals produce alkoxy and peroxy radicals with hydroxy or hydrogen ions.

Eq. 7. By abstracting hydrogens from adjacent molecules, RH, the alkoxy and hydroxyl radicals are terminated, but additional radicals form in the molecules that had their hydrogen abstracted ($2R\cdot$).

III. Fragmentation and termination

alkoxy radical
$$-CH_2-CH=CH-CH-CH=CH- \qquad + \quad \cdot OH \tag{8}$$
$$\overset{|}{O\cdot}$$

aldehyde   alkyl radical
$$-CH_2-CH=C-CH \qquad + \quad \cdot CH=CH- \tag{9}$$
$$\overset{\|}{O}$$

$$-CH_2-CH=CH-CH-CH=CH-$$
$$\overset{|}{O-CH=CH-}$$

Eq. 8. An alkoxy radical can be further oxidized and fragmented as a result of continued radical attacks on other carbons that are adjacent to the double bonds and result in the formation of bis-hydroperoxides (i.e., two —OOH groups form on one fatty acid); the fatty acid then fragments to form aldehydes and alkyl radical fragments.

Eq. 9. The alkyl radicals can react with other surrounding radicals, e.g., other alkoxy radicals, and terminate to form an oxygen-linked bridge.

Figure 1. The three phases of free radical chain reactions in polyunsaturated fatty acids

double bonds in the middle of its 20-carbon chain length (Panganamala, 1977). The PGs, HETEs, HPETEs, and leucotrienes are extremely powerful regulatory substances that help control the cardiovascular system tissue blood flow, coagulation mechanisms, diameter of bronchi, cyclic nucleotide (cAMP,

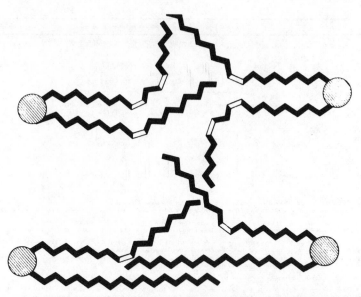

Figure 2. Diagramatic representation of phospholipid molecules arranged as a bilayer, with their lipoidal "tails" extending toward each other. The circles are the hydrophilic, polar head groups of these phospholipids. The midzone of the membrane is lipoidal. The black zig-zag lines are the fatty acids and their unsaturated (double) bonds are in white. They are shown in the cis (123° angle) isomeric form

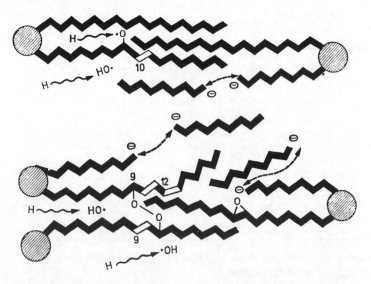

Figure 3. Schematic demonstration of free radical reactions occurring among the polyunsaturated fatty acids in the membrane phospholipids. Basically, the reactions of Figure 1 are represented in this figure. There is a fragmentation, abnormal peroxide bridges, and other abnormal shapes induced in the molecules

Liquid O_2 held between the pole pieces of a super-cold electromagnet; this magnetic susceptibility of oxygen demonstrates the free radical nature of ordinary O_2, which is caused by the molecular orbitals of O_2:[20]

$\sigma 2s$	$\overset{*}{\sigma}2s$	$\pi 2p$	$\pi 2p$	$\sigma 2p$	$\overset{*}{\pi}2p$	$\overset{*}{\pi}2p$
(↑↓)	(↑↓)	(↑↓)	(↑↓)	(↑↓)	(↑)	(↓)

* = anti-bonding orbitals

Figure 4. The free radical-like aspects of molecular oxygen are demonstrated

cGMP) synthesis, and promotion mechanism in carcinogenesis (see Tables 1 and 5 and Figure 5) (Samuelsson, Paoletti, 1982; Murad, Arnold, Mittal, & Braughler, 1979; Vesely, Watson, & Levey, 1979).

Free radical pathologic reactions can have many consequences because of the membrane pathology induced by free radicals. Seven major categories of consequences at a molecular and cellular level lead to most of the pathology.

1. *With loss of membrane barrier functions,* the usual exclusion of Ca^{+2} from cells and the concentrating of K^+ inside cells is disordered; this affects excitable membranes in nerves and muscles. Also, influxes of Ca^{+2} stimulate more free radical reactions by activation of membrane phospholipase A_2 which cleaves arachidonic acid and other polyunsaturates from membrane phospholipids and thereby increases the "fuel supply" of these easily peroxidized molecules (Figure 5) (Samuelsson & Paoletti, 1982; Wieloch & Siesjo, 1982).

2. *Altered fluidity of membranes* may impair transmembrane transport across plasma and organelle membranes, as well as the normal fusions that occur

Table 4. Phospholipid dependent membrane proteins that can be inhibited by lipid peroxidation

Microsomes	Plasma membrane	Mitochondria
Prostaglandin synthetase system	NaK ATPase	Cytochrome oxidase
Hydroxylase system with cytochrome p450	Adenylate cyclase	Succinic dehydrogenase
NADH-cytochrome b5 reductase	Lectin binding glycoproteins and surface glycolipids	Monoamine oxidase
Steroid-glucuronyl transferase	5/-Nucleotidase	NADH cytochrome c/NADH-ubiquinone reductase
	RBC acetyl cholinesterase	Succinate-cytochrome reductase
UDP-glucuronyl transferase		ATP synthetase system
Phosphatidic acid phosphatase		Hexokinase
Phosphoryl choline transferase		Citric acid cycle enzymes
Glucose-t-phosphohydrolase		$NADPH_2^+$: NAD oxidoreductase
		GTP-dependent acyl Co-A synthetase
		Deoxycorticosterone 11-$_\beta$-hydroxylase
		D-$_\beta$-hydroxybutyrate dehydrogenase

Table 5. Summary of free radicals in pathology

- Trauma or ischemia in the brain or spinal cord; due to hemorrhage-induced, iron/copper catalysis of lipid peroxidation in trauma, or CoQ semiquinone/flavin radicals in ischemia, tissue destruction occurs.

  Platelet adherance/aggregation resulting in vasocontriction, micro-occlusions, and the build-up of atherosclerotic plaques is secondary to inhibition of PGI_2 (prostacyclin) synthesis by free radical produced lipid peroxides; PGI_2 maintains the endothelium as a "non-stick" surface and without it, the endothelium becomes as sticky as "flypaper"; platelet adherance/aggregation is constantly fostered by thromboxane A_2, an oxy-arachidonic acid product, and is countered only by PGI_2.

- Cholesterol free radical oxidation products damage the endothelium and are present in low density lipoproteins (LDL).

- Carcinogenesis, in both "initiation" and "promotional" events; metabolic activation of carcinogens proceeds via the endoplasmic reticulum and its hydroxylation mechanisms which can be facilitated by lipid peroxides; free radical intermediates of carcinogenic chemicals may add to critical biomolecules; some cholesterol free radical products are carcinogenic; "promotional" events involving mitosis may involve oxygen free radicals and lipid peroxides which stimulate guanylate cyclase to increase cGMP levels, which in turn activate specific kinases that facilitate rapid cell division.

- High dietary fat levels of cholesterol or polyunsaturates may exhaust endogenous antioxidants and result in the formation of cholesterol oxidation products or oxyarachidonic acid peroxides; some of these are carcinogenic and others will damage endothelium and accelerate atherosclerosis.

- Pathologic cross-linking, especially those induced by aldehydes.

- Loss of immuno-competence is linked to high polunsaturated fatty acid intake, and possibly to the increased oxy-arachidonic acid products that result; lymphocytes have highly unsaturated lipid membranes and are therefore quite senstitive to free radical injury.

- Alcohol (ethanol) produces free radicals during its dehydrogenation to acetaldehyde, and then again if the acetaldehyde is acted on by xanthine oxidase.

- Aldehydes, and in particular acetaldehyde (results from alcohol metabolism and is found in cigarette smoke and in heavily polluted air) combine stochiometrically with cysteine, a key cellular antioxidant, and reduce its levels.

- Alcohols, ketones, and aldehydes will add across double bonds, as in unsaturated fatty acids, by free radical addition mechanisms.

(Cont.)

Table 5 (Cont.)

- Environmental pollutants such as NO_2 are free radicals and will add to lipids in membranes; ozone will cause lipid peroxidation.

- Halogenated hydrocarbons such as carbon tetrachloride, chloroform, and halothane (widely used anesthetic) will form free radicals that will add to lipid biomolecules; ethanol and these substances act synergistically.

- Hyperoxia, as in administering oxygen to premature infants (leads to retrolental fibroplasia, a form of blindness), and to heart attack and stroke victims causes free radical damage; this is particularly severe with high pressure, or hyperbaric oxygen.

- Pharmaceutical agents, including chemotherapeutic drugs (adriamyin, cis-platinum, and bleomycin), produce pathologic free radicals that account, in part, for the absolute limits on the total cumulative dose that can be administered; other drugs with free-radical mediated toxicities include the tranquilizing phenothiazines.

- Infection with acute inflammatory reaction is mediated by the phagocytic oxygen free radicals, and the consequent production of free radical lipid/protein products that act as chemotactic agents.

- Fibrotic responses to inert inhaled particles such as asbestos, silica, and cotton dust follow the phagocytic free radical reactions that are incited by such substances.

- Ultra-violet irradiation initiates lipid free radical peroxidation, and also produces free radicals within thymidine resides in DNA.
  Ionizing radiations (x-rays, cosmic rays, and others) break bonds and produce ions as well as free radicals; the reactivity of free radicals and their chain reactions among membranes and DNA are the principal damaging mechanisms; a small amount of O_2 greatly enhances radiation injury, while the absence of O_2 protects.

- Hydroperoxyeicosatetraenoic acids (HPETEs) and hydroxyeicosatetraenoic acids (HETEs) are produced by free radical lipid peroxidation of arachidonic acid; these may cause vasospasm, and one group of derivatives, the leucotrienes, may cause bronchospasm, as in asthma.

(primary lysosomes with phagosomes, endoplasmic reticulum vesicles, or secretory vacuoles with plasma membrane) (Demopoulos et al., 1983).

3. *Inactivation of phospholipid dependent membrane enzymes and membrane receptors* (see Table 4) especially of central regulatory enzymes, results in their function being greatly disturbed by membrane pathology induced by free radicals; a number of receptor sites also depend on the integrity of the phospholipids and will show altered binding (Demopoulos, Flamm, Pietronigro, & Seligman, 1980).

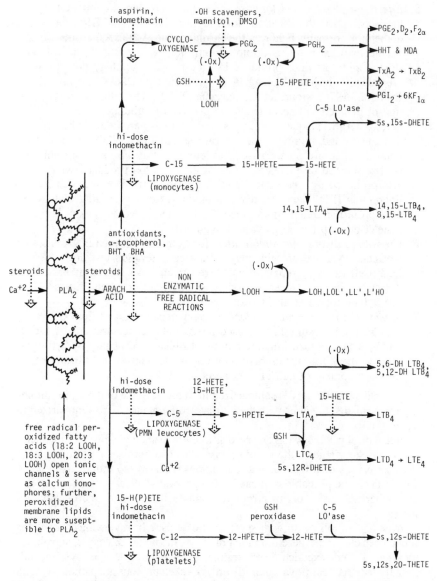

Figure 5. Arachidonate metabolism in free radical damaged CNS tissue, caused by the initial trauma or ischemia, and propagated by the influx of adhering platelets, and leucocytes

4. *Alteration of the nuclear membranes,* with spread of free radical damage from membrane lipids to the closely associated DNA occurs with membrane pathology which may also alter the nuclear pores that are the principal avenues of nuclear-cytoplasmic exchanges (Pietronigro, Seligman, Jones, & Demopoulos, 1976; Pietronigro, Jones, Kalty, & Demopoulos, 1978).

5. *Effects on blood vessel linings,* since lipid peroxides inhibit PGI₂ synthesis, which is the "Teflon" of endothelial surfaces. PGI₂ from endothelium normally balances the thromboxane A₂ (TxA₂) from platelets so that platelets do not clump, adhere, and "gum up" blood flow. Lipid peroxides produced by free radical pathology unfortunately are selective in just blocking PGI₂ synthesis (Moncada, Gryglewski, & Brunting, 1976; Moncada & Amezcua, 1979). The adherence/aggregation of platelets is one of the basic process of building up atherosclerotic plaques and is fostered by lipid peroxides. When platelets adhere and aggregate they release serotonin and thromboxane A₂, both of which are potent vasoconstrictors; occlusion due to thrombosis is also initiated by platelets. Cholesterol oxidation products, which are also produced by free radical pathology, are carried by low density lipoprotein (LDL) and are toxic to blood vessels by causing craters to develop in the endothelium; such defects then serve as a focus for platelet buildup (see Figures 6 through 10).

6. *Cross-links among macromolecules,* for example, between DNA bases or between DNA and protein, may have a configuration that does not lend itself to ready repair by DNA repair enzymes, and thus basic defects leading to cancer and other genetic injuries result (Ames, 1983; Pietronigro et al., 1978).

7. *Stimulation of guanylate cyclase* by oxygen radicals and lipid peroxides generally results in increased intracellular concentrations of cyclic GMP, which in turn initiates rapid cell division, probably by activating specific kinases; this may be a major mechanism in "promoting" the development of cancer (Murad et al., 1979).

Free radical pathology is summarized in Table 5. Some of the major initiating mechanisms, together with the ultimate consequences, are summarized in Table 6.

Free radical pathology has emerged as a central pathologic mechanism, analogous to Pasteur's germ theory of disease. Just as microbes were found to be the root causes of infectious and contagious diseases, so too are pathologic free radicals the probable root cause of degenerative diseases (cancer, occlusive atherosclerosis, organ atrophy, immune losses, and neurobehavioral losses).

What has all this to do with sports and exercise? In reviewing these fields it becomes clear that there is an area of sports medicine and exercise pathology which includes sudden death, trauma in the central nervous system, pulmonary edema, cardiovascular disorders, skeletal muscle pathology, and immunoincompetence that may be facilitated by free radical pathologic mechanisms.

Sources of Pathologic Free Radicals in Sports and Exercise

Trauma

Trauma to the central nervous system (CNS) is the most serious nonfatal consequence of sports or exercise and is commonly seen in young athletes as a

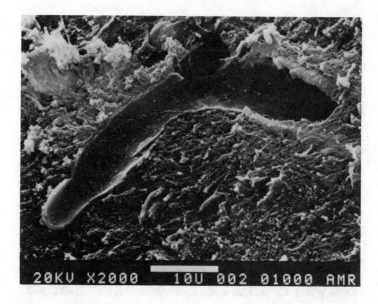

Figure 6. Scanning electron micrograph of a brain capillary. The magnification bar is 10 microns

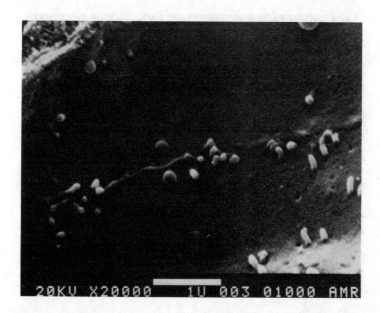

Figure 7. Higher magnification of the endothelial lining surface of the capillary in Figure 6. These are normal villous projections and openings of endothelial pores. The linear junction of two endothelial cells runs across the scanning electron micrograph

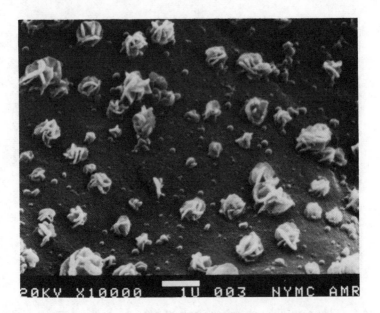

Figure 8. Platelets adhering to a free radical damaged artery in the brain

Figure 9. Higher magnification of the scanning electron micrograph in Figure 8, showing aggregation as well

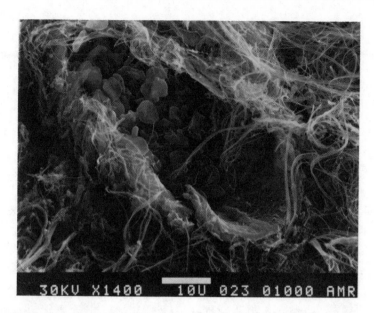

Figure 10. Occlusion of small artery in a free radical damaged spinal cord, composed largely of red blood cells

result of boxing, skiing, bobsledding, football, and similar activities. The long-term sequelae may be permanent paralyses (quadriplegia of all four extremities from cervical spinal injuries, or paraplegia of the lower extremities from thoracic spinal injuries, or various motor/sensory losses from brain trauma). In head injuries the losses may involve not only motor and sensory areas but also the centers for the special senses, communication, social behavior, learning, memory, and thought.

CNS trauma offers several aspects for study in sports medicine and exercise science aside from its serious sequelae. Anatomically there is a discrepancy between the immediate clinical, neurologic losses and the amount of initial tissue damage (Demopoulos, Flamm, Seligman, & Pietronigro, 1982; Demopoulos et al., 1984; Mitamura et al., 1981). Over a period of a few hours, the amount of tissue damage increases progressively as a result of secondary pathologic mechanisms that have been set in motion through the initial trauma. The same type of delay in tissue damage is seen in rhabdomyolysis following extensive muscle use (Hagerman, Hikida, Staron, Sherman, & Costill, 1984). Rarely is the CNS trauma sufficient to actually sever the spinal cord. In most cases the spinal cord is badly bruised but not cut.

Similarly, in head trauma there is an evolution of the anatomic damage, over hours, by secondary pathologic processes (Mitamura et al., 1981). This secondary pathology in CNS trauma adversely affects the microcirculation and is mediated by free radical reactions (Demopoulos, Yoder, Gutman, Seligman, Flamm, & Ransohoff, 1978). Since this secondary microcirculatory pathology evolves over a period of a few hours, there are therapeutic opportunities through the use of massive antioxidants (Demopoulos, Flamm, Seligman, &

Table 6a. Etiology of free radical reactions

Inciting Factors

1. *Oxygen Stresses*
Resulting from approximately 3% of mito-chondiral-consumed O_2 being converted to O_2^-. because only one electron is transferred, aberrantly, from CoQ as a "normal error."

Ground state O_2, analogous to the lethality of O_2 for anaerobic organisms, which are deficient in SOD and catalase.

Increases resulting from exertion, trauma, low blood flow states that allow CoQ autoxidation to accelerate so that O_2^-. production increases, inflammation with cellular exudation involving micro and macrophages that produce O_2^-., H_2O_2 and $^1O_2$ during phagocytosis accompanying allergic reactions or infections.

2. *Antioxidant Deficiencies*
Destruction by tobacco smoke (cigarettes, pipes, cigars, sidestream), alcohol and excessive exertion. Inadequate intake of ascorbic acid, alpha tocopherol, carotenoids, sulfhydryl and phenolic amino acids, botanic catechols, selenium, and zinc.

3. *Chemical Pathology of Diet*
Excess intake of total fats, polyunsaturated fatty acids, and cholesterol. Intake of preformed lipid peroxides from oils extracted from botanic specimens, and from animal fats that are stored as in the "...aging and tenderizing..." of beef and the aging of cheeses.

Deficiency of fibers from botanic specimens that are complex carbohydrates, and which serve to abosrb potentially toxic cholesterol oxidation products and bile salts, thus preventing re-absorption via the entero-hepatic circulation.

Free Radical Pathology
In membrane *lipids*, particularly polyunsaturated fatty acids and cholesterol.

In membrane associated DNA to produce irreparable adducts, and also to dislodge supercoiled DNA from its binding sites on the inside of the inner membrane of the nuclear envelope.

In membrane associated proteins that serve as regulatory enzymes and as receptors for hormones and neurotransmitters, e.g., Na-K ATPase, guanylate cyclase.

Pietronigro, 1982; Mitamura et al., 1981). Provided they are used early enough and in high enough doses these antioxidants may decrease paralyses and neurologic losses following sports injuries.

The exact mechanisms whereby free radical pathology is set in motion by trauma, and how these free radicals progressively disrupt the structure and function of the tissue, provide insights into how free radical pathology under

Table 6b. Pathogenesis

Molecular Pathology

Membrane Instability

Ions may "leak" into or out of special environments.

Water and other small molecules may diffuse more readily.

Connection between cells may "loosen" so that tight junctions of endothelial cells may destabilize, and junctions between glandular cells and organ linings may "leak"

Lipid Oxidation Products

The polunsaturated fatty acid, arachidonic acid, will be oxidized by free radical reactions into lipid peroxides (HPETEs, HETEs and leucotrienes), most of which cause vasoconstriction and poor blood flow.

Arachidonic acid will be oxidized and cyclized to prostaglandins (PGs), but since lipid peroxides can block PGI_2 synthesis, the predominant effect may be the production of PGs that constrict blood vessels and make platelets sticky.

Cholesterol oxidation products, carried in serum low density lipoproteins (LDL), damage the endothelial lining cells of blood vessels and form "craters."

Cholesterol oxidation products may be carcinogenic and can damage DNA.

DNA Damage

Cross links may form between bases.

Cross links may form between DNA and chromatin proteins which may not be reparable and lead to deletions of proteins and regulators.

Adducts between DNA and free radical products, such as aldehydes, may not be reparable and lead to deletions.

Alterations in Protein Structure

Enzymes that are dependent on membrane phospholipids, damaged possibly by free radicals, may be inhibited, such as Na-K ATPase cytochrome oxidase, and RNA polymerase.

Proteins that serve as receptors on the cell surface or in the cytoplasm, for neurotransmitters or for hormones, may be structurally altered and lose their "receptivity."

Pathology in Organ Systems

Cancer

DNA changes result in deletions of proteins and gene regulators, thereby altering structure and expressivity of DNA.

Peroxidized polyunsaturates and cholesterol oxidation products can damage DNA directly, as well as by malonaldehyde fragments, and by hydroxyl radicals and other active radical species that accompany the breakdown of metastable oxidation products.

(Cont.)

Table 6b (Cont.)

Lipid peroxides and O_2^-. stimulate guanylate cyclase so that cGMP levels rise and in turn cause cells to divide rapidly and often; this may be particularly operative during the "promotional" phases of carcinogenesis.

Polyunsaturates and prostaglandins suppress the immune system and allow tumorigenesis.

Alterations in protein receptors allow tumor cells to possibly escape controlling influences of hormones.

Changes in cell surfaces preclude normal "cell to cell" communications that help to maintain order.

Loss of manganese SOD in tumors allows for continued uncontrolled reactions of O_2^-., ← which generates ongoing free radical reactions in tumors, and continues to stimulate guanylate cyclase → cGMP → increase in cell division.

Occlusive Atherosclerosis
Platelets become sticky because production of thromboxane A_2 is accelerated by lipid peroxides; TxA_2 is also a potent vasoconstrictor.

Platelets adhere over lipid deposits in arterial linings because the endothelial lining over a fat deposit cannot make PGI_2, the "Teflon" of blood vessels; macrophages have ingested the fat in the blood vessel linings and in so doing elaborated O_2^-, H_2O_2 and $^1O_2$, all of which can cause lipid peroxidation; lipid peroxides specifically inhibit PGI_2 synthesis.

Platelet build-up initiates the coagulation process and leads to constantly increasing plaque sizes and finally arterial occlusion.

Organ Atrophy
Poor blood flow, caused by atherosclerosis and vasconstriction (both from free radical lipid peroxides), results in atrophic shrinkage of almost all organs during senesence, including the brain (goes from 1.5 kg to 1.0 kg) reproductive organs, heart, lungs, liver, muscle, and skeletal tissues.

Loss of receptor proteins in cells and on surfaces precludes stimulation of cells by normal trophic influences provided by hormones and neurotransmitters.

Immune Losses
Lipid oxidation products are immunosuppresive.

Poor blood flow leads to organ atrophy.

Behavior
Neurologic reflexes and circuits malfunction because of poor blood flow and failure of neurotransmitter secretion and absorption.

Psycho-social possibly due to altered endogenous opiate receptors which are influenced by ascorbic acid and other antioxidants.

circumstances not induced by trauma might adversely affect the structure and function of other tissues. For example, the evolution of rhabdomyolysis in marathon runners also requires hours to develop, through mechanisms that are not understood (Hagerman, et al., 1984). In short, trauma serves as a model for free radical pathology that may be initiated in other ways as in hyperoxia during sports and exercise (Taylor et al., 1983; Jenkins et al., 1984; Burton & Ingold, 1984).

The essential events in CNS trauma as mediated by free radical pathology are summarized in Table 7. Trauma to the CNS causes minute hemorrhages which release iron and copper into the tissues (Demopoulos, Flamm, Seligman, & Pietronigro, 1982). These metals greatly catalyze lipid free radical reactions known as lipid peroxidation. The iron and copper may speed peroxidation by 1,000,000 times (Demopoulos et al., 1983).

The rapid accumulation of lipid peroxides (LOOH) injures cell membranes (Figures 1-3) so that permeability barriers are lost, K^+ leaks out, Ca^{+2} leaks in, membrane enzymes such as Na^+-K^+ ATPase are inactivated (Table 6), and finally the LOOH adversely affects the complex balance among the prostaglandins (PGs), HPETEs, HETEs, and leukotrienes (Figure 5) (Hemler & Lands, 1980; Panganamala, 1977; Wieloch & Siesjo, 1982; Moncada & Amezuca, 1979; Demopoulos, et al., 1978). There is a special importance in the balance between PGI_2, which keeps the endothelium of vessels "nonsticky," and the thromboxane A_2, which makes platelets adhere and aggregate (Moncada et al., 1976; Moncada & Amezuca, 1979). The increased LOOH fosters increased synthesis of thromboxane A_2 and all of the PGs except for PGI_2, which specifically and unfortunately is inhibited by LOOH (Moncada et al., 1976; Moncada & Amezuca, 1979). This imbalance allows for the aggregation and adherence of platelets that are normally kept off the endothelium by PGI_2 (Demopoulos et al., 1978).

As free radical reactions continue, the tissue antioxidants such as ascorbic acid and glutathione (GSH) are consumed (Flamm, Demopoulos, Seligman, Poser, & Ramshoff, 1978; Rehncrona, Folbergrova, Smith, Siesjo, 1980). One of the principal regulators of arachidonate metabolism is 12-HETE. It can react and inhibit the synthesis of the PGs and the leukotrienes. However, GSH is required for 12-HETE synthesis (Chang, Nakao, Orimo, & Murota, 1982) and as GSH levels drop, less 12-HETE is formed (Table 8). As less of this "natural braking system" is produced, there is accelerated production of PGs (except PGI_2) and leukotrienes, driven by the increased LOOH levels and the low 12-HETE concentrations. The platelets make more thromboxane A_2 without a corresponding balanced production of PGI_2, and the net result is platelet aggregation and adherence. The increased adherence of platelets is so marked that it can be detected in the general circulation, as summarized in Table 9 (Hossman, Hossman, & Takagi, 1980; Auer & Ott, 1979).

As a result of increased production of leukotrienes, many white blood cells (WBCs) adhere to the vessels and damage them. Finally, the microcirculation is occluded by platelets and WBCs (see Figures 6 through 10). These are scanning electron micrographs of free radical damaged blood vessels in the CNS. It is these micro-occlusions that lead to the final disruption and death of the neural tissue.

Table 7. Summary of free radical pathology in CNS trauma

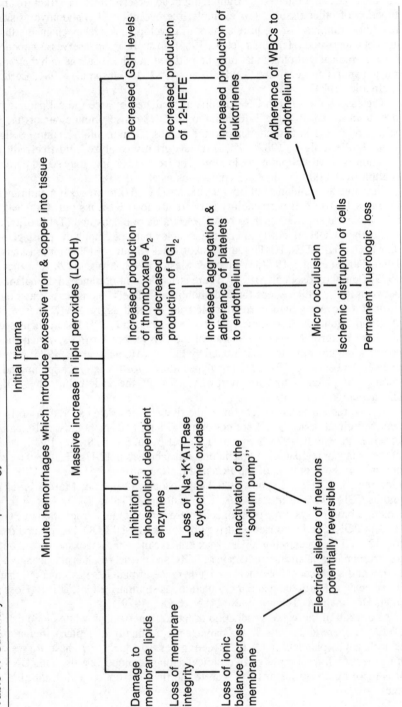

Table 8. Arachidonic acid free radical products (HETEs) from traumatized cat spinal cord

Group		A	AA[a]	B	C	D[b]	DI[a]	E	F	G
0 hrs	Av.	4.4	16.5	26.9	1.5	30.5	2.2	2.2	1.0	0.5
	SEM	4.4	5.1	13.6	1.1	27.5	1.1	0.4	0.3	0.5
3 hrs post injury	Av.	21.7	25.3	196.7	48.4	13.9	34.1	30.8	8.3	14.6
	SEM	8.3	3.3	18.2*	10.1*	6.1	8.1*	10.4	7.0	7.3
5 hrs post injury	Av.	22.2	57.2	298.3	26.7	17.3	59.3	13.0	9.5	12.1
	SEM	4.2*	19.4	81.8*	4.7*	10.8	25.5	8.8	4.9	5.0

[a]Peak A represents arachidonic acid, which is released from membrane phospholipids following the trauma.
[b]Peak D is a major control factor, 12-HETE. It has been definitively characterized by mass spectroscopy. The asterisked (*) values are statistically significantly different from the base line values at 0 hours ($p < .05$).

Table 9. Effects of treatment on platelet adhesiveness, in vitro following spinal cord injury

	Non-operated	Untreated	A & I (L)[a]	A & I (H)[b]	MPSS	Naloxone
% of platelets transmitted[c]	54% n = 4	16.4%[d] n = 6	23.6 n = 5	39.2%[d] n = 4	34.8%[d] n = 6	27.1% n = 6

[a]A & I (L) refers to the lower dose of 1.5 mg/kg/hr aminophylline and 1.5 μg/kg/hr isoproterenol.
[b]A & I (H) is the higer dose of 15 mg A and 15 μg I.
[c]% transmitted are those platelets that did *not* adhere to the glass microbeads filling a 7 cm tygon tube; arterial blood, without anticoagulant of any type, was passed through this disposable apparatus into an EDTA-containing vacutainer; the tygon tubing was then detached and a second sample was drawn into another tube; the platelets were counted directly from platelet rich plasma prepared in the Baker Plateletfuge; the difference in platelet counts between the two tubes, with and without passage through the microbeads, represents the percentage of platelets that were transmitted.
[d]Indicates significance ($p <0.01$) comparing A & I (H) to Untreated SCI, and MPSS to Untread SCI; also comparing Untreated SCI to Non-operated Controls. For details of surgical procedure for spinal cord injury see Demopoulos et al., (1982).

Experimental CNS trauma in cats has been treated acutely with various substances, most of which are of minor benefit. The striking exception is *very* high doses of glucocorticoids, such as methylprednisolone (MP). This substance functions as a potent lipoidal antioxidant when used in extraordinary doses, such as 30 mg/kg, intramuscular or intravenous (Seligman, Mitamura, Shera, & Demopoulos, 1979). This is equal to approximately 2,000 mg in the average human. Considering that 20 mg of MP is a highly effective dose for the general medical use of steroids, a dose of 2,000 mg is extraordinary, especially because somewhat smaller doses such as 1,000 mg (15 mg/kg) do *not* ameliorate CNS trauma. Further, this very high dose of 30 mg/kg must be administered within the first 1-2 hours to prevent permanent paralysis, as summarized in Table 10.

High concentrations of MP were first shown to have an optimum concentration range by Seligman, et al. (1979), in liposomes that were being damaged by free radical reactions. Subsequently, Demopoulos and others employed varying concentrations of MP and clearly demonstrated that 30 mg/kg of MP (a) prevented free radical damage to the traumatized CNS, (b) anatomically preserved the neural tissue, and (c) prevented permanent paralysis in 80% of

Table 10. Functional outcome following very high dose methylprednisolone treatment of feline spinal cord impact

No. cats		Paraplegia	Poor walker	Walker
10	15mg/kg, MPSS, i.v bolus 45 min after impact, plus 15mg/kg, MPSS, i.p. at 5 h, & bid x 7 days, i.p.	2	2	6
10	Saline	9	0	1

See Demopoulos et al., (1982) for details

the cats—in contrast to the permanent paralysis that developed in virtually all of the untreated injured controls.

In humans, CNS trauma has been treated with 15 mg/kg (reaching 1,000 mg in the average person) with little regard for the need to administer the drug within the first 1-2 hours. Most CNS trauma victims actually are not given any drug treatment for 8-24 hours. Consequently, and as expected, the delayed 1,000-mg MP treatment (15 mg/kg) has not been successful because it is too little, too late.

In any plans to use 30 mg/kg (2,000 mg in the average human), the precautions should include (a) using the drug at this dose for only 3-5 days and then cutting down to 15 mg/kg for another 3-5 days; (b) monitoring for bleeding from gastric or duodenal ulcers, and (c) observing for predisposition to infections as a result of steroid suppression of the immune system. Restricting such high doses to 3-5 days may help to decrease the complications.

Physiological Pathways

Table 11 lists the sources of pathologic free radicals arising during sport and extensive exercise. The increased rate of oxygen consumption is a major source because O_2 already is a diradical with unpaired electrons (see Figure 4).

In addition a certain proportion of molecular oxygen is not enzymatically reduced to water by the simultaneous transfer of four electrons via mitochondrial cytochrome oxidase. This proportion may be from 3% to 10%. As the

Table 11. Free radicals generated through sports and exercise

1. Increased intake of oxygen, which is a diradical (see Figure 4).
2. Intermediates from the partial reduction of oxygen (superoxide, $\cdot O_2^-$; hydrogen peroxide, H_2O_2; and hydroxyl radical, $\cdot OH$). Increased O_2 consumption still allows 3-10% of O_2 to form more of these intermediates.
3. Lactic acid production in stressed muscle, or in injured tissue coverts a weakly damaging free radical (superoxide, $\cdot O_2^-$) into a strongly injurious one (hydroxyl, $\cdot OOH$), as a result of the interaction of hydrogen ions (H^+), from lactic acid, and $\cdot O_2^-$. The reaction is:
$$H^+ + \cdot O_2^- \rightarrow \cdot OOH$$
4. Epinephrine and other catecholamines, which are produced in large amounts during sports and exercise, yield oxygen radicals when they are metabolically inactivated.
5. Poor circulation, as a result of trauma or as a result of other free radicals that impair blood flow, will incite further production of free radicals through the action of xanthine oxidase, or through the auto-oxidation of electron transport factors such as coenzyme Q.
6. Injuries and inflammatory reactions. Trauma can lead to the extravasation of blood and the introduction of iron and copper into tissues. These metals catalyze free radical reactions. Inflammation, with its infiltrates of white blood cells and macrophages, produces a spectrum of free radicals.
7. Increased exposure to certain air-borne pollutants, such as No_2 and O_3, which can incite free radical reactions in the lungs. Increases in ventilation/respiration carry more of these polluting free radicals into the respiratory tract.

rate of O_2 utilization increases, the absolute amount of molecular oxygen that is not handled by cytochrome oxidase rises. The noncytochrome oxidase reduction of O_2 always produces a variety of oxygen free radicals ($\cdot O_2^-$ and $\cdot OH$) and sometimes other activated states of oxygen ($^1O_2$) (see Tables 1 and 3).

At rest there are normally sufficient quantities of enzymes in the mitochondria, such as Mn-dependent superoxide dismutase (SOD) and catalase, to quench the oxygen radicals (see Table 2). Nonenzymatic, stochimetric antioxidants that extinguish free radicals on a one-for-one basis also abound within cells and function in concert with the enzymes SOD, catalase, and glutathione peroxidase. If more free radicals are produced as a result of increased oxygen utilization, the quantity of O_2 radicals may exceed the capacity of the available enzymes. This may result in free radical pathology as summarized in Tables 4 and 5.

Jenkins, Friedland, and Howald (1984) have recently reviewed the literature which demonstrates that catalase increases in response to training and repetitive contraction of muscles. The reviews suggested that catalase activity might correlate positively with the performance capacity of the muscle. They went on to study superoxide dismutase (SOD) in humans and rats.

Skeletal muscle tissue was obtained through needle biopsy in 12 healthy male subjects and was studied for SOD and catalase levels. The subjects were divided into a low aerobic capacity group ($\dot{V}O_2$ max below 60 ml/kg/min) and a high aerobic capacity group ($\dot{V}O_2$ max above 60 mg/kg/min). The high aerobic capacity group had significantly higher concentrations of catalase and SOD activities compared to the low aerobic capacity group. In further work, Jenkins showed that training in rats, enough to increase aerobic metabolism, caused a significant rise in catalase and SOD activities.

These authors also suggested that some individual human subjects may not be able to develop protective adaptations against oxidative free radical damage in their muscles. There are of course limits to how much extra SOD and catalase can be synthesized in a cell, and not everyone has the same capacity to promote increased endogenous SOD and catalase levels. The net result of deficient responses in the synthesis of SOD and catalase can be an excess production of $\cdot O_2^-$ beyond the protective levels of endogenous SOD and catalase. This situation then mimics oxygen toxicity which can cause injury to the brain, lungs, and other tissues.

Another source of sports-generated free radicals listed in Table 11 involves the acidic conversion of a weakly toxic radical $\cdot O_2^-$ into a highly toxic free radical, $\cdot OOH$, by the following equation (Singh, 1982)

$$\cdot O_2^- + H^+ \rightarrow \cdot OOH$$

The source of $\cdot O_2^-$ is from increased O_2 consumption and increased production of O_2^- radicals, while the source of hydrogen ions is lactic acid. These two would shift the equilibrium to the right and increase the production of the $\cdot OOH$ radical. At physiologic pH only about 1% of the $\cdot O_2^-$ will be present as $\cdot OOH$. As the pH drops, due to lactic acidosis, the level of $\cdot OOH$ will rise in tissues.

During competition the amount of catecholamines released is increased. The problem arises as these substances undergo metabolic degradation after they have had their desired effect. During enzymatic degradation of the catecholamines, $\cdot O_2^-$ and other oxygen free radicals are produced (Singal et al., 1982). Once again, if there are sufficient levels of SOD, catalase, and other antioxidants, there may be no harm. However, if $\cdot O_2^-$ and other radicals are produced in excess of the protective levels of SOD, catalase, and other antioxidants, then free radical pathology may ensue.

There is clearly a time factor to consider. If the catecholamine production is prolonged as a result of the additive effects of precompetition behavior, plus lengthy and aggressive competition, plus postcompetition emotional states, there may be a deficiency of the stochiometric, nonenzymatic one-on-one antioxidants, even in well trained individuals who have developed very high levels of SOD and catalase in their cardiac and skeletal muscles.

Catecholamines released in severe, emotional, painful stress have been shown to cause free radical lipid peroxidation in cardiac muscle (Meerson, 1980). Chance, Seis, and Boveris (1979) and Pla & Witschi (1976) have shown that lipid peroxidation products adversely affect the semipermeability of the cellular and subcellular membranes. These membrane changes lead to calcium influx into the myocardial cells (Fleckenstein, Janke, Doering, & Leder, 1974) which results in depletion of high-energy phosphates (like ATP) because the calcium activates certain ATPases and adversely affects mitochondrial phospholipase A_2 (PLA_2). This liberates increased amounts of arachidonic acid, which can then cascade into the PG, HETE, HPETE, and leucotriene pathways to disturb the microcirculation of the myocardium.

Vitamin E and zinc, used separately, are capable of scavenging the free radicals produced by catecholamines and to prevent the adverse membrane changes. Using vitamin E and zinc separately, Singal et al. (1982) were able to protect rat myocardial cells against catecholamine-induced mitochondrial swelling, myocardial cell necrosis, leucocyte infiltration, and high energy phosphate depletion. They attributed the protection to the antioxidant properties of their separate pretreatment regimens of vitamin E and zinc (Dhalla, Singal, & Dhillon, 1980).

Sudden, nontraumatic death in athletes and during exercise is often due to cardiac arrhythmias and occasionally to rupture of aneurysms in cerebral vessels. The cardiac arrhythmias may be induced by severe potassium depletion, greater than 70% narrowing of atherosclerotic coronary arteries, or by free radical mediated lipid peroxidative changes. Two of the three major causes of cardiac arrhythmias (K^+ depletion and lipid peroxidation) can be guarded against by providing adequate K^+, sufficient aerobic training to boost endogenous SOD and catalase, and supplementary, safe antioxidants including vitamin E. For the long term, it is also known that dramatic reduction in dietary cholesterol and other fats, and control of hypertension and of diabetes, will largely prevent occlusive atherosclerosis of the coronary arteries.

Another cause of sport/exercise-generated free radicals listed in Table 11 is poor blood flow (ischemia). In model systems of ischemia to the intestine, central nervous system, or heart, free radical pathology has been well demonstrated. The mechanisms include (a) the transformation of an enzyme, xanthine dehydrogenase, into xanthine oxidase, which is capable of generating superoxide radicals ($\cdot O_2^-$) from hypoxanthine and from acetaldehyde (Kellogg & Fridovich, 1975) and (b) the autoxidation of electron transport factors such as coenzyme Q.

During sports and exercise blood flow is preferentially shunted to the skeletal muscles at the expense of the intestinal tract and other organs. The severe gastrointestinal pains, cramps, and other disturbances that sometimes accompany sports and exercise may have a relationship to relative intestinal ischemia and the free radical pathology that this may induce.

"Hitting the wall" in long-distance runs may be indicative of some degree of cerebral ischemia occasioned by short-circuiting blood away from the extensive capillary networks. Other sources of ischemia may occur as a result of the increasing trend for high altitude mountain climbers to avoid using or carrying supplementary oxygen. J.B. West (1984) has recently reviewed human physiology at extreme altitudes on Mount Everest. He has documented significant neurologic changes, both transient and permanent, as a result of the prolonged, severe hypoxia resulting from not using supplementary oxygen.

The next item in Table 11, injuries and inflammatory reactions, has been largely covered in the preceding section on trauma. The last item in Table 11 deals with NO_2 and O_3 (ozone). Goldstein (1979) has shown that these air pollutants induce free radical damage to the lungs; however, protective adaptations are possible. Free radical controlling enzymes increase as a result of exposure to NO_2 and O_3 and serve to protect against pulmonary damage. These are gradual adaptations since these enzymes must be synthesized. In our opinion, this emphasizes the need for careful aerobic training.

Pathology of Endogenous Opioids and Blockage with Antioxidants

The brain and spinal cord produce a variety of opioids that have roles in normal neurophysiology such as helping to suppress sensations of pain. Opioids may also be associated with the positive emotional state termed "the runner's high." In addition, trauma to the CNS may involve excessive opioid release since the opiate antagonist, naloxone, ameliorates some of the damage and the consequent paralysis (Young, Flamm, Demopoulos, Tomasula, & DeCrescito, 1981).

Stress, whether from physical exertion, trauma, or neurobehavioral factors, results in the release of endogenous opiates through catecholamines and other stimuli (Willer, Dehen, & Cambier, 1981). For example, impact injuries to the spinal cord cause a massive sympathetic nervous system response which is thought to be followed by opioid release; naloxone treatment therefore ameliorates some of the damage. Physical exertion in animals is also associated with release of endogenous opioids (Shavit, et al., 1984).

These opioids have generally been viewed as having beneficial effects such as suppression of pain and the development of pleasant feelings. However, these substances share some of the same toxicities of the exogenous opioids such as morphine; for example, immunosuppression and neurosuppression.

Perhaps the most serious consequence of the opioids is the immunosuppression. For example, after Joan Benoit won the 1984 Olympic marathon, she succumbed to a prolonged period of infections that reportedly lasted 6 weeks. This is not uncommon in athletes nor in students at highly competitive schools. Students may go through their final exams and then "crash" after the last exam with recurrent infections.

The mechanism of immunosuppression by the opioids involves suppression of the natural killer (NK) lymphocytes (Shavit et al., 1984). These NK cells are a subset of the different types of protective lymphocytes and unfortunately they have opioid receptors (Mathews, Froelich, Sibbitt, & Bankhurst, 1983). No evolutionary or teleological reasons have been proposed for the presence of these opioid receptors on the NK cells, but they clearly are detrimental to individuals under stress from any of the multitudinous stress-inciting factors one encounters. When endogenous or exogenous opioids attach to the NK cells, the result is a significant inhibition of the protective biologic functions of the NK lymphocytes. This may help explain the increased rates of infection, and of cancer, in chronically stressed organisms.

The opioid receptors apparently depend for their configuration in part on sulfhydryl groups (-SH) (Marzullo & Hine, 1980). It is possible through the use of oxidation-reduction factors to alter the configuration of these receptors and thereby influence the binding of the opioids to the receptors. Ascorbic acid, a reducing antioxidant, can quite dramatically block the neurobehavioral effects of intravenous morphine in human subjects (Free & Sanders, 1979). This may be based on the interaction of the -OH groups of ascorbic acid and the -SH or disulfide (-S-S-) groups in the opioid receptors (Cox, Leslie, & Dunlap, 1980). Naloxone may also exert its effects on the sulfur groups in the receptors since it has been shown to be a lipoidal antioxidant. (Koreh, Seligman, Flamm, & Demopoulos, 1981). It has a group that has allylic hydrogen, and it is therefore capable in molecular terms of donating a hydrogen, the main mode of action of many antioxidants.

The opioids are not the only basis for stress-induced suppression of the immune system. Riley (1981) demonstrated that even relatively minor stress in rodents that received carcinogens would result in an increased secretion of corticosteroids, which then caused significant destruction of lymphocytes. This in turn was followed by an increase in the number of tumors that developed in response to the carcinogen. Controls that were not exposed to the stress did not have an elevation of serum corticosteroids, their lymphocytes remained normal, and they developed significantly fewer tumors in response to the same carcinogen.

The stressed athlete or exercising individual therefore has two separate mechanisms for immunosuppression: (a) the endogenous opioids and (b) the corticosteroids which may be endogenous in origin or sometimes exogenous.

Clinical Toxicities of Large Dose Anitoxidants and Other Nutrient Supplements

Today there is an increasing interest in self-help in order to achieve improved health levels. John Naisbitt pointed this out in his best-selling *Megatrends* (1984). He estimates that 100 million Americans carry out some form of exercise, one out of seven jogs on a regular basis, fat consumption has been cut markedly, there are 50% fewer male smokers over 40 years of age, alcohol consumption has seen a shift from distilled liquor to wine, and the number of health food stores has climbed from 1,200 in 1968 to 9,500 in 1982, with sales up to $2 billion in 1981.

There have been no medical studies on the potential toxicities or adverse drug interactions of regimens that include a wide spectrum of high doses of micronutrient supplements. Many potential toxicities were considered with ascorbic acid (vitamin C). It was thought that ascorbic acid might cause renal stones or frank acidosis, or predispose the high-dosing individuals to scurvy if they stoped taking it. Alpha tocopherol (vitamin E) was linked to the toxicities of the other fat soluble vitamins and it was also thought capable of causing hypertension in high doses.

This study investigated the possible toxicities of high doses of the several categories of micronutrient supplements when they are taken together, as well as with prescription drugs and nonprescription drugs.

Characterization of the Group

Table 12 lists the identification number, age, height, weight, and habits of the human subjects studied. Most of this group has been under study for 5 years (#31-70) and the remainder (#71-81) for 4 years. All took a variety of micronutrients in large doses, of their own accord. The purpose of this study was to determine what toxicities might be apparent.

Most of the subjects did not have serious medical problems and could be classified as essentially normal, but a few had symptoms of coronary atherosclerosis and other disorders. The patients with medical disorders provided a valuable group to test for drug interactions.

The social characteristics of the group were as follows: middle to upper income; most were college graduates and some were science graduate students, medical students, and university science faculty; occupations included business executives, physicians, research scientists, and leaders in the performing arts. Low-income groups and blue collar workers were not represented.

Micronutrient Consumption, Pharmaceuticals, and Diet

The list of substances used by this group is given in Table 13 and includes not only the micronutrients but also over-the-counter (OTC) preparations and prescription drugs. There were no predominant dietary patterns; most consumed a balanced diet while small numbers consumed up to 60% of their calories from fat and a few as low as 10% of their calories from fat.

This data and the dietary information was secured by medical questionnaires. Medical records and laboratory test results were obtained from the individuals' personal physicians. The range of doses of the listed substances usually consumed was itemized from the questionnaires and the medical records. The range of micronutrient doses was *generally* 500%-10,000% greater than the level of these micronutrients usually found in a balanced American diet. In general, OTC and prescription drugs were not used in larger-than-recommended doses. A small number of individuals used doses of some micronutrients as high as 20,000-40,000% above what is found in balanced diets; for example ascorbic acid has been consumed by a few of these individuals on a daily basis at levels of 10-20 grams orally, with some of it as the calcium salt; alpha-tocopherol has been used by some at levels of 2,000-5,000 I.U. per day.

Presently all the subjects are using relatively pure preparations with no, or minimal amounts of, excipients or oils after early studies revealed a major

Table 12. Human subjects using enhanced levels of micro-nutrients

ID#	Age	Weight	Height	Smoking History	Drinking History
31	39	175	6'4"	yes	non-drinker
32	39	117	5'3"	yes	non-drinker
33	52	153	5'9½"	no	moderate
34	53	160	6'1"	no	moderate
38	66	184	6'1"	yes	non-drinker
39	57	140	5'7¼	yes	non-drinker
41	66	162	5'11'	yes	non-drinker
42	72	156	5'8½"	yes	moderate
44	40	145	5'7"	yes	non-drinker
46	36	153	5'7"	no	non-drinker
48	65	160	5'8"	yes	non-drinker
49	68	115	5'	yes	non-drinker
50	39	215	6'2"	no	non-drinker
51	29	143	5'11"	no	moderate
55	57	150	5'10½	yes	non-drinker
58	39	115	5'7"	no	non-drinker
59	36	175	5'11"	no	non-drinker
61	45	150	5'8"	yes	non-drinker
62	36	195	5'7½"	yes	moderate
64	68	135	5'6½"	yes	non-drinker
66	40	210	5'10"	yes	non-drinker
69	52	200	6'4"	no	non-drinker
70	34	140	5'9"	yes	non-drinker
71	28	156	6'	no	non-drinker
72	49	175	5'8"	no	non-drinker
73	49	135	5'4"	no	non-drinker
74	23	160	5'10"	no	non-drinker
75	28	120	5'5"	no	non-drinker
76	30	120	5'3"	yes	non-drinker
77	38	160	5'10"	no	non-drinker
78	26	125	5'6"	yes	moderate
79	20	140	5'5"	no	non-drinker
80	20	110	5'3"	no	non-drinker
81	38	103	5'4"	no	non-drinker

Average age: 43.44 years
17 out of 34 are smokers
6 out of 34 are moderate drinkers

incidence of varied toxic reactions to micronutrient preparations that contained assorted excipients, binders, fillers, lubricants, oils, and some forms of residues from natural sources. Normally the manufacturing excipients and additives do not cause adverse reactions if only one or two tablets are taken. However, when multiples are taken to achieve a much higher dose, the excipients and additives mount and constitute a significant intake. The ascorbic acid is generally taken as encapsulated crystals together with most of the B-complex vitamins, and the alpha-tocopherol, especially at the very large doses, as the nonencapsulated, pure liquid acetate (DL-alpha tocopheryl acetate); the syn-

Table 13. Medications, drugs and vitamins consumed by human subjects

Alfalfa
Alpha Tocopherol (Vit. E)
Ascorbic Acid (Vit. C)
Ascorbyl Palmitate
Aspirin

Benactyzine
Benadryl
Beta Carotene
Bioflavonoids
Biotin
Birth Control Pills
Bromcryptine
Bromelains
Butylated Hydroxytolune (BHT)

Caffeine
Calamus (Herb)
Calcium
Cannabis
Choline Chloride
Chromium
Copper Sulfate
Cyanocobalamine (Vit. B12)

Deaner
Diapid
Diazepam
Digel
Digoxin
Dihydrocholecalciferol (Vit. D)
Dilaurly Thiodiproprionate
DL Phenylalanine
DMSO
DNA

Ethyl Alcohol
Fluoride (Mouth wash)
Folic Acid

GABA
Garlic
Hashish
Heparin
Hesperidin
Hydergine
Inositol
Iodine Compounds
Iron

L-Arginine
L-Cysteine
L-Lysine
L-DOPA
Lecithin
Lithium
LSD

Magnesium Compounds
Manganese Compounds
Multivitamins

Niacin
Niacinamide

PABA
Pantothenic Acid
Parsley
Pectin
Phenylethylamine
Phosphorus
Potassium Chloride
Potassium Gluconate
Propanolol
Psilocybin
Pyridoxine (Vit. B6)

Retinol
RNA
Rutin

Selenium
Sodium Bicarbonate

Testosterone
Theobromine
Thiamine
Thiodipropionic Acid
Thyroid Extract
Tryptophan

Vasopressin
Vegatamin

Zinc
Zyloprim

thesized form (DL-) was found to be especially palatable since it was odorless, tasteless, and virtually colorless—in contrast to the somewhat malodorous, nonpalatable, pale green natural form (D) that was as pure as economically attainable.

Specific Studies, Analyses, and Test Results

Table 14 lists the studies and analytical procedures carried out on the group. Approximately 25% of subjects were further studied with CAT scans, EEGs, psychometrics, computerized neurometrics, reflex times, stress tests, and respiratory functions. Subjects studied with these tests were those who generally took the highest doses of micronutrients for the longest time periods.

Table 15 summarizes the toxicity results. The majority of individuals who consumed large quantities of micronutrients that are commonly available with excipients, binders, fillers, lubricants, oils, and some form of residues from natural sources eventually reacted adversely to these materials.Most of these subjects were forced to discontinue use of these types of micronutrients and switched to relatively pure preparations in order to take large doses. When the micronutrients were supplied at the same and higher doses but in these relatively pure forms, the several adverse reactions disappeared (gastrointestinal aches, nausea, rhinitis, significant malaise, presistent diarrhea, prolonged headaches, and skin rashes). This group of reactions was attributed to the excipients and other additives because (a) substitution with relatively pure forms did not provoke the reactions; and (b) the reactions to the excipients and other additives occurred shortly after ingestion of preparations containing these substances and were not specific to the micronutrient.

Table 14. Studies on human subjects for toxicities and interactions of micronutrients/drugs

Medical	Laboratory Tests
Complete History	*Hematology:* MCV, MCHC, MCH
Physical Examination	Hgb, Hct, WBC, Differential,
Neurologist's Examination	Platelet count, Platelet
Gynecologist's Examination	adhesiveness with glass
	microbeads, PT, PTT
Special analyses	Serum chemistry: Glucose,
EEG	Cholesterol, Triglycerides,
Computerized Neurometrics	Uric Acid, BUN, Creatinine,
CAT Scan	SGPT, LDH, Alkaline phosphatase,
Phychometrics	total protein, A/G,
Reflex times	Bilirubin, Ca^{+2}, PO_4, Na_4, Na^{+} K^{+},
Respiratory functions	Cl^{-}, CO_2, T_3, T_4, HDL, and
Cardiovascular stress	LDL
tests	

Urinanalysis: Complete including sediment microscopy

*Performed on approximately 25% of the subjects.

Table 15. Toxicities resulting from high dose micronutrient preparations

Preparations with Additives Oils, and Natural Bases[a]	Preparations Without Additives, Oils, or Natural Bases[b]
• Severe epigastric and generalized abdominal pains[c] • Nausea[c] • Recurrent diarrhea[c] • Persistent headaches[c] • Severe malaise[c] • Rhinitis, serous[c] • All of the above were progressive[c]	• Restrosterinal pain secondary to swallowing large capsules, or loose powders of acidic vitamins without fludis, indicative of esophageal irritation[d] • Transient loosening of stools when abruptly starting on high doses of ascorbic adic; stops after 4-6 days of continued use • Niacin "flushes" when large doses, approximately 50 mg or more, were taken on an "empty stomach"[d]

[a]The additives are listed in Table 16; the oils included soybean, wheat germ and other similar oils; the natural bases included materials such as kelp and alfalfa.
[b]Pure, high quality micro nutrients were used, with *nothing* else added.
[c]These symptoms became progressively more severe with repeated use.
[d]The proper use of these pure preparations, to be taken with some type of fluid, after a meal, entirely eliminated retrosternal, esophageal irritation and niacin "flushes." The loosening of the stools, when abruptly initiating high dose ascorbic acid use, is self-limiting even with continued use.

The adverse reactions to the excipients and additives do not occur when only one or two tablets or capsules are taken. These reactions took place only after multiples of such supplements were taken in an attempt to reach high doses of the specific micronutrients.

The exact additive(s) responsible for the adverse, toxic reactions could not be identified from the present studies. In reviewing the types of materials employed, the spectrum is large and varies among different manufacturers. Table 16 is a partial listing of additives, obtained from the 16th Edition of Remington's Pharmaceutical Sciences, (Mack Publ. Co., Easton, PA, 1980, pp. 1553-1584). In addition, some manufacturers will add kelp, alfalfa, and other organic materials of unknown composition to provide a "natural base."

Aside from the apparent reactions to the excipients and additives, no substantive adverse reactions could be attributed to the pure forms of the micronutrients except for the following: (a) Retrosternal discomfort in approximately 10% of the group when acidic forms of micro-nutrients were consumed *without* some type of fluid; esophageal irritation has been reported with ascorbic acid and generally occurred when large capsules were swallowed *without* fluid. Advice to take the materials with some water obviated this type of reaction even in one individual with a hiatus hernia; attempting to swallow large quantities of ascorbic powder with little or no fluid intake also produced this symptom. (b)Niacin *flushes* when quantities of 40-50 mg of niacin were consumed on an empty stomach; these flushes consisted of reddening of the face and arms and lasted for 5-15 minutes; the flushing was irregular and did not occur consistently at such doses, even on an empty stomach; flushes could be prevented by just taking the supplement after a meal or snack. (c) Transient

Table 16. Additives for tablets, capsules and pills*

Diluents	Binders
for preparations with small quanitites of active material, e.g. 500 micrograms of vitamin B-12:	Starch, including corn starch
	Sugars
	Acacia gum
Dicalcium phosphate	Sodium alginate gum
Calcium sulfate	Irish moss extract gum
Lactose	Panwan gum
Kaolin	Ghatti gum
Mannitol	Mucilage of siapol husks
Sodium chloride	Carboxymethylcellulose
Dry starch	Methylcellulose
Powdered sugar	Polyvinyl pyrrolidone
Calcium carbonate	Veegum
Magnesium carbonate	Larch arbogalactan
Lubricants	Binders may comprise 10-20% of the formulation by weight
to improve the rate flow of the powders in the machines:	*Disintegrators*
	Sodium lauryl sulfate
Talc	Corn starch
Magnesium stearate	Potato starch
Calcium stearate	Veegum HV
Stearic acid	Methylcellulose
Hydrogenated vegetable oils	Carboxymethylcellulose
Lubricants may comprise 1-5% of the formulation weight	Agar
	Bentonite
	Cellulose
	Natural Sponge
	Cation-exchange resins
	Alginic acid
	Guar gum
	Citrus pulp

*From the 16th Edition of *Remington's Pharmaceutical Sciences* (Mack Publishing Co., Easton, PA 1980, pp. 1553-1584).
Coloring agents and flavoring agents have not been included.

loosening of the stools when large doses (5-6 grams/day) of ascorbic acid were started suddenly; this generally stopped after 4-6 days of continued use.

These minor reactions were entirely eliminated in the group by advising that some water be taken with the acidic substance, that niacin doses should be kept to 25-30 mg or less each time it was taken, and that the supplements be consumed after meals.

In evaluating the medical records and the data from the questionnaires, there was no evidence of interference with the enhanced use of micronutrients listed in Table 13. In the course of the study, no subjects who were taking para amino benzoic acid were give prescriptions for sulfa drugs, and there were no Parkinsonian patients; pyridoxine interferes with the L-DOPA used in treating Parkinsonism.

Hypothetical concerns that large doses of pure vitamin C might cause urinary oxalate stones or serious acidity in the blood or urine were unfounded, and discontinuance of high doses of vitamin C did not appear to lead to scurvy. There was no instance of blood pressure rising in any of these subjects, nor of any distinctive bleeding tendencies, despite the consistent use of high doses of pure vitamin E. Previous concerns voiced by others in regard to vitamin E may have been associated with the so-called natural source vitamin E which is significantly contaminated with peroxidized lipids. To date most of the subjects have maintained their high intakes of antioxidants, vitamins, and calcium using the basic regimen as outlined in Table 17. The total daily doses that have been regularly consumed by 20 subjects without toxicities for 5 years are listed in Table 18.

Other subjects in the original study group have not been consistent in their intakes over the past 5 years and have either gone significantly above or below these ranges in an irregular manner.

Table 17. Micronutrient Supplements

1. Capsules, free of all excipients and additives containing, per capsule:

Ascorbic acid	800 mg	(1,300% of RDA)
Calcium pantothenate	120 mg	(1,200% of RDA)
Pyridoxine/vitmin B-6	40 mg	(2,000% of RDA)
Thiamine HCL/vitamin B-1	40 mg	(100% of RDA)
Niacin/vitamin B-3	20 mg	(100% of RDA)
Riboflavin/vitamin B-2	4 mg	(235% of RDA)
Cyanocobalamin/vitamin B-12	200 mcg	(3,333% of RDA)

   One to two capsules are taken after each meal, with fluids, and one to two between lunch and dinner total 4-8/day.

2. Pure liquid DL-alpha tocopherol acetate/vitamin E. This is a viscid, clear, odorless, tasteless, pale yellow liquid at normal room temperatures. This is the pure synthetic form, which is more pure than generally available vitamin E from so-called "natural sources." 600-2,400 I.U are taken at bedtime.

3. Pure beta carotene, free of BHT, BHA, ascorbyl palmitate and other substances, is taken at doses of 15-60 mg/day, at bedtime. When suspended in liquid alpha tocopherol acetate and encapsulated in a soft gel, the beta carotene will not oxidize since hydrophobic suspending mediums seem to protect the carotene against air oxidation. This is a desirable source for any vitamin A that may be required since the production of vitamin A from beta carotene stores is strictly regulated and can *not* be produced in excess. 15 mg carotene could produce up to 25,000 I.U. of vitamin A, if needed.

4. Capsules, free of all excipients and additives, containing per capsule:

reduced glutathione	50 mg
ascorbic acid	200 mg (300% of RDA)

   One to two capsules are taken after each meal, with fluids, and one to two between lunch and dinner; total 4-8/day.

5. Capsules of calcium carbonate, containing 250 mg of calcium (25% of RDA), together with 125 I.U. of vitamin D (30% of RDA). Two to four such capsules, per day, are taken to provide 50-100% of the calcium RDA. The proportions of vitamin D have been found to ensure the absorption of the calcium.

Table 18. Micronutrient Consumption

Micronutrient	Daily dose		
Ascorbic acid	4000	—	8000 mg
Calcium pantothenate	480	—	960 mg
Pyridoxine	160	—	320 mg
Thiamine	160	—	320 mg
Niacin	80	—	160 mg
Riboflavin	16	—	32 mg
Vitamin B-12	800	—	1600 mcg
Alpha tocopherol	600	—	2400 I.U.
Beta carotene	15	—	60 mg
Glutathione	200	—	400 mg
Calcium	500	—	1000 mg
Vitamin D	250	—	500 I.U.

An additional group of 15 consistent subjects has been added during the past 2 to 4 years, and toxicities have not been detected in their regular daily consumption of the listed ranges, employing the battery of analytic tests in Table 14.

Among the consistent users, now totaling 35 subjects ranging from 2 to 5 years of micronutrient use, a number of them exercise vigorously. Two have been long-distance runners for more than a decade, two are intermediate runners, and four engage in moderate to extensive weight training. There have been no adverse effects on their physical activities.

Toxicities of Micronutrients

Some general principles of toxicology may help to explain why the micronutrients in Table 17 are not toxic, and why the following substances in this section are or can be toxic. The major principle is whether the substance is stored and thereby capable of gradually building up to toxic levels. In general, the nontoxic materials taken in high doses listed in Table 17 are rapidly excreted in the urine, except for vitamin E and beta carotene. Vitamin E, although lipid soluble, is excreted within 24 hours and does not accumulate. Beta carotene will accumulate with time and is the only high dose substance listed in Table 17 that does so. Fortunately, the long-term safety of this material has been demonstrated through its use for many years in the treatment of a photosensitizing congenital porphyria disorder (Mathews-Roth & Kass, 1970). It has been administered to these patients in doses of several hundred milligrams per day, to the point of turning their skin yellow-orange, with no significant persistent toxicity. Therefore, despite its storage capability, beta carotene is not toxic. This is not surprising; many life forms use beta carotene and its analogues as a natural, endogenous body colorant.

Vitamins
Certain vitamins are toxic. The fat soluble ones such as A,D, and K are toxic when the recommended daily allowances (RDA) are exceeded several fold on a long-term basis. These vitamins are stored and high tissue concentrations

build up when the RDA is exceeded. In Table 17, the vitamin D consumed by the study subjects is approximately at the RDA.

Among the water-soluble vitamins, there are reports of the toxicities of folic acid when there is just a minor excess beyond the RDA of 400 micrograms. In pregnant or lactating women the RDA is 800 mcg. Folic acid in high doses has the capacity to cause lesions in the brain (Schwartz, Whetsell, & Mangano, 1983). It is noteworthy that the self-medicated human subjects studied have generally not remained on any folic acid supplement. They had subjective, poorly defined responses to folic acid that could not be characterized consistently.

Vitamin B-6 (pyridoxine) has been reported to cause toxicities, but only when taken at extraordinary doses beyond 2,000 mg every day for 3 months (Schaumberg et al., 1983). The RDA is 2 mg and these large doses are therefore, 100,000% above the RDA. The reported toxicity above 2,000 mg daily consumption was a consistent neuropathy involving the peripheral nerves. When these doses were discontinued the neurologic disturbances cleared up. None of the present group of human subjects have exceeded 500 mg/day, which is well below the 2,000-mg threshold for toxicity.

Degraded forms of vitamin B-12 may be toxic. Vitamin B-12 becomes a potentially toxic substance when it is chemically reduced or acted upon by vitamin C and/or iron (Herbert, 1981). Therefore, mixtures containing vitamin C and vitamin B-12 must be specially formulated to prevent significant chemical interactions in the capsule. Once ingested, there is no interaction in the stomach because of the low pH and the binding of the B-12 to absorption factors.

Antioxidants

The antioxidants listed in Table 17 are safe and include vitamins C and E, beta carotene, glutathione, and some of the B-complex vitamins. Butylated hydroxy toluene (BHT) is an antioxidant that is useful in small quantities, in prepared foods and in packaging, to retard lipid peroxidation (rancidity). When consumed directly at doses of 500-750 mg per day for several months, there is some suggestion from the data of the present study that damage to the liver occurs. Enzymes that leak out of damaged liver cells enter the circulation and can be detected. These include elevations in LDH, SGOT, and SGPT. Discontinuing or decreasing the amount of BHT ingested allowed these enzyme elevations to revert back to normal levels.

Coenzyme Q (CoQ) has appeared on the market recently. It is an important factor in energy production when it is located within the inner membrane of mitochondria. However, when given as a supplement it enters many cell membranes where it can autoxidize and produce superoxide radical ($\cdot O_2^-$) (Demopoulos & Flamm, 1981). No reasonable toxicity studies have been performed despite the fact that laboratory animals receiving high doses develop toxicities. CoQ has been used extensively in Japan, but no one has followed up or inquired as to adverse reactions. It can generate considerable free radical pathology in vivo and may do so following supplementation. The particular risk with this material in the sport and exercise sciences is that it may be mistaken as an ergogenic aid in view of its role within mitochondria. However, there is no indication that supplemental CoQ can enter the inner mitochondrial membranes, nor whether a disproportionate, unbalanced increase in this location would be safe. The electron transport factors are held to strict proportions and this is an essential feature of energy production. The introduction of an excess of an active quinoid compound such as CoQ into electron transport is known to be capable of damaging mitochondria and thus could be the opposite of an ergogenic aid.

Another antioxidant, the amino acid cysteine, makes use of its thiol group (-SH) to quench free radicals. In so doing, however, it may form the disulfide (-S-S-) cystine. Cystine is not very soluble and may precipitate in the kidneys if there is poor hydration. Cysteine would not be a suitable antioxidant in sports and exercise, due to frequent dehydration. A better source of the thiol group is glutathione. This is a tripeptide and the middle amino acid is cysteine. Glutathione is absorbed as the tripeptide from the G-I tract because none of the digestive enzymes attack the two specific aminopeptide bonds, and the pH of the stomach is not low enough after a meal to hydrolyze the bonds. Glutathione will not precipitate in the kidneys and it is recycled enzymatically. This latter aspect modifies the view of the stochiometric, one-on-one antioxidants. Glutathione is stochiometric, but since it can be recycled back to its antioxidant form by enzymes it can be used repeatedly as long as there are hydrogen donors around such as NADH and ascorbic acid.

Aside from its being a recyclable antioxidant, glutathione is used extensively to aid in the detoxicifiction and urinary excretion of many substances, including pollutants and metabolites of pharmaceuticals.

Minerals

These substances have also burst upon the commercial market with various implied claims. The only mineral that absolutely needs to be supplemented is calcium because the average American is deficient in it. The calcium requirements have recently been increased to 1,500 mg/day. This amount is found in 1 1/2 quarts of milk or the equivalent in cheeses. Clearly this amount of cholesterol-laden material cannot and in fact is not taken by the average American. While the calcium requirement can be met by 1 1/2 quarts of skim milk, most people are not likely to drink that much skim milk every day.

Calcium supplementation is necessary; without it, serious osteoporosis develops at an accelerated rate. Adding vitamin D in a suitable ratio aids in the absorption of the calcium. A final point is that calcium carbonate is the preferred source over calcium phosphate or other salts. There is no evidence that Americans in reasonably good health have any mineral deficiency other than calcium. Magnesium deficiencies can develop, but this is seen in cancer patients undergoing therapy and in those with other serious disorders. The idea that if calcium is taken there must be matched amounts of magnesium is not based on controlled scientific observations.

Manganese deficiency has not been demonstrated, nor have copper, zinc, or selenium deficiencies been documented in reasonably healthy Americans. A distinction should be made between minerals that are necessary for metabolism and minerals that should be supplemented. The average American does not have mineral deficiencies that would require supplements other than calcium. If a mineral deficiency other than calcium is suspected, a medical examination and laboratory tests are called for. If the tests are postive a doctor's prescription and continuing medical surveillance is required until the deficiency is corrected.

The reason for caution concerning noncalcium minerals is their potential for toxicity. Most of them can accumulate and eventually reach toxic levels, as has already occured with iron. It took 15 to 20 years and developed because American women were convinced they had to replace the small monthly loss that occurred. By now, many women have over-ironized themselves and suffer from a form of diabetes and arthritis. Selenium will cause liver damage when it reaches toxic levels, and zinc can cause atherosclerosis at toxic concentrations. The same is true for copper.

The basic problem in taking noncalcium mineral supplements therefore centers about the potential build-up over the next 15 to 20 years to toxic levels, as has occurred with iron.

Single Amino Acids and Limited Combinations

Amino acids, like tryptophan, can be toxic because metabolites such as serotonin and quinolinic acid may form. Ingested tryptophan can produce serotonin throughout the body and cause substantial changes in the physiology of the intestines, blood vessels, heart, and brain. Quinolinic acid is an excitatory metabolite of tryptophan and causes focal damage to the cerebral cortex. In the initial group of human subjects, one middle-aged female developed repetitive, crippling excitatory behavior in response to using tryptophan. She promptly discontinued this supplement, which she was taking on her own. This adverse reaction occurred within a few hours in response to her starting this amino acid. It occurred on two occasions; there were no other obvious causative factors.

Other amino acids, such as ornithine and arginine, with or without tryptophan, may cause a release of pituitary hormones including growth hormone and prolactin. Both of these pituitary hormones can accelerate the growth of cancers, and prolactin may also lead to breast development in males.

Phenylalanine, tyrosine, and L-DOPA (now available as a nonprescription food supplement from certain bean extracts) as amino acid supplements, may lead to increased and unbalanced production of catecholamines (epinephrine, norepinephrine, and DOPAmine). In our opinion, this may aggravate cardiac arrhythmias and heighten blood pressure.

Neurotransmitter Precursors

These substances are available commercially with implied claims, some suggesting beneficial neurologic changes. These can be particularly misinterpreted by athletes and exercising individuals hoping to avoid neurologic fatigue or to improve coordination and reflex times. There are no controlled scientific studies for such claims.

Choline is taken in the hopes of increasing the acetyl-choline content of the brain, but doses required to do this are upwards of five to six grams daily, and even then it is not certain that neurologic gains are made. Lecithin is also used to enhance acetylcholine levels since lecithin contains choline. However, lecithin also contains polyunsaturated fatty acids which have been found to be peroxidized (rancid) in multiple commercial retail preparations.

The most dangerous precursor studied is dimethyl amino ethanol (DMAE), which becomes choline with the addition of one more methyl group. It is found in certain foods and therefore has been sold as a food supplement. In the experience of the human subjects studied, four found that DMAE produced extreme hostility at low doses (100-200 mg/day) and one young adult had a grand mal seizure after one dose of 100 mg. This individual was thoroughly studied by EEG, CAT scans of the brain, neurologic exams, and blood and urine tests, and followed for 2 years. No other cause for the grand mal seizure was found. He was not put on any anticonvulsant medications but instead was followed very closely on a daily basis for 2 years. There have been no repeat episodes. This is a well documented instance of DMAE-induced convulsion. According to some of the original patent literature of 25 years ago, DMAE caused convulsions in all the rodents studied. Further, an abstract reported that EEG tracings of several humans taking DMAE showed the induction of increased amplitudes of brain waves.

Unsaturated Oils

Polyunsaturated oils such as those found in lecithin, wheat germ oil, soy oil, fish body oils, liver oils, eicosapentaenoic acid (EPA), and blue-green algae all turn rancid very rapidly. Analyses of retail products containing these types of oils revealed significant lipid peroxidation, as summarized in Table 19. These lipid peroxides are rancid and can participate in a variety of free radical reactions since they are absorbed after ingestion and then circulate. It is difficult to prevent the lipid peroxidation of these oils because molecular oxygen dissolves in them very readily, and their molecular structure makes them susceptible to oxidative rancidity.

Steroids from Botanic Sources

Dehydroepiandrosterone (DHEA) can be readily extracted from Mexican yams. These tubers are not edible but have been grown for their high DHEA content. DHEA is somewhat androgenic and various implied claims have been made for it. It is a steroid, and among individuals who have used it consistently there is evidence that it may accelerate growth of the prostate in middle-aged males.

The example of DHEA is applicable to other botanically derived steroids. Just because they are natural doesn't mean they are any less toxic than the anabolic steroids produced by pharmaceutical companies. The final outcome is still the same: immunosuppression, growth of the prostate, osteoporosis, massive imbalances of the entire endocrine system, and atrophy of the adrenals and of the testes.

Discussion

The foregoing data and hypotheses indicate that free radical pathology may be a relevant new area in sports medicine and exercise science, particularly because theoretical methods involving antioxidants and diet may help to control this pathology and help to reduce the extent of some harmful sequelae of sports and exercise.

Trauma to the brain and spinal cord initiate free radical pathology which then amplifies the extent of the injury by causing secondary damage in the microcirculation. As the microcirculation becomes plugged through free rad-

Table 19. Lipid peroxidation products[a] in retail preparations[b] of micronutrient supplements

Type of Product, Generic	nMoles MDA/ml or/gm
D-Alpha Tocopherol Acetate in Soft Gel Capsules with Plant Oil[b]	432-867/ml
Blue-Green Algae[b]	290-292/gm
Lecithin preparations	487-563/ml
Eicosapentanoic Acid from Fish Oil[b]	585-916/ml
Evening Primrose Oil[b]	27-34/ml
Multi-Vitamin Tablets[b]	401-479/gm
Pure DL-Alpha Tocopherol Acetate	0.783/ml (same as blank)

[a]Malondialdehyde, a fragmentation product of extensive lipid peroxidation, was measured by the thiobarbituric acid test.
[b]The retail preparations were obtained from two different stores specializing in vitamins, minerals, amino acids, and other supplements. The stores were at busy locations to ensure short shelf storage. Four brands were used for item 1, two brands for item 2, two brands for item 3, three brands for item 4, two brands for item 5, and two brands for item 6. The utility of some of these substances is not always clear.

ical reactions, larger volumes of tissue become ischemic (Figures 6-10). As a result, larger areas may dysfunction or undergo necrosis.

It is possible to blunt the rapidly expanding free radical chain reactions caused by trauma, but the number of antioxidant molecules required is large since the chain reactions branch. In reliable experimental model systems of CNS trauma, extremely high doses of injected glucocorticoids such as methlyprednisolone can halt most of the anatomic damage and prevent complete paralysis in approximately 80% of the injured animals that have been treated. The doses used (30 mg/kg/day for 3-5 days) were far beyond the usual pharmacologic dose and were actually antioxidant doses that have been previously demonstrated for this particular substance (Seligman et al., 1979).

Serious paralytic and other neurologic losses following trauma may be alleviated in the future with high doses of methylprednisolone if used within the first 1 to 2 hours. Thus far, only doses of 15 mg/kg (about 1 gram) have been used in CNS trauma in humans. This is below the antioxidant dose of 30 mg/kg and is of no benefit in animal models or in patients. Humans would require about two grams a day, intramuscularly or intravenously, to benefit from the antioxidant properties of methylprednisolone. To date, only animal models have been studied with this high dose; no controlled human studies have been reported.

CNS trauma and other instances of free radical pathology, such as use of beta carotene to blunt the radical reactions in patients with a rare porphyria disorder demonstrate the need for high doses. In treating the photosensitive porphyrias the dose of beta carotene is in the range of 300 mg/day and results in an orange-yellow coloration of the skin. The large doses are required because once an antioxidant molecule quenches a free radical, that antioxidant is no longer effective unless it is recycled. Glutathione is an example of an antioxidant that can be recycled by an enzyme (glutathione reductase), while alpha tocopherol (vitamin E) can be recycled from its quinone form (=0) back to its active alcohol form (-OH) by ascorbic acid (vitamin C).

Another lesson from CNS trauma and free radicals is the need to use appropriately soluble antioxidants (Ortega, Demopoulos, & Ransohof, 1972). Free radical reactions occurring within the lipoidal midzone of cell membranes can best be reached by lipoidal antioxidants. Methylprednisolone enters the cell membranes quite rapidly, which is one of the reasons for its high dose efficacy in trauma. In other model systems of brain injury, a water-soluble antioxidant had little value compared to the lipid-soluble antioxidant.

In nontraumatic situations, the high intake and increased utilization of oxygen during athletics and exercise creates free radicals and may induce pathology, especially if there has not been sufficient training to gradually build up the concentration of the free radical scavenging enzymes, superoxide dismutase (SOD) and catalase. There are no shortcuts to training, and aerobic fitness may really translate biochemically into the SOD and catalase content of the heart and other organs (Jenkins et al., 1984).

SOD and catalase are enzymes. Since they are proteins they must be manufactured within the cell. This means that appropriate chemical signals such as increased levels of the respective substrates, the superoxide radical ($\cdot O_2^-$), and hydrogen peroxide (H_2O_2) must trigger the relevant DNA codes to produce more messenger RNA, which then leads to increased production of the specific proteinaceous enzymes. SOD and catalase supplements taken by mouth cannot be helpful because their protein structure is instantly destroyed by the acidity of the stomach and the digestive enzymes in the gastrointestinal tract. As more is learned about SOD and catalase, athletes, coaches, and exercising individuals should be on guard against oral supplements of SOD and catalase. These can be no more effective than insulin taken by mouth. Insulin is a protein, and its efficacy for diabetics is based on sterile injections of pure materials.

Whether the simple, stochiometric types of one-on-one antioxidants may be useful as oral supplements in sports medicine and exercise science is a logical question, but the answer requires controlled scientific studies that have not yet been done. Hypothetically this is a valid concept and stochiometric antioxidant supplements may in fact help SOD and catalase to carry out their protective functions.

The first step in testing such a hypothesis is to have available a nontoxic antioxidant regimen that can be subjected to scientifically controlled studies for efficacy. Of the multitude of antioxidants and metabolic cofactors, several have been tested and a number have been found to be nontoxic in high doses in the present ongoing medical studies which are now past the 5-year mark.

The clinical toxicity study reported in the present work has delineated, as one of its ramifications, what may be a reasonable program to be tested. It includes vitamin C and vitamin E, which are thought to provide a measure of synergism in preventing lipid peroxidation (Leung, Vang, & Mavis, 1981). Interactions between the two have been documented and one way they may function in vivo is for the vitamin C to aid the recycling of vitamin E after it has been oxidized to alpha tocopheryl quinone:

ascorbic —OH   O= alpha   ascorbic =O HO-alpha
               +   →   +
acid —OH   tocopheryl   acid —OH   tocopherol
                      quinone

Ascorbic acid could regenerate two molecules of oxidized vitamin E. The residuum will be oxidized dehydro-ascorbic acid which may be recycled by donations of hydrogen (H) from hydrogen carriers:

dehydroascorbic = O   ascorbic —OH
                      + 2 NADH →   + 2 NADH
acid   = O   acid —OH

A continuing flow of hydrogen from active metabolism (the Krebs cycle, and H transport) assures a steady supply of H to regenerate ascorbic acid which may then regenerate alpha tocopherol. Antioxidant regimens therefore include vitamin C, vitamin E, and beta carotene to scavenge a variety of water-soluble and lipid-soluble free radicals. In addition, cofactors are supplied that may aid in the metabolic flow of hydrogen.

Among the newest antioxidants available is glutathione. This tripeptide is nontoxic and serves as follows:

1. As a direct antioxidant;
2. As a cofactor for glutathione peroxidase which mutes potentially harmful lipid peroxides (LOOH) into the corresponding lipid hydroxides (LOH) (Smith, Tappel, & Chow, 1974);
3. As a detoxifying agent, to conjugate with varied toxic substances to aid in their urinary excretion;
4. Its sulfhydryl (-SH) group may keep the opioid receptors in the reduced state, analogous to the effects of ascorbic acid, and thereby prevent endogenous opioid binding to nerve cells and lymphocytes, thus preventing neurosuppression and immunosuppression.

The present studies suggest that prospective, scientifically controlled studies that would test the hypothesis that antioxidant vitamins help prevent some of the harmful sequelae of sports and exercise should be done with substances that are free of excipients and additives. These latter materials are toxic and debilitating when taken in large doses (Rawlins, 1981; Bachman, 1978). Therefore, perhaps only pure preparations should be used.

Those micronutrient supplements that have demonstrable or potential toxicities such as BHT, Coenzyme Q, tryptophan, phenylalanine, tyrosine, arginine, ornithine, selenium, zinc, eicosapentaenoic acid (EPA), fish body oils, liver oils, lecithin, choline, and dimethyla minoethanol (DMAE) should not be employed in prosepctive studies until specific doses, dosage regimens, and stable, pure forms have been tested and found to be nontoxic for the great majority of the people. We believe that diet may be the most important factor to help control some of the free radical pathologic sequelae of sports and exercise.

Decreasing drastically the intake of all types of fats will accomplish several things:

1. The intake of preformed, already peroxidized lipids will be decreased; many of the fats we eat are not fresh and have been aged for weeks, months, and even years (i.e. meats and cheeses).
2. There will be an abrupt decrease in the number of susceptible fat molecules that can participate in or sustain lipid free radical chain reactions. This includes the polyunsaturated fatty acids as well as cholesterol; the latter is also easily peroxidized and yields free radical products that can injure blood vessels or cause cancer.
3. The availability and concentration of fat-soluble antioxidants will be increased; large depots of fat serve to decrease the availability and concentration of antioxidants by keeping them in body fat.
4. Lipid-soluble antioxidants that might have been present in the organism's original fat source are either taken out or oxidatively destroyed during processing and storage; oxidized antioxidants may be quite toxic, and this occurs because there are no living, metabolic pathways to regenerate the oxidized antioxidants, for example the antioxidants in the fat of hamburger.

In determining what should be eaten, we believe the answer is complex carbohydrates as in grains, plus fresh fruits and vegetables. Legumes are the ideal source of proteins, not milk, cheeses, and meat; calcium and vitamin D requirements are best met through a supplement so that dairy products can be entirely avoided. Fresh fruits and vegetables have abundant antioxidants, separate and aside from vitamin C and beta carotene. They contain phenols and catechols that are excellent antioxidants and which should be considered in planning total antioxidiant consumption in future research.

While the many benefits of sport and exercise have accrued to the participants, so too have the occasional pathologic sequelae including CNS damage, cardiac arrhythmias, susceptibility to infections, muscle damage, and traumatic arthritis. The present studies offer some avenues for further research into alleviating some of these harmful sequelae.

References

American College of Sports Medicine. (1984). *Position stand on the use of anabolic-androgenic steroids in sports.* (pp. 13-18).

Ames, B. (1983). Dietary carcinogens. *Science,* **221**, 1256-1264.

Auer, M.L., & Ott, E. (1979).Disturbances of the coagulatory system in patients with severe cerebral trauma. II. Platelet function. *Acata Neurochirurgica,* **49**, 219-226.

Babior, B.M. (1982). The enzymatic basis for O_2^- production by human neutrophiles. *Canadian Journal of Physiology and Pharmacology,* **60**, 1353-1358.

Bachman, E. (1978). Biochemical effects of gum arabic, gum tragacanth, methylcellulose, and carboxmethylcellulose-Na in rat heart and liver. *Pharmacology,* **17**, 39-49.

Borgeat, P., deLaclos, B.F., Picard, S., Vallerand, P., & Sirois, P. (1982). Double dioxygenation of arachidonic acid in leucocytes by lipoxygenases. In B. Samuelsson & R. Paoletti (Eds.), *Leucotrienes, and other lipoxygenase products* (pp. 45-51). New York: Raven Press.

Boveris, A. (1977). Mitochondrial production of superoxide radical and hydrogen peroxide. In M. Reivich, R. Coburn, S. Lahin, & B. Chance (Eds.), *Tissue hypoxia and ischemia. Advances in experimental medicine and biology* (Vol. 78 pp. 67-82). New York: Plenum.

Boveris, A., Cadenas, E., & Stoppani, A.O.M. (1976). Role of ubiquinone in the mitochondrial generation of hydrogen peroxide. *Biochemistry Journal,* **156**, 435-444.

Bulkley, G.B. (1983). The role of oxygen free radicals in human disease processes. *Surgery,* **94**, 407-411.

Burton, G.W., & Ingold, K.U. (1984). B-carotene: an unusal type of lipid antioxidant, *Science,* **224**, 569-573.

Chance, B., Seis, H., Boveris, A. (1979). Hydroperoxide metabolism in mammalian organs. *Physiology Review,* **59**, 527-605.

Chang, W.C., Nakao, J., Orimo, H., & Murota, S. (1982). Effects of reduced glutathione on the 12-lipoxygenase pathways in rat platelets. *Biochemistry Journal,* **202**, 771-776.

Cox, B.M., Leslie, F.M., & Dunlap, C.E., III. (1980). The use of ascorbate as a probe of opioid receptor structure: evidence for two independent mechanisms of receptor destruction by ascorbate. *Journal of Receptor Research* **1**, 329-354.

Demopoulos, H.B. (1973). Control of free radicals in biologic systems. *Federation Proceedings* (Federation of American Society of Experimental Biology), **32**, 1903-1908.

Demopoulos, H.B., & Flamm, E.S. (1981). Possible pathology induced by CoQ10. In K. Folkers, & Y. Yamamura (Eds.), *Biochemical and clinical aspects of coenzyme Q* (pp. 373-384). New York: Elsevier/North Holland Biochemical Press.

Demopoulos, H.B., Flamm, E.S., Pietronigro, D.D., & Seligman, M.L. (1980). The free radical pathology and the microcirculation in the major central nervous system disorders. *Acata Physiologica Scandinavica* (Suppl. 492). 91-119.

Demopoulos, H.B., Flamm, E.S., Seligman, M.L., & Pietronigro, D.D. (1982). Oxygen free radicals in central nervous system ischemia and trauma. In A.P. Autor (Ed.), *Pathology of oxygen,* (pp. 127-155). New York: Academic Press.

Demopoulos, H.B., Flamm, E.S., Seligman, M.L., Pietronigro, D.D., Tomasula, J., & DeCrescito, V. (1982). Further studies on free radical pathology in the major central nervous system disorders. *Canadian Journal of Physiology & Pharmacology,* **60**, 1415-1424.

Demopoulos, H.B., Pietronigro, D.D., Flamm, E.S., and Seligman, M.L. (1980). The possible role of free radical reactions in carcinogenesis. *Journal of Environmental Pathology and Toxicology,* **3**, 273-303.

Demopoulos, H.B, Pietronigro, D.D., Seligman, M.L. (1983). The development of secondary pathology with free radical reactions as a threshold mechanism. *Journal of the American College of Toxicology,* **2**(3), 173-184.

Demopoulos, H.B., Seligman, M.L., Schwartz, Tomasula, J., & Flamm, E. (1984). Molecular pathology of regional cerebral ischemia. In A. Bes, P. Braquet, R. Paoletti, & B.K. Siesjo (Eds.), *Cerebral ischemia* (pp. 259-264). Amsterdam: Elsevier.

Demopoulos, H.B, Yoder, M., Gutman, E.G., Seligman, M.L., Flamm, E.S., & Ransohoff, J. (1978). The fine structure of endothelial surfaces in the microcirculation of experimentally injured feline spinal cords. *Scanning Electron Microscopy,* **2**, 677-679.

Dhalla, N.S., Singal, P.K., & Dhillon, K.S. (1980). Mitochondrial functions and drug-induced heart disease. In M.R. Bristow (Ed.), *Drug induced heart disease* (Vol. 5, pp. 39-61). New York: Biomedical Press.

Flamm, E.S., Demopoulos, H.B., Seligman, M.L., Poser, G.R., & Ransohoff, J. (1978). Free radicals in cerebral ischemia. *Stroke,* **9**, 445-447.

Fleckenstein, A., Janke, J., Doering, H.J., & Leder, O. (1974). Myocardial fiber necrosis due to intracellular Ca overload—A new principle in cardiac pathophysiology. *Recent Advances Studying Cardiac Structure and Metabolism,* **4**, 563-580.

Free, V., & Sanders, P. (1979). The use of ascorbic acid and mineral supplements in the detoxification of narcotic addicts. *Journal of Psychedelic Drugs,* **11**, 217-222.

Gardner, T.J., Stewart, J.R., Casale, A.S., Downey, J.M., & Chambers, D.E. (1983). Reduction of myocardial ischemic injury with oxygen-derived free radical scavengers. *Surgery,* **94**, 423-427.

Goldstein, B. (1979). Combined effects of ozone and nitrogen dioxide. *Environmental Health Perspectives,* **30**, 87-89.

Hagerman, F.C., Hikida, R.S., Staron, R.S., Sherman, W.M., & Costill, D.L. (1984). Muscle damage in marathon runners. *The Physican and Sportsmedicine,* **12**, 39-46.

Hemler, M.E., & Lands, W.E.M. (1980). Evidence for a peroxide-initiated free radical mechanism of prostaglandin biosynthesis. *Journal of Biology and Chemistry,* **225**, 6253-6261.

Herbert, V. (1981). Vitamin B-12. *American Journal of Clinical Nutrition,* **3**, 971-972.

Hess, M.L., Manson, N.H., & Okabe, E. (1982). Involvement of free radicals in the pathophysiology of ischemic heat disease. *Canadian Journal of Physiology and Pharmacology,* **60**, 1382-1389.

Hossman, V., Hossman, K.A., & Takagi, S. (1980). Effect of intravascular platelet aggregation in blood recirculation following prolonged ischemia of the cat brain. *Journal of Neurology,* **222**, 159-170.

Imai, H., & Werthessen, N.T. (1980). Angiotoxicity of oxygenated sterols and possible precursors. *Science,* **207**, 651-653.

Jenkins, R.R., Friedland, R., & Howald, H. (1984). The relationship of oxygen uptake to superoxide dismutase and catalase activity in human skeletal muscle. *International Journal of Sports Medicine,***5**, 11-14.

Jokl, E. (1984). Olympic medicine and sports cardiology. *Annals of Sports Medicine,* **1**, 127-169.

Kellogg, E.W., III, & Fridovich, I. (1975). Superoxide hydrogen peroxide and singlet oxygen in lipid peroxidation by xanthine oxidase system. *Journal of Biology and Chemistry,* **250**, 8812-8816.

King, C.G., & Burns, J.J. (Eds.) (1975). Second Conference on Vitamin C. *Annals of the New York Academy of Sciences.*

Koreh, K., Seligman, M.L., Flamm, E.S., & Demopoulos, H.B. (1981). Lipid antioxidant properties of naloxone, in vitro. *Biochemical and Biophysical Research Communications,* **102**, 1317-1322.

Lawrence, J.H., Loomis, W.F., Tobias, C.A., & Turpin, F.H. (1946). Premilinary observations on the narcotic effects of xenon with a review of values for solubilities of gases in water and oils. *Journal of Physiology,* **105**, 197-204.

Leung, H.W., Vang, M.J., & Mavis, R.D. (1981). The cooperative interaction between vitamin E and vitamin C in suppression of peroxidation of membrane lipids. *Biochimica et Biophysica Acta,* **664**, 266-272.

Marzullo, G., & Hine, B. (1980). Opiate receptor function may be modulated through an oxidation-reduction mechanism. *Science,* **208**, 1171-1173.

Masterton, W.L., & Slowinski, E. (1977). *Chemical Principles* (p. 203 and Plate 5) Philadelphia: Saunders.

Mathews, P.J., Froelich, C.J., Sibbitt, W.L. & Bankhurst, A.D., Jr. (1983). Enhancement of natural cytotoxicity by beta-endorphin. *Journal of Immunology,* **130**, 1658-1662.

Mathews-Roth, L.C., & Kass, E.H. (1970). Beta-carotene as a photoprotective agent in erythropoietic protoporphyria. *New England Journal of Medicine,* **282**, 1231-1235.

McCay, P.B., & King, M.M. (1980). Vitamin E: Its role as a biologic free radical scavenger and its relationship to the microsomal mixed-function system. In L.J. Machlin (Ed.), *Basic and clinical nutrition* (Vol. I, pp. 289-317). New York: Marcel Dekker.

McCord, J.M., & Roy, R.S. (1982). The pathophysiology of superoxide: Roles in inflammation and ischemia. *Canadian Journal of Physiology and Pharmacology,* **60**, 1346-1352.

Meerson, F.Z. (1980). Disturbances of metabolism and cardiac function under the action of emotional painful stress and their prophylaxis. *Basic Research in Cardiology* **75**, 479-500.

Mitamura, J.A., Seligman, M.L., Solomon, J.J., Flamm, E.S., Demopoulos, H.B., & Ransohoff, J. (1981). Loss of essential membrane lipids and ascorbic acid from rat brain following cryogenic injury and protection by methylprednisolone. *Neurological Research*, **3**, 329-344.

Moncada, S., & Amezuca, C. (1979). Prostacyclin, thromboxane A$_2$ interactions in hemostasis and thrombosis. *Haemostasis*, **8**, 252-265.

Moncada, S., Gryglewski, S., & Brunting, S. (1976). A lipid peroxide inhibits the enzyme in blood vessel microsomes that generates from prostaglandin endoperoxides the substance (prostaglandin X) which prevents platelet aggregation. *Prostaglandins*, **12**, 715-737.

Murad, F., Arnold, W.P., Mittal, C., & Braughler, J.M. (1979). Properties and regulation of guanylate cyclase and some proposed functions for cyclic GMP. *Advances in Cyclic Nucleotide Research*, **11**, 175-181.

Naisbitt, J. (1984). The new health paradigm. *Megatrends* (pp. 146-152). New York: Warner Books.

Ortega, B.D., Demopoulos, H.B., & Ransohoff, J. (1972). Effect of antioxidants on experimental cold-induced edema. In H.J. Reulen & K. Schurmann (Eds.), *Steroids and brain edema* (pp. 167-175). New York: Springer Verlag.

Panganamala, R.V. (1977). Differential inhibiting effects of vitamin E and other antioxidants on prostaglandin synthetase, platelet aggregation and lipoxidase. *Prostaglandins*, **14**, 261-271.

Parks, D.A., Bulkley, G.B., & Granger, D.N. (1983). Role of oxyen-derived free radicals in digestive tract diseases. *Surgery*, **94**, 415-422.

Pearson, D., & Shaw, S. (1982). *Life extension*. New York: Warner Books.

Petkau, A. (1982). Introduction: Free radical involvement in physiological and biochemical processes. *Canadian Journal of Physiology and Pharmacology*, **60**, 1327-1329.

Pietronigro, D.D., Jones, W.B.G., Kalty, K., & Demopoulos, H.B. (1978). Interaction of DNA and liposomes as a model for membrane-mediated DNA damage. *Nature*, **267**, 78-79.

Pietronigro, D.D., Seligman, M.L., Jones, W.B.G., & Demopoulos, H.B. (1976). Retarding effects of DNA on the autoxidation of liposomal suspensions. *Lipids*, **11**, 808-813.

Pla, G.L., & Witschi, H. (1976). Chemicals, drugs, and lipid peroxidation. *Annual Review in Pharmacology and Toxicology*, **16**, 125-141.

Pryor, W.A. (Ed.) (1976-1980). *Free radicals in biology* (Vol, 1-3). New York: Academic Press.

Rawlins, M.D. (1981), Adverse reactions to drugs. *British Medical Journal*, **282**, 974-976.

Rehncrona, S., Folbergrova, J., Smith, D.S., & Siesjo, B.K. (1980). Influence of complete and pronounced incomplete cerebral ischemia and subsequent recirculation on cortical concentrations of oxidized and reduced glutathione in the rat. *Journal of Neurochemistry*, **34**, 477-486.

Riley, V. (1981). Psychoneuroendocrine influence on immunocompetence and neoplasia. *Science*, **212**, 1100-1109.

Samuelsson, B., & Paoletti, R. (Eds.). (1982). *Leukotrienes and other lipoxygenase products*. New York: Raven Press.

Schaumberg, H., Kaplan, J., Windebank, A., Vick, N., Rasmus, S., Pleasure, D., & Brown, J.B. (1983). Sensory neuropathy from pyridoxine abuse: a new megavitamin syndrome. *New England Journal of Medicine*, **309**, 445-448.

Schwartz, R., Whetsell, W.O., & Mangano, R.M. (1983). Quinolinic acid: An endogenous metabolite that produces axon-sparing lesions in rat brain. *Science*, **219**, 316-318.

Seligman, M.L., Mitamura, J., Shera, N., & Demopoulos, H.B. (1979). Corticosteroid (methylprednisolone) modulation of photoperoxidation by UV light in liposomes. *Photochemistry & Photobiology, 29*, 549-558.

Shavit, Y., Lewis, J.W., Terman, G.W., Gale, R.P., & Liebeskind, J.C. (1984). Opioid peptides mediate the suppressor effect of stress on natural killer cell cytotoxicity. *Science, 223*, 188-190.

Singal, P.K., Kapur, N., Dhillon, K.S., Beamish, R.E., & Dhalla, N.S. (1982). Role of free radicals in catecholamine-induced cardiomyopathy. *Canadian Journal of Physiology and Pharmacology, 60*, 1390-1397.

Singh, A. (1982). Chemical and biochemical aspects of superoxide radicals and related species of activated oxygen. *Canadian Journal of Physiology & Pharmacology, 60*, 1330-1345.

Smith, P.J., Tappel, A.L., & Chow, C.K. (1974). Glutathione peroxidase activity as a function of dietary selenomethionine. *Nature, 247*, 392-393.

Spector, R. (1977). Vitamin homeostasis in the central nervous system. *New England Journal of Medicine, 296*, 1393-1398.

Taylor, A.E., Martin, D., & Parker, J.C. (1983). The effects of oxygen radicals on pulmonary edema formation. *Surgery, 94*, 433-438.

Vesely, D.L., Watson, B., & Levey, G.S. (1979). Activation of liver guanylate cyclase by paraquat—possible role of superoxide anion. *Journal of Pharmacology and Experimental Therapy, 209*, 162-164.

West, J.B. (1984). Human physiology at extreme altitudes on Mount Everest. *Science, 223*, 784-788.

Wieloch, T., & Siesjo, B.K. (1982). Ischemic brain injury: The importance of calcium, lipolytic activities, and free acids. *Pathology & Biology, 30*, 269-177.

Willer, J.C., Dehen, H., & Cambier, J. (1981). Stress-induced analgesia in humans: Endogenous opioids and naloxone-reversible depression of pain reflexes. *Science, 212*, 689-691.

Young, W., Flamm, E.S., Demopoulos, H.B., Tomasula, J., & DeCrescito, V. (1981). Effect of naloxone on post-traumatic ischemia in experimental spinal contusion. *Journal of Neurosurgery, 55*, 209-219.

15

Dangers, Detection, and Control of Doping in Sport

Svein Oseid
THE NORWEGIAN COLLEGE OF PHYSICAL EDUCATION AND SPORT
OSLO, NORWAY

Thor Ole Rimejorde
THE NORWEGIAN CONFEDERATION OF SPORTS
RUD, NORWAY

In 1963 the European Council defined *doping* as

> the administering or use of substances in any form alien to the body or of physiological substances in abnormal amounts and with abnormal methods, by healthy persons with the exclusive aim of obtaining an artificial and unfair increase of performance in competition.

Since then many professional committees have attempted to define the doping problem more clearly, but without much success. At their 1972 meeting in Helsinki, the Joint Nordic Committee for Scientific Athletics Research adopted a simpler definition:

> Doping is the administration of medication or the *use by other means* [italics added] *of artificially increasing an athlete's competitive performance.*

Added to the definition was the phrase *by other means;* this indicated that the use of different methods as well as the use of drugs to artificially increase competitive performance should be included in the definition. However, because such methods as blood transfusions, oxygen inhalation, hypnosis, and electric stimulation of muscles are difficult to control, they will not be included on the doping list.

Why Do Athletes Use Drugs?

The growing impression over the last 20 years has been that many athletes will do anything to win, not only in competitive countries like the United States, but perhaps even to a greater extent, in societies where success in sports is used politically and is socially and economically rewarded. Among high-level competitors, there is little question that drug use is considered an adjunct to training, diet, and psychological preparation for optimizing performance. Artificial agents include anabolic steroids and other hormones, central nervous system stimulants, sympathomimetics, tranquillizers, beta-blockers to reduce tremor, and autotransfusion of blood in an attempt to increase oxygen-carrying capacity and endurance. The doping list also contains many other drugs, but they play a relatively minor role in this context.

The purpose of this presentation is to illuminate the dangers and side effects of using drugs, and to discuss the detection and control of doping in sport. The aim is to try to further athletic traditions and to maintain an ethical attitude towards the goals and means of athletics by condemning the use of stimulating agents.

Why Prohibit Doping?

Doping is prohibited for the following important physical, ethical, and legal reasons:

Physical reasons
- Acute health hazard, potentially fatal.
- Potential chronic disability, possibly fatal.

Ethical reasons
- The use of doping agents is unethical to the concept of athletics.
- Use can lead to addiction that can result in ethical and social degeneration.

Legal reasons
- It defies The Norwegian Confederation of Sports' statutes.
- Certain doping agents are also illegal according to the narcotics laws in many countries and use, therefore, may be punishable by law.

Dangers of Doping in Sport

Only two groups on the doping list will be considered: Group A, psychomotor stimulant drugs, and Group E, anabolic steroids. Dangers and potentially harmful side effects of narcotic analgesics are obvious and will not be further discussed.

The health hazards involved in using central nervous system stimulants are loss of appetite, which may eventually lead to an anorexic condition, anxiety, insomnia, various psychological disturbances, drug addiction, and death by exhaustion during training or competition. In reducing the signals of physical fatigue, it is possible to stress the cardiovascular system to ultimate collapse. Drug addiction, therefore, is a serious problem. Several cases in which athletes of various disciplines have used and misused amphetamines have ultimately resulted in the use of even more potent drugs like heroin. This is what we are up against in the drug scene of the 1980s.

Potential harmful side effects of anabolic steroids in children are acceleration of the closure of epiphyses leading to lessened ultimate height and precocious puberty. In women the masculinizing effects are of the greatest concern, that is, increased facial hair, deepening of the voice, and clitoral hypertrophy.

All of these effects are largely irreversible. If taken by pregnant women, steroids may inhibit the development of a female embryo, cause pseudohermaphroditism, and even cause death of a fetus.

In adult men gynecomastia may develop, and a reduction in circulating levels of testosterone and gonadotrophins occurs, leading to testicular atrophy and oliogospermia. Increase in libido may be purely psychological; the opposite effect has also been reported. Common problems are acne and a tendency toward baldness.

More general side effects have been reported in several athletes, independent of age and sex. These side effects include the following: body weight gain, increased incidence of injuries to joints and tendons of the lower extremities, salt and water retention, increase of blood pressure, lowered HDL-cholesterol with risk of cardiovascular disease, decrease in glucose tolerance, abnormalities in liver function (disturbances of liver enzymes, development of jaundice), development of liver tumors (after long-term drug use), increase in aggressive behavior, increased irritability, and occasional psychotic behavior.

The most serious concern is not the use itself, but the quantities involved. Large doses of anabolic steroids for prolonged periods of time will always carry the risk of permanent alterations. The ultimate concern is the use of these steroids by prepubertal children and women.

Doping Control

In 1971 the Norwegian Sports Assembly stated its concern about the methods being used to increase performance level. The sports board's procedure program for the 1973-76 period revealed that the use of stimulating agents during sports competitions were to be controlled. As a result, in 1976 the Norwegian Confederation of Sports General Assembly decided to institute regular doping control for anabolic steroids.

The terms stated that the control measures be carried out (a) at selected Norwegian championships, (b) on Norwegian athletes prior to departure for international meets, and (c) as random controls on Norwegian athletes in international meets and at various times during the year.

In 1979, the control measures were extended to include all athletes regardless of age, sex, athletic discipline, or individual performing capacity.

By 1980 the doping control programs were extended to include all drugs and agents adopted by the International Olympic Committee (IOC) medical commission list.

Since 1980 it has become obvious that some sports (such as power lifting, weight lifting, and throwing events in track and field) were more loaded with drug problems than other sports—hence, the term *loaded sports*. Such facts were considered by the Norwegian Confederation of Sports and led to another decision made by the General Assembly in 1982 to

1. intensify the random control for both anabolic steroids and central nervous system stimulants;
2. direct the controls more specifically towards the sports and individual exercises known to be loaded;
3. increase the random controls during the training period;
4. demand that disqualified athletes submit to doping control regularly during the period of suspension; and
5. increase the sports confederation's budget for doping control.

By January 1, 1984, 21 positive cases on Norwegian athletes were registered at doping controls. Since 1977 400-600 test have been made annually. The Norwegian Confederation of Sport has also guided and assisted its special federations in connection with international championship competitions in Norway, and doping controls have also been carried out at international meets in Norway (after acceptance by the relevant international sport federation) through the same Norwegian sport federation.

At the initiative of some top Norwegian athletes—among them winners and medalists in Olympic events and world championships—the project "Top level athletics without doping" was launched. These athletes wished to prove that it was possible to reach the top without using stimulant drugs or hormones. Before the 1980 Winter Olympics, 17 controls were performed during 9 months. Altogether, 104 individual tests (87 male, 17 female) were given and all tests were negative. A similar number of winter athletes were controlled before the 1984 Winter Olympics, and these tests were also negative. An even more extensive program was instigated during the last few months to control athletes in more than 20 different sports in preparation for the 1984 Summer Olympics in Los Angeles.

Preventive Measures (*Antidoping*)

Experience has shown that in addition to regular random controls, information programs and actions to influence attitudes are equally important. The ten most important tasks are to

1. provide information about the health hazards of doping;
2. provide information about the limited value of most doping agents in in creasing performance;
3. attempt to produce ethical attitudes toward the goals and means of sport to directly lead to condemnation of doping and other artificial means used to achieve better results;
4. prepare and distribute exact and detailed lists of different doping agents, stating both the chemical composition and trade name of the various drugs in alphabetical order and in accordance with international resolutions;
5. work toward a stricter control over doctors' prescriptions of medication classified as doping;
6. demand that more severe action be taken toward athletes, coaches, and leaders having been found guilty of introducing doping agents to athletes;

7. institute and support practical and regular doping tests at the national level by putting financial means at the organizer's disposal;
8. cooperate with the custom officials to prevent substantial import of drugs;
9. cooperate with the police authorities to prevent distribution of narcotics and doping agents; and
10. provide more details about the Norwegian antidoping programs that have been published (Oseid, 1984; Rimejorde, 1983).

Control and Detection of Doping in Sport

The aim must be to establish regular doping control at national and international competitions for drugs listed as group A to D (psychomotor stimulant drugs, sympatomimetic amines, miscellaneous central nervous system stimulants, and narcotic analgetics) on the IOC list of forbidden substances. For anabolic steroids and testosterone, regular random doping control in the training period must be established at all national and international levels. The only way to curtail the misuse of hormones in sport is to persuade all international federations to acknowledge the amount and extent of hormone use, and to institute random controls at the national level.

Problems-What Are We Up Against?

Even with regular doping control and extensive antidoping campaigns, several problems must still be recognized. Negative attitudes toward control and detection of doping in sport still exist among athletes, for most athletes fanatically believe that hormone drugs have a positive effect. Most athletes are convinced that using drugs will enable them to train harder (intensity) and longer (duration), and that they will show a more rapid increase in competitive performance.

A serious problem is the existence of different lists of doping agents in different international federations as well as different prescription rules and attitudes in various countries. Different sanctions are also practiced by the international federations. As our society tends to develop into a drug society, this will draw an even thinner line between doping and therapy. Consequently, a more realistic and up-to-date list of drugs should be compiled with the exclusion of such drugs as the sympatomimetic amines (Group B) and drugs listed under miscellaneous central nervous stimulants (Group C) as suggested in Sweden by Björkhem, Eriksson, and Sjöquist (1984). This view is strongly supported by the Norwegian Confederation of Sports; it together with the Swedish authorities suggests to concentrate the control programs on psychomotor stimulant drugs and hormones (anabolic steroids, testosterone, and human growth hormone).

Finally, we must also be aware of the fact that many athletes attempt to foil detection by changing the pH of the urine with alkaline substances and by changing the specific gravity of the urine with diuretics. Attempts have been made to dilute the specimens by scooping from the toilet bowl, as well as to insert plastic bags with surrogate donor's urine in the vagina of female athletes. Remote attempts to catheterize and install surrogate donor's urine in the bladder have also been reported.

General Conclusions

The future of doping in sports is uncertain, but we must strive to obtain mutual international agreement about the necessity of efficient doping control, not only at international competitions, but also randomly at national levels.

Our information programs must be extensive and realistic, and we must move forward with ongoing vigilance to protect sport as well as athletes from being degraded.

Many questions remain unanswered, but the goal of responsible leadership is clear: to eradicate abuse and assure good health for our athletes.

References

Björkhem, I., Ericksson, B., & Sjöquist, F. (1984). Dopinganalyser-Preventiv medicin eller bara toppidrottsjippo? *Läkartidningen, 81*(19), 1925-1926.

Oseid, S. (1984). Doping and athletes—Prevention and counseling. *Journal of Allergy and Clinical Immunology, 73*, 735-739.

Rimejorde, T.O. (1983). Guidelines for doping controls and anti-doping work. Oslo: Education Department, The Norwegian Confederation of Sports.

16

Nutritional Habits of Active and Inactive Women Participating in an Osteoporosis Study

Joanne L. Slavin
UNIVERSITY OF MINNESOTA
ST. PAUL, MINNESOTA, USA

Pam V. York and Judy M. Lutter
MELPOMENE INSTITUTE FOR WOMEN'S HEALTH RESEARCH
ST. PAUL, MINNESOTA, USA

Although all adults lose bone as they grow older, some adults suffer excessive loss that results in osteoporosis. White, postmenopausal women are at particular risk in developing osteoporosis (National Institute, 1983). By age 65, about 25% of white, postmenopausal women have bone fractures related to osteoporosis. The medical costs of treating osteoporosis and caring for patients with fractures related to osteoporosis are astronomical.

Hormones, exercise, and diet are all important in preventing osteoporosis. Estrogen therapy is effective in slowing bone loss but is associated with an increased risk of uterine cancer (Recker, Saville, & Heaney, 1977). The increased stress on bone caused by exercise may slow bone loss (Smith, Khairi, Norton, & Johnston). Smith, Reddan, and Smith (1981) demonstrated a significantly higher bone mineral content in aged females who exercised over a 3-year period compared to a sedentary group of postmenopausal women. Calcium intake is the most important dietary consideration in the prevention and treatment of osteoporosis. In a comprehensive review of calcium supplemental trials, Heaney, Recker, and Saville (1978) concluded that calcium supplementation caused decreased bone loss. Other dietary factors also affect calcium status and ultimately bone mineral content. Vitamin D is needed for the absorption of calcium; lactose (the main carbohydrate in milk) also enhances calcium absorption (Armbrecht & Wasserman, 1976). High-protein diets (Linkswiler, Zemel, Hegsted, & Schuette, 1981) can increase urinary calcium excretion while both dietary fiber and phytate (Allen, 1982) may inhibit absorption of calcium.

The objective of the present study was to examine differences in nutrient intakes in active and inactive women recruited to participate in a long-term osteoporosis study. This paper describes their baseline nutritional data.

Methods

Subjects:

Fifty-seven inactive women and 54 active women, ages 47 to 76, were recruited by the Melpomene Institute and were initially placed in an active or inactive group. Active women were recruited at local running races and at Melpomene Institute seminars. Inactive subjects were recruited through a news piece on a local television station. Descriptive data are presented for 57 inactive women and 54 active women.

As activity data were further analyzed, the subjects' activity levels did not clearly fall into two categories. Therefore, the following six activity categories were developed (see Table 1):

1. Sedentary
2. Very low
3. Low active
4. Moderately active
5. Very active
6. Intensely active

For the purposes of nutrient analysis, Levels 1 and 2 were considered "low" (N=28), 3 and 4 "medium" (N=32), and 5 and 6 "high" (N=37).

Nutrient Analysis

All women completed a detailed, 12-page questionnaire, including sections on general health history, menstrual history, menopause history, physical activity, nutrition and weight history, drug and nutrient supplement usage, and lifestyle information. All participants submitted a 3-day diet record, including 2 weekdays and 1 weekend day. The women were instructed to choose days that were representative of typical eating patterns. The diet record forms clearly stated the importance of carefully describing the food, the method of preparation, and the portion size. Participants were also reminded to include condiments, snacks, and nutritional supplements. Nutrients in the diets were calculated with the NUTALLY computer program, (Department of Food Science and Nutrition, University of Minnesota) based on USDA Handbook #8. Nutrient values for fast foods, food mixtures, and other recipes were included in the data base.

Analysis of variance was used to determine differences in nutrient intakes between the low-, medium-, and high-activity groups.

Table 1. Activity level classifications of subjects

1. SEDENTARY
   - Very low daily household activity
   - Occasional flights of stairs, usually fewer than 2 to 3/day
   - Walks generally less than 4 blocks/day
   - No activity leading to a sweat
   - Usually feels activity is impaired by specific health problems or general conditions of "old age"
   - Level of inactivity constant all-year-round
2. VERY LOW
   - Consists mainly of everyday living requirements—a few flights of stairs, a few blocks of walking, a relatively low level of housework
   - Usually no activity leading to a sweat
   - Usually had been more active in younger years but level has progressively dropped off with advancing age, loss of spouse, and increasing health problems viewed as inhibiting activity
3. LOW ACTIVE
   - Maintains household and family
   - No steady formal activity, however, occasionally enjoys activities such as bowling, a bike ride, a walk, some golf
   - Activity seasonal—increases in the summer months and drops to near zero in the winter
   - Participation at any given time of short duration—less than ½ hour
4. MODERATELY ACTIVE
   - Usually engages in very little "formal" athletic activity but leads a life that keeps her "on the go"
   - Frequent walks, several flights of stairs
   - Activities include golf, mild calisthenics or stretching, walking, and doubles tennis
   - More interested in activity year-round, but no running, "hard" biking, or cross-country skiing
   - Aerobic activity but at a low cardiovascular stress level
   - Length of any given activity—½ to 1 hour
5. VERY ACTIVE
   - Participates regularly, several times a week, in athletic activities
   - Generally includes both group and individual activities
   - Actively incorporates activity into lifestyle as a complement to everyday activities.
   - Usually competes at some level in one or more activities
   - Usually changes sports depending on the season
6. INTENSELY ACTIVE
   - Participates in aerobic activity at a high level (probably to 70% of maximum heart rate) for an hour or more at a time, 5 to 7 days per week
   - High level of activity as much a part of everyday living as all other aspects of life
   - Sustains activity level all-year-round; often continues the same activity or activities all-year-round or substitutes similar activities in similar amounts
   - Almost always competes in an activity
   - Tends not to use advancing age or health problems as reason for slowing down

Results

Although the average height was the same at 64.5 in. for each group, the average weight was 145 lbs for the inactive group and 133 pounds for the active group. The participants were asked to describe their weight (see Table 2.) Only 7% of the inactives considered themselves "just right," with 42% reporting "slightly over" and 37% "over." More than 50% of the active women thought they were "slightly over" while approximately one-third of the active women thought their weight was "just right."

About 60% of the women reported consuming a "balanced, four food group diet." Active women (22%) were more likely to say they ate a diet that was "higher in carbohydrate, lower in fat and protein" than inactive women (15%). Only 2% of the women described their diet as "modified vegetarian."

The more active women consumed more calories. The Recommended Dietary Allowance (RDA) for females aged 51-75 years is 1,800 kcal, with a range of 1400 to 2200 kcal (National Research, 1980). Mean calorie intakes fell within the recommended range for all activity levels (see Table 3). All groups consumed about 17% of their calories as protein. There was no significant difference between the groups in the percentage of calories from fat and carbohydrate.

Mineral intakes of the subjects generally exceeded the RDA (see Table 4). For the low- and medium-activity group only calcium intake was less than the RDA. For the low-activity group, more than 75% of the women consumed less than the RDA for calcium. Of the 28 women in the low-activity group,

Table 2. Self-descriptions of weight

Description	Inactive %	Active %
Underweight	5.3	1.9
Slightly Under	7.0	1.9
Just Right	7.0	31.5
Slightly Over	42.1	51.9
Over	36.8	11.1

Table 3. Calorie intakes

Activity rating	N	Calories	Protein	Fat (g)	Carboyhdrate
Low	28	1745 ± 480	76 ± 18 (17%)*	68 ± 24 (35%)	213 ± 68 (48%)
Medium	32	1751 ± 418	71 ± 17 (16%)	70 ± 23 (36%)	202 ± 61 (46%)
High	37	2047 ± 523	85 ± 22 (17%)	76 ± 30 (33%)	253 ± 80 (49%)

*Percent of calories from each nutrient. Values are $\bar{X} \pm$ SD.

only 3 consumed more than 1,000 mg of calcium daily. The average calcium intake for the medium-activity group was less than for the low-activity group. More than 65% of the medium-activity group women consumed less than 800 mg of calcium daily, and only 2 women consumed more than 1,000 mg calcium daily. About 40% of the high-activity group consumed less than the RDA for calcium, and 18 of 37 women in the group consumed more than 1,000 mg of calcium daily.

For all activity groups, phosphorus intakes were higher than calcium (see Table 4). Calcium to phosphorus ratios for the three groups were 1:1.56, 1:1.53, and 1:1.50, respectively.

Vitamin intakes of all groups exceeded the RDA (see Table 5). Many of the women also consumed vitamin supplements, but the intakes were variable. For example, in the low-activity groups, daily vitamin C intake ranged from 23.5 mg to 388.3 mg.

Discussion

In general, more active women consume more calories yet seem to have less difficulty controlling their weight. Blair et al. (1981) reported that runners consume more calories than control subjects yet weigh significantly less. In their sample of 27 female long-distance runners, 35 to 59 year old, runners consumed 42 kcal/kg body weight daily while control subjects consumed 27 kcal/kg. The percentage of calories from fats, carbohydrates, and protein did not differ between active and inactive females in this study or in the Blair study.

Table 4. Mineral intakes

| Activity rating | Calcium | Phosphorus | Mineral, mg | | |
			Iron	Sodium	Potassium
Low	757 ± 287 (95%)*	1185 ± 323	13 ± 5	3110 ± 1452	2487 ± 659
Medium	737 ± 189 (92%)	1125 ± 263	13 ± 4	3043 ± 1132	2716 ± 646
High	1032 ± 523	1550 ± 477	14 ± 4	3052 ± 1289	3613 ± 986

*Mean values of all other nutrients are greater than 100% of the RDA.
Values are $\bar{X}$ ± SD.

Table 5. Vitamin intakes

Activity rating	Vitamin A IU	Thiamin mg	Riboflavin mg	Niacin mg	Vitamin C mg
Low	5909 ± 5571	1.2 ± 0.3	1.5 ± 0.4	20.2 ± 5.4	134 ± 75
Medium	5858 ± 4388	1.1 ± 0.4	1.5 ± 0.4	19.6 ± 7.0	128 ± 49
High	7575 ± 5323	1.5 ± 0.6	1.9 ± 0.7	19.7 ± 6.7	168 ± 67

Values are $\bar{X}$ ± SD.

We had originally planned to place our subjects into active and inactive groups, but such a division was difficult. Many of the active women were involved in exercise that required minimal energy expenditure. Women in the inactive group often performed manual work or engaged in hobbies such as square dancing.

On the average, the diet quality of the subjects was quite good. Average intake of all vitamins exceeded the RDA. The women attended a nutrition education session after their diets had been analyzed and the computer printouts of the nutrient analysis were returned.

The vitamin A content of the women's diets was highly variable between subjects and days. About 50% of the women in the low-activity group consumed the RDA for vitamin A, although the average intake of vitamin A exceeded the RDA.

Some studies have shown that women should consume 1,000 to 1,500 mg of calcium daily to prevent bone loss (Heaney et al., 1982; Heaney, Recker, & Saville, 1978; Marcus, 1982). In our study, only 3 of 28 low-activity women, 2 of 32 medium-activity women, and 18 of 37 high-activity women consumed more than 1,000 mg of calcium daily. Therefore, it appears that the higher levels of calcium intake recommended by many scientists to prevent osteoporosis are not likely unless women are consuming higher calorie diets or taking supplements.

Besides low calcium intake, other aspects of the womens' diets could negatively affect calcium status. A dietary ratio of Ca:P of 1:1 or 2:1 is often recommended to enhance calcium bioavailability (Marcus, 1982). For all subjects, the Ca:P ratio was between 1:1.5 and 1.1.6, a value similar to most American diets (Chinn, 1981). Further, the women consumed more than the RDA for protein, which has been shown to increase urinary excretion of calcium (Linkswiler et al., 1981). Many of the women were also consuming bran cereals or other fiber supplements that could further limit calcium absorption (Slavin & Marlett, 1980).

The original intent in selecting these subjects was to determine if exercise helped prevent bone loss in postmenopausal women. We found, however, that active women eat significantly more food than inactive women and, as a result, tend to ingest more calcium. To examine the role of exercise in the prevention of osteoporosis by comparing an active and inactive group will be difficult because diet will be a confounding factor. Studies that have shown active women to have larger bone masses than inactive women can be criticized because active women are most likely consuming more calcium (Brewer, Meyer, Keele, Upton, & Hagan, 1983). Calcium intakes and intakes of other nutrients that affect calcium absorption will need to be controlled when studying the effect of exercise on bone loss.

References

Allen, L.H. (1982). Calcium bioavailability and absorption: A review. *American Journal of Clinical Nutrition, 35*, 783-808.

Armbrecht, H.J., & Wasserman, R.H. (1976). Enhancement of Ca++ uptake by lactose in the rat small intestine. *Journal of Nutrition, 106*, 1265-1271.

Blair, S.N., Ellsworth, N.M., Haskell, W.L., Stern, M.P., Farquhan, J.W., & Wood, P.D. (1981). Comparison of nutrient intakes in middle-aged men and women runners and controls. *Medicine and Science in Sports and Exercise,* **13**, 310-315.

Brewer, V., Meyer, B.M., Keele, M.S., Upton, S.J., & Hagan, R.D. (1983). Role of exercise in prevention of involutional bone loss. *Medicine and Science in Sports and Exercise,* **15**, 445-449.

Chinn, A.I. (1981). *Effects of dietary factors on skeletal integrity in adults: Calcium, phosphorus, vitamin D, and protein* (Report prepared for FDA Contract 223-79-2275). Bethesda, MD: Life Sciences Research Office, FASEB.

Heaney, R.P., Gallagher, J.C., Johnston, C.C., Neer, R., Parfitt, A.M., & Whedon, G.D. (1982). Calcium nutrition and bone health in the elderly. *American Journal of Clinical Nutrition,* **36**, 986-1013.

Heaney, R.P., Recker, R.R., & Saville, P.D. (1978). Menopausal changes in calcium balance performance. *Journal of Laboratory and Clinical Medicine,* **92**, 953-963.

Linkswiler, H.M., Zemel, M.B., Hegsted, M., & Schuette, S. (1981). Protein-induced hypercalciuria. *Federation Proceedings,* **40**, 2429-2433.

Marcus, R. (1982). The relationship of dietary calcium to the maintenance of skeletal integrity in man—An interface of endocrinology and nutrition. *Metabolism,* **31**, 93-102.

National Institute of Arthritis, Diabetes, and Digestive and Kidney Disease. (1983, April). *Osteoporosis: Cause, treatment, prevention* (NIH Publication No. 83-2226).

National Research Council. (1980). *Recommended dietary allowances (9th ed.)* Food and Nutrition Board.

Recker, R.R., Saville, P.D., & Heaney R.P. (1977). Effect of estrogens and calcium carbonate on bone loss in post-menopausal women. *Annals of Internal Medicine,* **87**, 649-655.

Slavin, J.L., & Marlett, J.A. (1980). Influence of refined cellulose on human bowel function and calcium and magnesium balance. *American Journal of Clincial Nutrition,* **33**, 1932-1939.

Smith, D.M., Khairi, M.R.A., Norton, J., & Johnston, C.C. (1976). Age and activity effects on rate of bone mineral loss. *Journal of Clinical Investigation,* **58**, 716-721.

Smith, E.L., Reddan, W., & Smith, P.E. (1981). Physical activity and calcium modalities for bone mineral increase in aged women. *Medicine and Science in Sports and Exercise,* **13**, 60-64.

17

Utilization of Ergogenic Aids and the Attitude Toward Safety in Marathon Runners

Guy Thibault
QUEBEC SPORTS SAFETY BOARD
TROIS-RIVIERES, QUEBEC, CANADA

Jean Lambert, Michéle Rivard, Jean-Marc Brodeur, and Béatrice St-Jacques
UNIVERSITY OF MONTREAL
MONTREAL, QUEBEC, CANADA

The popularity of road running has increased so rapidly that the safety problems of runners are not yet well documented. It has been suggested that most of these problems in marathon running are related to the importance that some individuals place on their performance (Croteau, 1982). The purpose of this study, therefore, was to further document safety problems in marathon running. In three different surveys, runners were questioned on the popularity of some ergogenic aids, on the occurence and consequences of running injuries, and on their attitude when faced with these injuries.

Survey 1

Method

A random sample of 2,359 subjects was selected among the 6,673 Quebec runners registered in the 1982 Montreal International Marathon. During the week preceding the race, the runners were asked to complete a questionnaire

This study was supported by the Quebec Sports Safety Board, Government of Quebec.

on the ergogenic aids and the medicinal drugs they planned to use before and during the marathon. (Ergogenic aids are defined here as any substances or techniques that can potentially increase running performance.) The questionnaire was confidential and consisted of 53 questions. However, only 1,123 individuals returned a properly completed questionnaire (47.6% response rate).

Table 1 shows the characteristics of the average respondent; these characteristics closely correspond to those of the typical North American runner, the vast majority of whom are males of higher income and education levels than the average population (Who is the American runner? 1984).

Results

The popularity of the different ergogenic aids is seen in Table 2. Ten percent of the runners did not plan to drink water during the race. The majority (61%) of the respondents followed the glycogen overloading diet (Bergstrom, Hermansen, Hultman, & Saltin, 1967). Among these respondents 68% were on the so-called classic overloading diet, which includes a long run followed by 3 days low and 3 days high carbohydrate intake. However, 23% were on a "modified overloading diet." This is a "normal" diet followed by 3 days high-carbohydrate intake.

In comparing the data of this survey with the results collected from Quebecers in the Canada Health Survey (Statistics Canada, 1981), the following observations were revealed: male marathon runners consume less alcohol than non

Table 1. The average respondent to Survey 1

Male (90%)	X̄	Female (10%)	X̄
31 years old		*28 years old*	
Francophone	(85%)	Francophone	(79%)
Married	(58%)	Single	(54%)
No children	(51%)	No children	(72%)
High school or more	(66%)	High school or more	(77%)
Work: full time	(75%)	Work: full time	(51%)
Income > $20,000	(60%)	Income > $10,000	(56%)
Running for 4 years	(X̄)	Running for 3 years	(X̄)
Already ran a marathon	(66%)	Never ran a marathon	(52%)

Table 2. Popularity of some ergogenic aids

Water during the race	90%
High-carbohydrate breakfast before the race	83%
Glycogen overloading diet	61%
Medicinal drugs 2 days before interview	35%
Coffee or tea before the race	32%
Glucose and salt solutions during the race	27%
Vitamin plus mineral pills	20%
Ointments	12%

runners, whereas the alcohol consumption rate is similar in Quebec female runners and nonrunners; marathon runners sleep better, the difference being more important to females than to males; and, 94% of the marathon runners are nonsmokers as opposed to 52% and 58% of male and female Quebecers, respectively.

Compared to their respective reference group described in the Canada Health Survey, female runners have a similar medicinal drug consumption rate (42% vs 44%), whereas men runners consume more (35% vs 26%). Vitamin and mineral pills and ointments were 2.5 and 3 times more popular, respectively, among runners than in the general population. The most popular medicinal drugs (8%) were analgesics, similar to that observed in the general population.

Survey 2

Method

Among the 7,102 Quebec participants entering the 1983 Montreal International Marathon, 560 individuals were randomly selected to complete a questionnaire on their attitude toward safety and utilization of different hypothetical ergogenic drugs. These drugs were differentiated by their popularity, their legality, and their potential hazard to health. The questionnaire was confidential, contained only six questions, and had a response rate of 98.2%.

Most respondents (58%) had run at least one marathon. Their reasons for participation were to improve fitness (56%), to show a good performance (18%), or to have fun (14%). While 22% of the marathon runners had no performance goal, 11% wanted to finish the race; 18% aimed at a sub-4:10 hr marathon, 27% at a sub-3:40 hr, and 14% at a sub 3:10 hr. The runners rated the achievement of their goal as being extremely important (15%), very important (20%), or important (43%).

The reaction of the runner, when faced with all the symptoms of an upcoming heat stroke, was assessed by the following question:

> If you realize at the 40th kilometer that you can achieve the goal you set for yourself, in spite of the heat that has been bothering you for the last 10 kilometers, will you:
> 1. Keep the same pace to try to achieve your goal even if you have all the symptoms of an upcoming heat stroke?
> or
> 2. Slow down to make sure you complete the race without any incident even if it means that you will not achieve your goal?

Runners' attitudes toward the utilization of ergogenic aids was assessed by the following question:

> Suppose the eight pills illustrated below can significantly improve your performance on a marathon (15 min for 4:00 hr and more; 8 minutes for between 3:00 hr and 4:00 hr; 5 minutes for 2:30 hr and less), which one would you be willing to take considering the characteristics of each one in terms of popularity, legality, and hazard to your health?

Pills # 1, 2, 3, and 4 are used by many runners:

Pill #1: legal and not hazardous to your health
Pill #2: legal but hazardous to your health
Pill #3: not hazardous to your health but illegal
Pill #4: hazardous to your health and illegal

Pills # 5,6,7, and 8 are used by a few runners:

Pill #5: hazardous to your health and illegal
Pill #6: not hazardous to your health but illegal
Pill #7: legal but hazardous to your health
Pill #8: legal and not hazardous to your health

The runners could choose as many pills as they wished or could answer that they would not use any pill.

Results

Figure 1 illustrates the attitude of respondents toward their safety in warm weather conditions and toward the utilization of ergogenic aids. Despite the symptoms of an upcoming heat stroke, 12% of the 550 respondents claimed that they would keep their pace to try to achieve their goal rather than slow down for a safer race. As expected, this percentage was greater among those motivated to marathon participation because of the desire to show a good performance (25%). However, the percentage is still high in those who claimed they ran for fun (16%).

Only 25% of the runners surveyed would utilize a pill which could significantly improve their performance even if the pill were legal, popular, and not hazardous to their health. The percentage of runners attracted by the pill is further reduced to 11% if the drug is not popular and to 4% if it is illegal; none would risk endangering their health.

The comparison in Figure 1 of runners from different performance goal groups illustrates that individuals most likely to risk heat stroke are above-average runners. More than 1 out of 4 marathon runners who aimed at a sub-3:10 hr race would risk a heat stroke, whereas only 19% of sub-3:40 hr and sub 4:10 hr marathoners would do so. This trend between runners of different performance goals is not observed with regard to the attitudes toward the utilization of ergogenic aids.

Survey 3

Method

Six months after the 1983 Montreal International Marathon, a random sample of 195 individuals was selected among the 852 runners consulting medical services during the race. A second sample was selected consisting of 169 marathon runners who participated in the same race without consulting medical services. These groups were questioned by telephone interview about their injuries during training and during the race.

**Performance goal affect attitude towards
risking heat stroke but not towards
utilization of drugs**

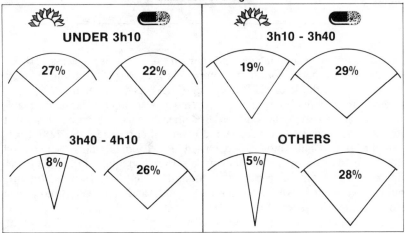

Figure 1. Attitude toward risking heat stroke and utilization of ergogenic aids

Results

The majority of the 364 respondents (195 consulted and 169 did not consult) claimed they followed their training program "rigorously" or "very rigorously." The total amount of kilometers covered each week was between 9 and 230 with an average of 69 km/week. The training frequency was under four times per week for only 16%, and four to five times per week for 79% of the runners interviewed.

About 1 out of 5 runners (21%) was injured during the training period for the marathon. The most frequent injuries and their location are shown in Table 3. Of the 76 runners injured during preparation for the marathon, 69% consulted a physician. In 44% of these cases, cessation of training was the suggested treatment. However, more than 1 out of 3 (35%) respondents who were requested to stop running disobeyed such advice and only lowered their training volume. Moreover, 36% of the runners injured during the training period were still injured the day of the race and ran the marathon despite their injuries.

During the race, 19% of the runners who suffered an injury did not stop for medical assistance even though 12 first-aid stations were located and well indentified along the course. Runners claimed they did not stop because they did not feel it was necessary (38%) or because the pain was tolerable (32%). Reported cases were "overuse injuries" (43%); "different ailment" (39%),

Table 3. Running injuries during training

Diagnosis	%	Location	%
Tendinitis	24%	Knee	42%
Sprain	17%	Leg	21%
Charley horse	14%	Ankle	19%
Periostitis	12%	Foot	14%

such as headache, general fatigue, or heat injury; and "other problems" (18%), such as a charley horse, sprain, or cramps. The locations of these injuries were the foot (26%), the knee (22%), the leg (20%), and the thigh (19%).

Fifty percent of the 240 runners surveyed who were injured during the marathon claimed their symptoms disappeared after the race. Of those injuries that persisted, 63% completely disappeared 1 week after the race, and 22% disappeared after 1 month. Only 15% persisted after 1 month, and 10% persisted after 6 months. One out of 2 runners who suffered an injury during the marathon consulted a physician before resuming training; 28% resumed training within a week, 36% within 1 week to 1 month, and 33% within more than 1 month after the race.

Discussion

The most common and severe problems in marathon running are overuse injuries and heat stroke; these may occur whenever the structures or the functions of the runner are submitted to a stress exceeding the amount of stress the runner's genotype and phenotype will allow (Clement, Taunton, Smart, & McNicol, 1981). Overuse running injuries may be related to internal factors such as malalignment of lower segments or inappropriate physical fitness or maturation. Overuse injuries can also be associated with intrinsic factors such as bad equipment, poor technique, or an inappropriate training program (Stanish, 1984).

Runners' dependency toward their activity has been described in terms suggesting it may be a pathological situation (Leehey, Yates, Shisslak, 1983). Some runners may lose confidence in their physician who may suggest the most "painful" treatment—*rest*.

Indeed, more than 1 out of 3 respondents actually disregarded their physician's advice to stop training. These runners all claimed they did not listen to their physician's advice because they felt their doctor "knew nothing about running."

Data collected in this study provides additional insight about the runners' attitudes toward their sport in relationship to their safety. It is rather paradoxical that relatively few runners would utilize a legal, popular, and safe pill that could significantly improve their performance; this pill basically has the characteristics of the ergogenic aids that the majority of the respondents claimed they used in Survey 1. It is also surprising that 1 out of 4 runners who aimed at a sub-3:10 hr marathon would risk a heat stroke with well-known consequences, whereas none of the 550 respondents of Survey 2 would use a dangerous pill.

Explanations for this phenomenon may be that the samples in Survey 1 and 2 were different, that some people may have doubted the confidentiality of the questionnaire, or that the runners' answers may have been influenced by the somewhat frightening aspect of the term *pill*. However, our explanation of this paradox is that the running community has developed its own value system for what it regards as healthy living habits and physical efforts. Hence, some runners are prepared to do anything to show a good performance as long as it is through effort during training, through pain during the race, or through techniques that are broadly recognized as part of common runners' habits before a race.

The comments obtained from runners during the telephone interview revealed the importance of running in their lives. This attitude of runners toward their training and performance should be considered when teaching them the potential hazards of heat stroke and overtraining. The adverse effects of "overdoing it" must be explained in terms of impact not only on health but on future performance. Ideally, elite athletes whom runners highly regard should deliver the message, instead of so-called specialists.

References

Bergstrom, J., Hermansen, J., Hultman, E., & Saltin, B. (1967). Diet, muscle glycogen and physical performance. *Acta Physiologica Scandinavica, 71,* 140-150.

Clement, D.B., Taunton, J.E., Smart, G.W., & McNicol, K.L. (1981). A survey of overuse running injuries. *The Physician and Sportsmedicine, 9,* 47-58.

Croteau, F. (1982). L'hypertermie lors du marathon de Montréal en 1981. *L'Union Medicale du Canada, 111,* 413-416.

Leehy, K., Yates, A., & Shisslak, C.M. (1983). Running—An analogue of anorexia? *The New England Journal of Medicine, 5,* 251-255.

Stanish, W.D. (1984). Overuse injuries in athletics: A prospective *Medicine and Science in Sports and Exercise, 16,* 1-7.

Statistics Canada. (1981). *The Health of Canadians, Report of the Canada Health Survey* (Document No 82-538E).

Who is the American runner? (1984, August). *Runner's World,* pp. 46-51, 156, 158, 160, 162, 164, 168.

18

Motor Development and Performance of Children and Youth in Undernourished Populations

Robert M. Malina
UNIVERSITY OF TEXAS
AUSTIN, TEXAS, USA

A significant percentage of children and youth in developing countries live under conditions of chronic undernutrition. Undernutrition is a complex concept ranging from the most severe to the more common mild states. The world's most common form of undernutrition is protein-energy malnutrition (PEM). In Latin America, for example, it was estimated that 71 million (25% of the population) were affected by malnutrition in the mid-1970s. The majority were children; about 61% (28.3 million) of the preschool population under 5 years of age suffered from some degree of PEM (Inter-American Development Bank, 1979).

Implications of chronic undernutrition for growth and performance are reasonably well documented: high risk of mortality (especially infant and preschool), stunted physical growth, reduced muscle mass, delayed motor development, and reduced levels of physical activity, working capacity, and efficiency (Malina, 1984; Spurr, 1983, 1984). This paper considers the implications of undernutrition for the motor performance of children and youth. The development and refinement of skillful performance in movement activities is a major developmental task of childhood and youth. Further, it is often through fundamental and specialized motor skills that many childhood experiences within a specific culture are mediated.

The primary focus of this report is on children and school-age youth, although motor development during infancy and early childhood are briefly considered. Comprehensive literature is available on the consequences of undernutrition on the growth and development of preschool children, specifically those with PEM. Severe PEM is associated with high infant and preschool mortality. School age children in areas with a high incidence of PEM can be viewed as survivors of an early childhood characterized by intense nutritional and infectious disease stress, these being the primary contributors to preschool mortality in the developing areas of the world.

Severe PEM

Motor development, in general, and the attainment of motor skills such as sitting, standing alone, and walking independently are delayed in severe PEM, (i.e., marasmus, kwashiorkor, and undifferentiated forms.) Reduced motor nerve conduction velocities and changes in muscle tissue, that is, reduced fiber size, potassium, and energy metabolism are also associated with severe PEM. The persistence of changes associated with severe PEM varies with the timing, severity, and duration of the nutritional stress. Although motor nerve conduction velocities show normalization with nutritional rehabilitation in cases of severe PEM, data for muscle tissue and motor development indicate persistent deficits during childhood. Further, follow-up studies of youngsters hospitalized for severe undernutrition early in life indicate long-term persistence of motor and perceptual deficits (Malina, 1984).

Mild-To-Moderate PEM

Children reared under marginal nutritional circumstances and not hospitalized probably experience changes in muscle mass and metabolism and perhaps in neurointegrative processes. These children, who subsequently comprise the school age and productive adult population, are generally shorter and lighter than better nourished individuals of the same ethnic group and show changes in body composition, specifically reduced lean body and muscle mass (Jelliffe & Jelliffe, 1969; Satyandrayana, Naidu, & Rao, 1979; Spurr, Barac-Nieto, & Maksud, 1978; Viteri, 1971). Because muscle strength is proportional to its cross-sectional area, reduced muscle mass in undernourished individuals should result in an absolute reduction in static and dynamic muscular strength. Further, dynamic strength (power) underlies performance in many motor tasks—for example, dashes, jumps, and throws—and involves motor coordination in addition to strength.

There is an extensive cross-cultural literature which considers motor development during the first 2 years of life in chronically undernourished populations. The evidence indicates satisfactory motor progress during the first year in most groups, for example, Mayans and East Indians, and precocity in others, for example, Africans (Malina, 1977, 1984). A developmental lag in motor proficiency toward the end of the first year and during the second year is commonly observed in these samples from developing areas of the world. This lag may be related to the break in continuity of rearing at weaning, to the effects of marginal nutritional status, and to the reduced levels of physical activity. Also, toward the end of the first year and during the second year stunting in physical growth becomes especially apparent. As an example, development of several motor items of the Gesell scale are shown in Figures 1 and 2 for rural Guatemalan Mayan (Cakchiquel) preschool children. Gross and fine motor achievements of the Mayan children are indicated relative to the Gesell reference sample. The Mayan infants compared favorably with the reference sample during the first 6 to 9 months of life, but progressively lagged behind later in infancy and especially during the second and subsequent years. Variation with specific motor items was apparent and may reflect cultural unfamiliarity with test procedures. Further, stranger-anxiety affects older infants and children and must be noted; it may make testing or observing motor behavior quite difficult, masking the true motor characteristics of the children.

Using the McCarthy Scale of Children's Abilities, Ashem and Janes (1978) compared the performance of a sample of rural and urban Ibadan children, 2.5 to 6.0 years of age. Well-nourished (urban, private school, "well off")

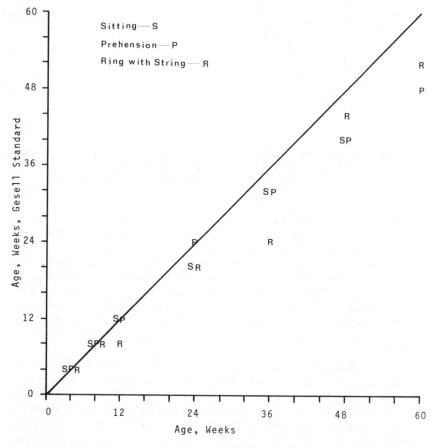

Figure 1. Development of gross (sitting posture) and fine (prehension and handling a ring with a string) motor abilities in rural Guatemalan Mayan infants. Drawn from the data of Wug de Leon, de Licardie, and Cravioto (1964)

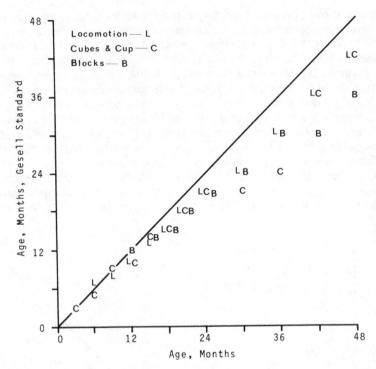

Figure 2. Development of gross locomotor and fine motor (placing cubes in a cup and building with blocks) abilities of rural Guatemalan Mayan infants and children. Drawn from the data of Wug de Leon et al. (1964)

children were compared to urban and rural "poor" children classified as reasonably nourished and malnourished on the basis of stature and weight. Performance on the perceptual and motor subscales was best in the well-nourished, intermediate in the reasonably nourished, and poorest in the malnourished children (see Table 1). Variation in specific items of the scale, however, should also be noted. Among 4- and 5- year-old lower socioeconomic status children in São Paulo, Rocha Ferreira (1980) reported consistently poorer motor performance among the undernourished (1st degree, Gomez scale) compared to children classified as average and above average (see Table 2).

The preceding two studies grouped children on the basis of their growth status in stature and/or weight. Stature and weight are significantly related to gross motor performance (Malina, 1975). Because children in populations nutritionally at risk are consistently shorter and lighter than reference data, body size should be considered in analyses of motor development and performance.

Among rural Guatemalan Ladino children, Lasky and colleagues (1981) considered the relationships of several anthropometric dimensions to scores on the motor subscale of a Composite Infant Scale at 6, 15, and 24 months of age. Weight had a greater effect on motor development than length. Partial

Table 1. Mean perceptual and motor performances, and deviation scores for selected subtests of the McCarthy Scale of Children's Abilities for children, 2-6 years of age, grouped by nutritional status*

Variables	Well nourished (N = 45)	Reasonably nourished (N = 28)	Malnourished (N = 55)
Performance:			
Perceptual	55.1	42.0	36.4
Motor	61.1	48.1	41.3
Deviation Scores:			
Block Building	0.13	-0.22	-1.57
Tapping Sequence	0.22	-0.98	-1.66
Drawing a Design	3.18	-2.00	-1.68
Counting and Sorting	-0.05	0.06	-2.29
Leg Coordination	2.02	0.43	-0.88
Arm Coordination	2.14	3.34	-0.21

*Adapted from "Deleterious effects of chronic undernutrition on cognitive abilities" by B. Ashem and M. Janes, 1978, *Journal of Child Psychology*, **19**. Adapted with permission.

Table 2. Mean motor performances of nursery school children, 4-5 years of age, from the lower socioeconomic stratum of São Paulo, grouped by nutritional status (Gomez scale)[a]

Motor items	Above average (N = 25-35)	Nutritional status average (N = 63-71)	undernourished[b] (N = 23-30)
Standing Long Jump, cm	81.8	75.9	63.3
20 Meter Dash, sec	6.05	6.03	6.27
Dynamic Balance, points[c]	3.6	3.2	2.9
Static Balance, % passing	89	82	77

*Adapted from Estado nutricional e aptidão fisica em préescolares. By F. Rocha, 1980, Dissertação de Mestrado, Universidade de Sao Paulo. Adapted with permission.
[b]1st degree undernutrition on the Gomez scale.
[c]A composite score based on 11 tests scored on a pass-fail basis and weighted.

correlations between weight and motor performance, controlling for length, were $r=0.19$, 0.11, and 0.19 at 6, 15, and 24 months of age, respectively. Thus, for the same length, heavier youngsters generally performed better than lighter youngsters. After statistically controlling for length and weight, none of the other anthropometric variables added significantly to the variation in motor development at these three ages.

At the school ages, Malina and Buschang (1985) considered the motor performance of 350 Zapotec Indian children, 6 through 15 years of age, who were raised under conditions of chronic mild-to-moderate undernutrition. The children were from a rural, subsistence agricultural community of approximately 1,700 in southern Mexico. Their absolute body size and levels of performance in tests of running, jumping, throwing, and grip strength were significantly below those for better nourished American children. When performances were corrected for the size difference between the undernourished and better nourished samples (plotted relative to stature or weight rather than age), grip strength in both boys and girls was slightly, but consistently less per unit body size over the age range. The performance of Zapotec boys was generally commensurate with their smaller body size in the dash between 6 and 9 years and in the standing long jump between 6 and 12 years, but at the older ages, performance was below that expected for body size. The latter observation may reflect a delayed adolescent spurt with its concomitant gain in muscle mass and strength. Among girls, performance in the dash was considerably less per unit body size. The girls performed on the jump commensurately with their reduced body size between 6 and 10 years, and then well below that expected for their size. In contrast to the run and jump, performance of Zapotec children in the ball throw for distance was greater than expected for their reduced body size.

The pattern of second order partial correlations shown in Table 3 between motor performance and age, height and weight in Zapotec children was generally similar to that for well-nourished children (Malina, unpublished; Rarick & Oyster, 1964; Seils, 1951). Stature had a low, positive, significant correlation with performance on the run, jump, and throw in both sexes after controlling for the effects of age and weight. Correlations between stature and strength, controlling for age and weight, were lower for boys than for girls. Partial correlations for weight, controlling for age and stature, were consistent only for the dash, indicating a low, significant negative relationship. Even in moderately malnourished children, this would seem to suggest a small negative effect of body weight on running speed. Weight had a low, significant positive correlation with grip strength in both sexes, and with the distance throw only in boys older than 9 years of age, after controlling for age and stature. This would seem to emphasize the role of absolute body mass in strength and

Table 3. Second-order partial correlations between age and body size, and motor performances of Zapotec school children

Motor items	Stature, controlling for age and weight		Weight, controlling for age and stature	
	boys	girls	boys	girls
35-yd dash[a]	+0.26 [c]	+0.32[c]	−0.19[c]	−0.17[b]
Standing long jump	+0.24 [c]	+0.21[c]	−0.04	+0.01
Distance throw:				
< 9 years	+0.18	+0.35[c]	+0.04	−0.06
≥ 9 years	+0.23 [c]	+0.23[b]	+0.24[c]	+0.01
Right-grip strength	+0.13 [b]	+0.26[c]	+0.28[c]	+0.30[c]
Left-grip strength	+0.07	+0.22[c]	+0.39[c]	+0.37[c]

Note. Adapted from "Growth, strength, and motor performance of Zapotec children, Oaxaca, Mexico" by R.M. Malina and P.H. Buschang, 1985, *Human Biology,* **57**, 163-181.
[a]Signs for the dash were inverted as a lower score is a better performance.
[b]$p < .05 > .01$
[c]$p < .01$

ball throwing for distance. The latter is a coordination and power task. We also attempted to evaluate the effects of other body dimensions (e.g., specific lengths, breadths, circumferences, and skinfolds) on the motor performance of the Zapotec school children. After removing the effects of age, stature, and weight, few of the anthropometric dimensions added significantly to describing the remaining variation in motor performance. Hence, body size per se was the significant factor influencing performance of school children living under marginal nutritional circumstances. These observations are consistent with those for rural Guatemalan children at 6, 15, and 24 months of age (Laskey et al., 1981).

Malina, Shoup, and Little (1985) considered the same performance items in a sample of approximately 85 Manus schoolchildren, 6 through 15 years of age, from Peri village in Papua New Guinea. Peri village, which had a population of 550 in 1980, is located on the south coast of Manus Island in the Admiralty Archipelago off the northern coast of New Guinea. The population of Peri village can be characterized as mildly undernourished. Heights, weights, and grip strength were similar to those of Zapotec children from Mexico. However, running and jumping performance were considerably better in the small sample of Manus than in Zapotec children and similar to well nourished children. Throwing performance was similar in both Manus and Zapotec boys but less than well-nourished boys. Manus girls, on the other hand, performed better in the throw than both the Zapotec and well-nourished girls.

Strength per unit body size was similar in the well-nourished, Zapotec, and Manus children. However, running and jumping performance per unit body size were considerably better in the Manus compared to the well-nourished and Zapotec children. Both undernourished samples had better throwing performances per unit body size than the well-nourished children.

The pattern of second order partial correlations between motor performance and age, height, and weight in Manus children (see Table 4) was generally similar to that for the undernourished Zapotec children and for well-nourished children. Except for grip strength in boys, height had a significant positive effect on motor performance after age and weight were statistically controlled.

Table 4. Second-order partial correlations between age and body size, and motor performances of Manus school children

Motor items	Stature, controlling for age and weight		Weight, controlling for age and stature	
	boys	girls	boys	girls
35-yd dash[a]	+0.40[c]	+0.25	−0.14	−0.52[c]
Standing long jump	+0.44[c]	+0.57[c]	−0.15	−0.18
Distance throw	+0.33[b]	+0.34[b]	+0.33[b]	−0.07
Grip strength	+0.26	+0.39[b]	+0.70[c]	+0.38[b]

Note. Adapted from "Growth, strength, and motor performance of Manus children" by R.M. Malina, R.F. Shoup, and B.B. Little, 1985, submitted for publication.
[a] Signs for the dash were inverted as a lower score is a better performance.
[b] $p < .05 > .01$
[c] $p < .01$

On the other hand, body weight had a negative effect on the run and jump and a positive effect on strength after age and height were statistically controlled. Weight was positively related to throwing in boys, but not in girls.

The preceding comparisons of undernourished and well-nourished children indicate several similarities and contrasts. The direction of correlations between age, height, and weight on one hand, and performance on the other, are generally similar, but the magnitude varies. Grip strength per unit body size is reasonably similar in the three samples, while the undernourished children throw better per unit body size. The mild-to-moderately malnourished Zapotec children do not run and jump as well per unit size compared to better nourished children, while the mildly undernourished Manus children run and jump better per unit size. Hence, it is difficult to apply observations from one undernourished population to another. Nutritional status is a variable concept and needs to be more precisely defined. Patterns of physical activity per se and types of activities need more consideration. Further, it should be emphasized that performance on such motor tasks is influenced by motivational and perhaps competition factors, and subtle cultural differences are undoubtedly significant.

Ghesquiére and Eeckels (1981) reported similar trends for primary school African boys in Kinshasa, Zaire. The growth and performance of 197 boys, 6 through 12 years of age, resident in an impoverished "shanty town" outside of the city were compared to that of boys attending a private school in the city. The former were shorter and lighter and presumably experienced nutritional and disease stress during infancy and early childhood. They also performed less well in grip strength, a medicine ball throw, the vertical jump, and the 50-m dash. However, when performance was expressed relative to body weight, the boys from the shanty town performed slightly but consistently better than those from the private school. Differences were most notable from 7 through 10 years and reduced at 11 and 12 years in the run, jump, and throw. The differences, however, were consistent across all ages for grip strength.

Data for other samples of undernourished children and youth are most available for grip strength (Acevedo, 1955; Burma Medical Research Council, 1968; De, Debnath, Dey, & Nagchaudhuri, 1980; Ishiko, 1967; Parizkova & Merhautova, 1973; Sabogal, Molina, & MacVean, 1979), with fewer studies of motor performance (Brandt & Broekhoff, 1981; Burma Medical Research Council, 1968; Ishiko, 1967; Parizkova & Merhautova, 1973). Body size is ordinarily not considered in the analyses, while social class, socioeconomic status, and/or height and weight are commonly used as a proxy for nutritional status.

Undernourished samples ordinarily show less absolute strength. However, when strength is expressed relative to body weight (using mean values in most instances), the data indicate generally similar values, thus emphasizing the role of body size differences between the better nourished and the undernourished. It should also be noted that the type of dynamometer used is often not reported, and the use of different dynamometers limits comparisons across studies.

Motor performance data among the marginally malnourished are more variable. Parizkova and Merhautova (1973), for example, reported no differences in running (50-m dash and 300-m run) between poor Tunisian boys from "modest, but sufficient living conditions" and "privileged" boys 11 years of age, although the latter were about 5 kg heavier and 3 cm taller. However, the poor boys performed better in the standing long jump.

Brandt and Broekhoff (1981) reported poorer performances in the shuttle run, pull-ups, distance throw, and sit-ups among 4th, 5th, and 6th grade (about 10 to 12 years of age) coastal, highland, and urban Morobe boys of Papua New Guinea compared to the AAHPERD norms, but better performances in the standing long jump and 600-yd run. Performance on the 50-yd dash was only slightly below the norms. Body size differences among the samples, however, were not considered in the analysis, and the Morobe boys were, on the average, shorter and lighter than United States reference data. Burmese youth of both sexes, 15 through 17 years of age, also performed poorly compared to the AAHPERD norms on most items of the youth fitness test except on the standing long jump (Burma Medical Research Council, 1968). Differences were small for the 600-yd run and 50-yd dash, while Burmese boys exceeded the norms for the pull-ups, and Burmese girls were well below.

Among a sample of approximately 30 Japanese boys, 7 through 15 years of age, from an isolated, nutritionally stressed area in northern Japan, Ishiko (1967) reported motor performances that were generally within the normal range of variation for Japanese urban boys. However, the majority had running, jumping, and throwing performances that were well below the median for the better nourished urban boys. Differences were most apparent in the jump and run, for which about one half of the boys had performances below the lower percentile limits for the better-off urban boys. Although the data were presented graphically, it would appear that the isolated, nutritionally stressed boys were performing commensurately with their smaller statures.

Given the lesser heights and weights and the jumping and running performances of the Morobe boys and Burmese youth, these results are consistent with the observations reported earlier for Peri village. The samples of Papua New Guinea and Burmese children and youth jump and run consistently better than would be anticipated from their small body size. The data for isolated Japanese boys, on the other hand, appear consistent with those for Zapotec children in Mexico.

The preceding are limited largely to the relationships and effects of height and weight on strength and motor performance in undernourished samples of children and youth. Note, however, that the degree of undernutrition among the samples varies considerably, and with few exceptions, most samples could be classified as mildly undernourished.

Chronic undernutrition is also associated with changes in body composition (Cheek, Habicht, Berall, & Holt, 1977; Spurr et al., 1978; Viteri, 1971). Studies of well nourished children indicate a significant effect of lean body mass (LBM) and body fat on performance that is independent of the influence of height and weight (Boileau & Lohmann, 1977; Malina, 1975). In an attempt to consider the relationships between body composition and motor performance in undernourished children, the body composition of Zapotec and Manus boys 9 through 15 years of age was predicted from skinfolds (Malina, Shoup, & Little, 1985; Malina & Little, 1985). Prediction equations for body density were developed from a sample of 95 lower socioeconomic status Mexican-American boys, 9 through 14 years of age (Zavaleta & Malina, 1982).

Body density was converted to relative fatness, which was subsequently used to calculate lean body and fat mass. The limitations of these procedures are recognized; nevertheless, they do provide an estimate of body composition.

Relationships between absolute LBM in two samples of well-nourished boys were virtually identical with those observed in undernourished Zapotec boys, while those in the Manus were higher (see Table 5). In contrast, relationships between relative fatness and performance were different in the undernourished compared to the well-nourished boys. Among the latter, relative fatness exerted a negative influence on events which require the displacement of body weight, that is, the dash and jump. On the other hand, correlations for Zapotec boys were low, indicating no relationship between relative fatness and running and jumping performance and a low-positive effect on throwing performance. Among the small sample of Manus, relative fatness showed a significant positive effect on performance in all three tasks.

Table 5. Correlations between absolute lean body mass and relative fatness and motor performance in well-nourished and undernourished boys

| | Well-nourished: | | | | Undernourished | | | |
| | Indiana[a] | | Illinois[b] | | Zapotec[c] | | Manus[d] | |
Motor item	LBM	% fat	LBM	% fat	LBM	% fat	LBM	% fat
Dash[e]	.56	− .55	.57	− .37	.50	.04	.79	.39
Jump	.57	− .44	.65	− .44	.64	.07	.77	.31
Throw	.63	− .16			.83	.26	.92	.71

Note. Data compiled from [a]"Body composition relative to motor aptitude for preadolescent boys" by A.H. Ismail, J.E. Christian, and W.V. Kessler, 1963, *Research Quarterly,* **34**, 462-470. Relationship of somatotype and body composition to physical performance in 7-to-12-year-old boys" by M.H. Slaughter, T.G. Lohman, and J.E. Misner, 1977, *Research Quarterly.* **48**, 159-168. [c]"Body composition, strength, and motor performance in undernourished boys" by R.M. Malina and B.B. Little, in R.A. Binkhorst, H.C.G. Kemper, and W.H.M. Saris (Eds.), *Children and Exercise XI,* (pp. 293-300). 1985, Champaign, IL: Human Kinetics. [d]"Growth, strength and motor performance of Manus children" by R.M. Malina, R.F. Shoup, and B.B. Little, 1985, submitted for publication.

Table 6. Correlations between absolute lean body mass and relative fatness and grip strength in well-nourished and undernourished boys

Samples		LBM	% Fat
Well-nourished	New York[a]	.91	
	Texas[b]	.91	.05
Undernourished:	Zapotec[c]	.80	.35
	Manus[d]	.96	.76

Note. Data compiled from [a]"Toward a new dimension in human growth" by G.B. Forbes, 1965, *Pediatrics,* **36**, 825-835. [b]"Growth and body composition of Mexican-American boys 9 through 14 years of age" by A.N. Zavaleta and R.M. Malina, 1982, *American Journal of Physical Anthropology,* **57**, 261-271. [c]"Body composition, strength, and motor performance in undernourished boys" by R.M. Malina and B.B. Little, in R.A. Binkhorst, H.C.G. Kemper, and W.H.M. Saris (Eds.), *Children and Exercise XI,* (pp. 293-300). 1985, Champaign IL: Human Kinetics. [d]"Growth, strength, and motor performance of Manus children" by R.M. Malina, R.F. Shoup, and B.B. Little, 1985, submitted for publication.

Correlations between estimated body composition and grip strength in two undernourished samples and two better nourished samples are shown in Table 6. Correlations for absolute LBM were high, although that for Zapotec boys was the lowest. The latter are more undernourished than the Manus, especially in terms of animal protein intake. The lower correlation between LBM and grip strength in Zapotec boys may be indicative of the effects of chronic protein deficiency on the integrity of muscle tissue. In contrast, relative fatness had a significant relationship with strength in the undernourished samples, but no relationship in the better nourished Mexican-American boys.

Changes in body composition under conditions of mild-to-moderate undernutrition apparently do not alter the relationship between lean body mass and performance compared to well-nourished children. However, relationships are changed between fatness and performance. The lack of an influence of relative fatness on performances involving the displacement of body mass in moderately undernourished boys, that is, the dash and jump, may be suggestive of a threshold level above which an excessive percentage of fatness exerts a negative influence on performance. On the other hand, a higher percentage of body fat may be indicative of relatively better nutritional status within a sample of undernourished boys. Estimated absolute and relative fatness are related to an absolutely larger LBM in the two samples of undernourished boys. Thus, relative fatness is an indication of a larger LBM and may be a good predictor of static strength and throwing performance in the undernourished samples. Both tasks are dependent on absolute body size, including LBM.

Implications

The adaptive significance of small body size and reduced LBM under conditions of chronic protein and energy undernutrition is frequently discussed within the context of natural selection, that is, size reduction relaxes the pressure on food available to the population, allowing more individuals to survive and maintain the population over time (Stini, 1972, 1975). It is also reported that reduced size and LBM do not impair physical performance and functional efficiency (Frisancho, Velasquez, & Sanchez, 1975; Parizkova & Merhautova, 1973; Stini, 1972). To the contrary, superior functional efficiency in association with reduced body size has been postulated:

> There is a real advantage, then, in developmental adjustments producing smaller but well-proportioned and functionally unimpaired males. The problem is not as easily resolved in the case of females (Stini, 1975, p.31)

The evidence presented herein suggest that it is premature to conclude that reduced body size and LBM under conditions of nutritional stress are an adaptive advantage. Static strength when expressed per unit body size is generally similar in undernourished and well-nourished samples. The motor performance data, however, are equivocal when expressed relative to body size. Nevertheless, a reduction in body size and LBM is more often associated with an absolute reduction in muscular strength and in performance of tasks requiring speed and power.

Static strength and motor performance are indicators of only one aspect of physical fitness: motor fitness. The other aspect of fitness, organic fitness, or physical working capacity, has not been considered. Spurr (1983, 1984) presents and excellent overview of physical working capacity in undernourished populations. Maximal oxygen consumption per kilogram of body weight does not differ in marginally malnourished and well-nourished boys. The malnourished, however, do have stunted growth and reduced absolute oxygen intakes, which prompted Spurr (1983, p.28) to conclude that "there does not appear to be any basic deficit in muscle function in marginally malnourished children—only in the quantity of muscle available for maximal work." Implications of reduced muscle mass for motor performance are obvious. The undernourished may perform well for their reduced size, but they generally do not perform as well as better nourished children and youth.

References

Acevedo, M.E. (1955). Contribucion al estudio de medidas antropometricas en el escolar Chileno. *Revista Chilena de Education Fisica,* **22**, 1101-1104.

Ashem, B., & Janes, M.D. (1978). Deleterious effects of chronic undernutrition on cognitive abilities. *Journal of Child Psychology and Psychiatry,* **19**, 23-31.

Boileau, R.A., & Lohman, T.G. (1977). The measurement of human physique and its effect on physical performance. *Orthopedic Clinics of North America,* **8**, 563-581.

Brandt, T.R., & Broekhoff, J. (1981). Physical fitness and motor skills of coastal, mountain, and urban Morobe boys of Papua New Guinea. *ICHPER Research Synposium, 24th World Congress on Health, Physical Education and Recreation, Manila* (pp. 119-131). Manila: Philippine Council on Health, Physical Education and Recreation.

Burma Medical Research Council. (1968). *Physical fitness of the Burmese.* Rangoon: Burma Medical Research Institute.

Cheek, D.B., Habicht, J.P., Berall, J., & Holt, A.B. (1977). Protein-calorie malnutrition and the significance of cell mass relative to body length. *American Journal of Clinical Nutrition,* **30**, 851-860.

De, A.K., Debnath, P.K., Dey, N.K., & Nagchaudhuri, J. (1980). Respiratory performance and grip strength tests in Indian school boys of different socio-economic status. *British Journal of Sports Medicine,* **14**, 145-148.

Frisancho, A.R., Velasquez, T., & Sanchez, J. (1975). Possible adaptive significance of small body size in the attainment of aerobic capacity among high-altitude Quechua natives. In E.S. Watts, F.E. Johnston, & G.W. Lasker (Eds.), *Biosocial interrelations in population adaptation* (pp. 55-64). The Hague: Mouton.

Forbes, G.B. (1965). Toward a new dimension in human growth. *Pediatrics,* **36**, 825-835.

Ghesquiére, J., & Eeckels, R. (1981). *Sante, developpement physique et capacite motorique des enfants de l'ecole primaire de Kinshasa.* Paper presented at XVᵉ Colloque des Anthropologistes de Langue Francaise, Université Libre de Bruxelles.

Inter-American Development Bank (1979). Nutrition and socio-economic development of Latin America. Washington, D.C.: Inter-American Development Bank.

Ishiko, T. (1967). Comparison of physical fitness between urban and secluded children. In G. Hanekopf (Ed.), *Kongressbericht. XVI Weltkongress für Sportmedizin in Hannover* (pp. 770-774). Berlin: Aerzte Verlag.

Ismail, A.H., Christian, J.E., & Kessler, W.V. (1963). Body composition relative to motor aptitude for preadolescent boys. *Research Quarterly,* **34**, 462-470.

Jelliffe, E.F.P., & Jelliffe, D.B. (1969). The arm circumference as a public health index of protein-calorie malnutrition of early childhood. *Journal of Tropical Pediatrics,* **15** (Monograph 8), 177-260.

Lasky, R.E., Klein, R.E., Yarbrough, C., Engle, P.L., Lechtig, A., & Martorell, R. (1981). The relationship between physical growth and infant behavioral development in rural Guatemala. *Child Development, 52*, 219-226.

Malina, R.M. (1975). Anthropometric correlates of strength and motor performance. *Exercise and Sport Sciences Reviews, 3*, 249-274.

Malina, R.M. (1977). Motor development in a cross-cultural perspective. In D.M. Landers & R.W. Christina (Eds.), *Psychology of motor behavior and sport. Volume II. Sport psychology and motor development* (pp. 191-208). Champaign, IL: Human Kinetics.

Malina, R.M. (1984). Physical activity and motor development/performance in populations nutritionally at risk. In E. Pollitt & P. Amante (Eds.), *Energy intake and activity* (pp. 285-302). New York: Alan R. Liss.

Malina, R.M., & Buschang, P.H. (1985). Growth, strength and motor performance of Zapotec children, Oaxaca, Mexico. *Human Biology, 57*, 163-181

Malina, R.M., & Little, B.B. (1985). Body composition, strength, and motor performance in undernourished boys. In R.A. Binkhorst, H.C.G. Kemper, & W.H.M. Saris (Eds.), *Children and Exercise XI* (pp. 293-300). Champaign, IL: Human Kinetics.

Malina, R.M., Shoup, R.F., & Little, B.B. (1985). Growth, strength and motor performance of Manus children, Papua New Guinea. Submitted for publication.

Parizkova, J., & Merhautova, J. (1973). A comparison of body build, body composition and selected functional characteristics in Tunisian and Czech boys of 11 to 12 years of age. *Anthropologie, 11*, 115-119.

Rarick, G.L., & Oyster, N. (1964). Physical maturity, muscular strength, and motor performance of young school-age boys. *Research Quarterly, 35*, 523-531.

Rocha Ferreira, M.B. (1980). *Estado nutricional e aptidão física em préescolares.* Dissertacão de Mestrado, Universidade de São Paulo.

Sabogal, F., Molina, B., & MacVean, R.B. (1979). Desarrollo fisico y cognoscitivo de niños Guatemaltecos, en funcion del nivel socioeconomico y del sexo. *Revista Latinoamericana de psicologia, 11*, 229-247.

Satyanarayana, M.B., Naidu, A.N., Rao, N. (1979). Nutritional deprivation in childhood and the body size, activity, and physical work capacity of young boys. *American Journal of Clinical Nutrition, 32*, 1769-1775.

Seils, L.G. (1951). The relationship between measures of physical growth and gross motor performance of primary grade school children. *Research Quarterly, 22*, 244-260.

Slaughter, M.H., Lohman, T.G., & Misner, J.E. (1977). Relationship of somatotype and body composition to physical performance in 7- to 12-year-old boys. *Research Quarterly, 48*, 159-168.

Spurr, G.G. (1983). Nutritional status and physical work capacity. *Yearbook of Physical Anthropology, 26*, 1-35.

Spurr, G.B. (1984). Physical activity, nutritional status, and physical work capacity in relation to agricultural productivity. In E. Pollitt & P. Amante (Eds.), *Energy intake and activity* (pp. 207-261). New York: Alan R. Liss.

Spurr, G.B., Barac-Nieto, M, & Maksud, M.G. (1978). Childhood undernutrition: Implications for adult work capacity and productivity. In L.J. Folinsbee, J.A. Wagner, J.F. Borgia, B.L. Drinkwater, J.A. Gliner, & J.F. Bedi (Eds.), *Environmental stress: Individual human adaptations* (pp. 165-181). New York: Academic Press.

Stini, W.A. (1972). Reduced sexual dimorphism in upper arm muscle circumference associated with protein-deficient diet in a South American population. *American Journal of Physical Anthropology, 36*, 341-351.

Stini, W.A. (1975). Adaptive strategies of human populations under nutritional stress. In E.S. Watts, F.E. Johnston, & G.W. Laskers (Eds.), *Biosocial interrelations in population adaptation* (pp. 19-41). The Hague: Mouton.

Viteri, F.E. (1971). Considerations of the effect of nutrition on the body composition and physical working capacity of young Guatemalan adults. In N.S. Schrimshaw